Praise for *Breakdown: A Clinician's Experience in a Broken System of Emergency Psychiatry*

Lynn Nanos accurately describes the daily struggles that an emergency clinician confronts on the job. *Breakdown* hits on all the hot-button issues and challenges of today's crisis team environment, such as the proliferation of substance abuse in our society, the proper use of Section 12s and balancing the liberty rights of the individual with the protection of the community at large, managing the pressures of hospital emergency rooms faced with the daunting challenges of inadequate bed availability and the revolving door of psychiatric admissions due to shortened length of psychiatric hospital stays, and the ongoing process of forming appropriate and collegial relationships with police departments, group homes, and assorted State agencies, such as DMH. Nanos expertly examines some of the inherent and structural obstacles that confront an emergency clinician on her or his shifts. She further opines on some of the more controversial issues of the day, including outpatient commitment, but does so with the compassion and insight of a professional who has worked in the trenches of the field. I highly recommend *Breakdown* for anyone interested in the realities of emergency services work and how such work affects the community.

—ROBERT F. BROWN, J.D., ATTORNEY, PURSUING THE INSANITY
DEFENSE IN CRIMINAL CASES; ATTORNEY, REPRESENTING
PATIENTS AND HOSPITALS IN CIVIL COMMITMENT
HEARINGS ON INPATIENT UNITS; MOBILE EMERGENCY
PSYCHIATRIC CLINICIAN (PER DIEM), MASSACHUSETTS

Lynn Nanos has put together a precise compilation of factual information for anyone disturbed about how seriously flawed our mental health care system is today. This book brings to the forefront the steps that must be taken in order to help our most vulnerable members of society, the mentally ill. Nanos irrefutably hits the target in advocating for Assisted Outpatient Treatment. For anyone concerned, particularly those who work in the field helping those with mental health issues, *Breakdown* is a must-read.

—WILLIAM CHANIS, SERGEANT, CRISIS INTERVENTION TEAM,
WORCESTER POLICE DEPARTMENT, MASSACHUSETTS

Breakdown is an excellent synopsis of the plight of the mentally ill in the United States. It brings to the forefront the need for immediate change in the way treatment and services are afforded. As a career law enforcement officer, I applaud the author of *Breakdown* for her insight and dedication in promoting future positive changes with regard to treating mental illness.

—DONALD P. DESORCY, CHIEF,
MILLBURY POLICE DEPARTMENT, MASSACHUSETTS

Lynn Nanos guides readers in *Breakdown: A Clinician's Experience in a Broken System of Emergency Psychiatry* through our nation's shameful treatment of Americans with debilitating mental illnesses. Only someone with her in-the-trenches experience can articulate the flaws with such authority. Her dedication to helping throw-away patients trapped on a treadmill of hospitalizations, homelessness, and jails is heroic and inspiring.

—PETE EARLEY, AUTHOR, *CRAZY: A FATHER'S SEARCH
THROUGH AMERICA'S MENTAL HEALTH MADNESS* (2007
PULITZER PRIZE FINALIST); 2008 AMERICAN PSYCHIATRIC
ASSOCIATION AWARD FOR PATIENT ADVOCACY

Lynn Nanos, L.I.C.S.W., manages to capture the devastating consequences of untreated serious mental illness that families witness daily, using vignettes to document her interactions with her patients. *Breakdown: A Clinician's Experience in a Broken System of Emergency Psychiatry* is a well-researched look at the many problems that have plagued our broken mental health system for decades and offers evidence-based, practical solutions. This book is a must-read for anyone with the power to fix our broken system. As a mother who has witnessed first-hand the horrible suffering inflicted by a society which has abandoned its seriously mentally ill, I am so grateful to Lynn for having the strength and courage to write this book.

—Jeanne Allen Gore, parent of a young man who suffers from schizoaffective disorder, Coordinator and Co-Chair, Steering Committee, National Shattering Silence Coalition

We have been struggling to find effective and humane means for the care of the seriously mentally ill at least since the time of the Industrial Revolution. Despite this long history, the contemporary "system" of care in the United States is arguably worse than many of its predecessors, due to its fragmentation, disorganization, financial mismanagement, and inability to rise above polarized policy debates that are not backed by evidence. Lynn Nanos draws on her significant clinical experience and her deep knowledge of legal and policy backgrounds to give a moving first-hand account of the people who suffer in the current "system." She also provides practical and realistic proposals for how we might begin to make repairs.

—Michael B. Knable, D.O., Medical Director, Clearview Communities; Executive Director, Sylvan C. Herman Foundation; Psychiatric Advisory Board Chair, Treatment Advocacy Center

Author Lynn Nanos provides a gritty and extremely candid look at our dysfunctional mental health care system. Her extensive experience in this trying environment provides a view of that world that few ever see. If you've ever wondered "Why don't we do more for the mentally ill?" read this book and you'll understand.

—Mark K. Leahy, Executive Director, Massachusetts Chiefs of Police Association; Chief, Northborough Police Department, Massachusetts (retired)

Ms. Nanos speaks about the broken system that is supposed to treat devastating psychiatric illness from experience after working in the trenches for many years. It is concerned clinicians like her who are the only hope for finding solutions to this current mess of a treatment system.

—Jonathan Lieff, M.D., Clinical Assistant Professor of Psychiatry, Tufts University School of Medicine; former President, American Association for Geriatric Psychiatry; Distinguished Life Fellow, American Psychiatric Association

Author Lynn Nanos offers a much-needed description of the problems with our current mental health system through the eyes of her experience as a clinical social worker. Her compassion for the unmet needs of the patients shines through, as does her concerns for where the system is failing. She shows how that flawed system for those with severe mental illness makes it the most difficult for those who have the most difficulty. If anyone wonders why our jails, emergency rooms, and homeless shelters are overwhelmed with persons with mental illness, they would do well to read this book. It will open their eyes.

—Tim Murphy, Ph.D., Psychologist; Member of Congress— United States House of Representatives (retired) (drafted the Helping Families in Mental Health Crisis Act); Author, *Overcoming Passive-Aggression: How to Stop Hidden Anger from Spoiling Your Relationships, Career and Happiness*; Author, *The Angry Child: Regaining Control When Your Child is Out of Control*

Breakdown should be required reading for clinicians, legislators, mental health advocates, and families who want the best care for their loved ones with serious mental illness. Lynn Nanos vividly illustrates the unconscionably inadequate laws governing the treatment of seriously disturbed persons and offers sound remedies to address these flaws. While sensitive to civil liberties issues, Nanos argues persuasively that no persons with serious mental illness should have to die "with their rights on."

—Ronald W. Pies, M.D., Professor Emeritus of Psychiatry, State University of New York—Upstate Medical University; Clinical Professor of Psychiatry, Tufts University School of Medicine; Editor-in-Chief Emeritus, *Psychiatric Times*

In *Breakdown,* Lynn Nanos draws upon years of clinical experience to expose one of our society's most shameful injustices: the neglect of individuals with serious mental illness. By weaving together her own first-person account with historical, political, and legal background, Nanos issues a clarion call for the construction of adequate mental health services for our most vulnerable citizens.

—Dominic Sisti, Ph.D., Director, Scattergood Program for Applied Ethics of Behavioral Health Care, Department of Medical Ethics and Health Policy, Perelman School of Medicine, University of Pennsylvania; Assistant Professor of Medical Ethics and Health Policy, Philosophy, and Psychiatry, University of Pennsylvania

Lynn Nanos' book *Breakdown* is a welcome addition to those that seek to educate the public about America's mental health crisis—one that too many willfully neglect. And she offers a valuable perspective from the front lines of a broken treatment system, where psychiatrists and social workers are overwhelmed by people for whom fewer and fewer inpatient treatment beds are available. Many do not even know they are sick and, after being released to the streets, will wind up behind bars. Nanos sees clearly the consequences of failing to treat the most severely ill among us, and she understands why systemic reform is so badly needed, particularly in her state of Massachusetts— one of just three states without an Assisted Outpatient Treatment program—where there is little to prevent the most severely ill from cycling through our emergency rooms, homeless shelters, and jails. "One tragedy should be enough to sound alarms," Nanos writes. Indeed. Yet, human tragedies continue to befall people with serious mental illness and their families at a record clip. I can only hope that this book will open eyes, ears, and hearts to their suffering, motivating action.

—John Snook, J.D., Executive Director, Treatment Advocacy Center

Breakdown: A Clinician's Experience in a Broken System of Emergency Psychiatry is yet another excellent example of our badly broken mental illness treatment system. The author, Lynn Nanos, is a psychiatric social worker within the Massachusetts state system, which is one of the worst states. She clearly describes the failures of the system and consequent tragedies for the patients. I recommend her well-written book.

If there is a right to be sick, there is also a right to be rescued. This book hits the right balance in that delicate equation, written by someone in the trenches and on the front line with seriously mentally ill persons day after day. The book underscores forcefully that it is not the mental health system that is broken and in a "mess." Rather, it is the mental illness system that requires rescue from economic, political, and cross purposes polemic bickering. Meanwhile, families and an entire public continue to watch as seriously mentally ill persons continue to die, languish in prisons, or suffer on the street with their rights on. Lynn Nanos is a present-day Dorothea Dix pointing out the tragic obvious, and suggesting attainable, evidence-based, affordable remedies.

Lawmakers, policymakers, and others who are responsible for shaping national, state, and local systems of care and treatment of serious mental illnesses too often have no practical knowledge of the individuals who suffer the most devastating consequences of psychosis or mania. In *Breakdown,* Lynn Nanos educates us with real clinical vignettes that give voice to individuals whose illnesses prevent them from accepting medical treatment that can save their lives. This book provides a window into a world that most people will never see, making it a must-read for anyone who is interested in understanding and reversing the country's decades of neglect of our most seriously mentally ill citizens.

—MARY T. ZDANOWICZ, J.D., ATTORNEY, SPECIALIZING IN ADVOCACY FOR THE SERIOUSLY MENTALLY ILL POPULATION; FORMER EXECUTIVE DIRECTOR, TREATMENT ADVOCACY CENTER

Breakdown:
A Clinician's Experience in a Broken System of Emergency Psychiatry

Lynn Nanos, L.I.C.S.W.

Breakdown: A Clinician's Experience in a Broken System of Emergency Psychiatry
Published by Lynn Nanos, Natick, Massachusetts

•   •   •

Publisher's Cataloging-In-Publication Data
(Prepared by The Donohue Group, Inc.)

Names: Nanos, Lynn.
Title: Breakdown : a clinician's experience in a broken system of
    emergency psychiatry / Lynn Nanos, L.I.C.S.W.
Description: Natick, Massachusetts : Lynn Nanos, [2018] | Includes
    bibliographical references.
Identifiers: ISBN 9780692168424
Subjects: LCSH: Psychiatric emergencies. | Mentally ill--Care. |
    Psychiatric hospital care--United States. | Alternatives to psychiatric
    hospitalization--United States.
Classification: LCC RC480.6 .N36 2018 | DDC 616.89025--dc23

•   •   •

International Standard Book Number: 9780692168424
Library of Congress Control Number: 2018909280

•   •   •

Cover illustration by Ivan Potter-Smith

Dedication

For seriously mentally ill people who need
help but lack the capacity to request it.

Acknowledgments

THANK YOU TO MY HUSBAND, Peter D. Nelson; my mother, Penelope Nanos; and Peter's parents, Patricia and Jeffrey Nelson, for their unwavering support. Thank you to my deceased father, Athanasios Nanos, for teaching me the value of hard work. Thank you to my brother, Chris Nanos; his wife, Luisa Nanos; Peter's sister, Kay Lindsay; and her husband, Tim Lindsay, for their consistent praise. Thank you to my sister, Georgine Nanos, for her medical knowledge and coaching. Thank you to my little nephews, Erik, Nathan, Tommy, Luke, and James; and my little niece, Julia, for brightening this project with humor. Thank you to my friend and cousin, George Nanos, for his computer technology expertise. Thank you to my closest friends for their love.

Thank you to the advocates for seriously mentally ill people, many of whom are family members or close friends of them, for inspiring me to write this book. Thank you to the seriously mentally ill patients for reminding me of the importance of compassion and for teaching me about mental illness.

Thank you to the government officials who have contributed to improving the mental health system. Thank you to the police officers who risk their lives daily to help this population.

Thank you to the mental health professionals who advocate for improvements of the system as well as to the professionals who care about this population. Thank you to the places of employment that have given me the clinical opportunities that have enabled me to write this book.

Table of Contents

Breakdown

Preface

I BEGAN MY CAREER IN PSYCHIATRY as a social work intern. In my final internship toward obtaining a Master of Science degree in social work, I worked at Rockland Psychiatric Center in New York State from the fall of 1996 to the spring of 1997. There, I began practicing my clinical skills in the service of patients who were on a locked inpatient psychiatric unit operated by the New York State Office of Mental Health. As I eagerly oriented myself to the unit, I began therapeutically engaging with the patients. I was interested in learning about their lives. I inquired about what had happened to get them admitted, what their current treatment goals were, and what their plans were for after discharge. I soon found that these patients believed that being on this unit was based on a huge misunderstanding and that they didn't need to be there. I discussed this with my supervisor, who told me, "No one here is mentally ill." Her statement didn't mean that she was part of the antipsychiatry camp that believes mental illness doesn't exist and that medication is largely unhelpful. She meant that the patients didn't believe they were ill.

Breakdown

Psychosis, defined as a loss of connection with reality, is a core feature of schizophrenia. Many of the patients at Rockland Psychiatric Center were psychotic and had lived on this inpatient unit for well over ten years. One of the patients with the most psychosis had been there for twenty-three years. My main role was to determine if they were clinically ready to be discharged to less restrictive settings. I helped prepare patients for interviews with unsecured residential programs on the hospital grounds. I also escorted patients to vocational programs outside on the grounds of the hospital.

Immediately after obtaining my graduate degree, I sampled a variety of other professional social work settings, but I missed working with patients on inpatient psychiatry. I then became an inpatient psychiatric social worker. My appreciation of the interdependence between clinical assessments and making referrals to outpatient treatment providers grew. I used many resources within the psychiatric system and myself to facilitate safe discharge plans. With my ability to be highly organized, thorough, and hardworking, I made appropriate clinical referrals for patients. I learned about the system and its patients from the nurses and psychiatrists who had far more experience than I did.

I gradually realized that there was a common theme among the cases involving the most psychosis on inpatient. Many of these patients lacked awareness of their psychosis, especially regarding delusions. When patients are unaware of their illness, they have anosognosia. These patients can be more challenging to work with because they don't believe that they need any help. Why would they? From their perspective, they're not ill. When patients don't want help, psychiatrists must decide if they are obligated to hold these patients against their will. Despite not having the authority to determine this, my clinical knowledge base grew. Some patients who were getting discharged were not ready to get discharged.

I noticed that some patients were more likely than others to be discharged prematurely. The most convincing evidence of this was that they were quickly readmitted. If we had gotten it right the first time, the patients would have remained stable in the community for months, if not years. When I think about the psychotic patients with anosognosia, I cannot recall anyone who was discharged from inpatient psychiatry at the appropriate time.

Some family members lashed out at me when I was an inpatient psychiatric social worker. I didn't take it personally and did know they were at a point beyond frustration. There were many times when I couldn't think of anything to say to them besides, "My hands are tied. There's nothing further I can do. The doctor is ordering the discharge, not me. I know you're angry." Some family members told me that they couldn't blame me for their seriously mentally ill loved ones being prematurely discharged again. Instead, they blamed the psychiatrists. I quietly blamed some of them, too, but mostly blamed the system.

Discharging a patient prematurely can have disastrous consequences as the story of one patient who refused treatment will illustrate. While I was working as an inpatient social worker, a patient on my caseload who was paranoid and delusional refused to accept medication because he did not believe that he was mentally ill. He refused to sign a release of confidentiality for me to communicate with his mother even though they resided together. She knew he was on the unit, so I just supportively listened to her concerns. She told me that he had been increasingly distant from her over the past several months, despite her attempts to converse with him. When he did talk to her, she had difficulty understanding what he meant because he was so vague and refused to elaborate. He spent most of his days locked in his bedroom without any structure, occupational productivity, or social ties. Once in the past year, he had slapped her across the face, an action that seemed to her to be unprovoked. This was not how he had functioned previously. She wanted to help him, but he didn't allow her to.

I passed these concerns on to the rest of the team, including his psychiatrist, and suggested that he might be a candidate for an extended stay. The psychiatrist acknowledged these concerns, which perhaps contributed to her decision to refrain from discharging him for another two days. He was eating and sleeping adequately, could formulate sentences lucidly, wasn't suicidal, and wasn't homicidal. He requested a discharge, and the psychiatrist concluded that he didn't qualify for a further inpatient stay. I knew enough not to press or raise concerns about this with the psychiatrist. She had a great deal of power over the nurses and especially over the social workers. If I were to disagree with her plan to discharge the patient, she would have disregarded me.

Shortly after this patient's discharge, he used a knife to stab his mother to death. I did not foresee that he could become that violent. Although he had slapped her previously, there was no evidence available to me that this was due to untreated mental illness. The main reason for his admission was not violence. I don't believe that any member of the treatment team could have predicted his mother's death at his hands. If he had believed that he was mentally ill, he might have accepted treatment and stayed on the unit. With more time on the unit, there would have been more opportunity for the treatment team to evaluate him. Perhaps he would have allowed us to fully communicate with his mother. It can be difficult to have a one-sided conversation with no ability to give information to a patient's family member. There were many questions about this case that couldn't be answered. In just four days, it was impossible to know even a small fraction of the course of his illness and his relationship with his mother.

I want to do anything possible to prevent this type of tragedy from happening again. If this book makes a small dent for the better, I'll be fulfilled. When legislators are educated about the system, change is more likely to occur. Overly restrictive inpatient commitment criteria often result in insufficiently short stays.

This tragedy planted the seeds of my motivation to learn and share with others as much as possible about the connection between untreated psychosis and violence. It strengthened my humanitarian mission. Unfortunately, seriously mentally ill people are violent with family members all too often. A research study found that 86 percent of the targets of violence inflicted by its mentally ill participants were family members or friends.[1] This statistic is not surprising, given that close emotional connections typically coincide with increased chances of acting on the most visceral of impulses.

I wanted to have more influence over the treatment of patients and eventually left the inpatient setting because I wasn't clinically challenged enough. My primary role on inpatient had been to plan for discharges based on the clinical leadership of the psychiatrists or advanced nurse practitioners. In this realm, I learned about the hierarchy of disciplines, since psychiatrists were the ultimate decision-makers on these units. They had, and still have, the most power and order all discharges in hospitals. However, I often earned credibility, built trust, and influenced psychiatrists when it mattered most.

After working on inpatient psychiatric units, I joined an emergency services team. I like clinical work. However, I find that it is nearly impossible to change the mental health system as a clinician within my place of employment. Professional disciplines are ranked in sharp hierarchy in mental health care. Decisions are largely driven from the top in clinical settings. I have no power to create or change policies because I am not an administrator. I've rarely met an administrator who, when making decisions, appeared to consider feedback about management operations from lower-ranking staff members. This has been especially true for professionals who are not psychiatrists. Social workers are highly trained professionals. Perhaps their expertise should be incorporated more in the decision-making process.

Emergency work involves observing patients functioning outside of hospitals for many years. Undoubtedly, many of these patients are safe. Nevertheless, some of them are not operating safely and need more help. Some attempt or complete suicide in response to severe depression. Others refuse to eat because they believe that their neighbors are poisoning their food. Some seriously harm others in response to auditory hallucinations that command them to act. Others seriously injure other people, or cats and dogs, because of paranoid delusions.

In my many years of emergency psychiatric experience, I have independently researched the mental health system on a macro level and directly connected to top advocates throughout the United States. I wanted to learn why the length of inpatient stays were too short, why the readmission rates were so high, and why patients were being readmitted sicker than ever before. In the last few years, I've had the good fortune of acquiring an extensive network of friends who advocate for the seriously mentally ill population. Many of them are family members or friends of such people. They had encountered a divergence of choices—they could either advocate for change in the system or let the system do them in. Some of them have continued to advocate for improvements in the mental health system long after their family members or friends have gone missing, became estranged, or died because of serious mental illness. Their horror stories—not only about the tragedies that took place but also about the barriers to accessing decent care for their sick loved ones—are evidence that the system is broken. They fight tirelessly for adequate treatment.

Those who bravely chose the path of advocacy are heroes. Their tragic stories inspire me to join their fight. They remind me to be courageous when I authorize involuntary transfers to the hospital for patients who, I expect, will be discharged too soon. I am taking my outrage about the injustices I've seen as a clinician and turning it into positive energy through this book. It's not only a book that I *want* to share with as many people as possible; it's a book that I *need* to share.

I come to present the strong claims of suffering humanity. I come to place before the Legislature of Massachusetts the condition of the miserable, the desolate, the outcast. I come as the advocate of helpless, forgotten, insane, and idiotic men and women; of beings, sunk to a condition from which the most unconcerned would start with real horror; of beings wretched in our Prisons, and more wretched in our alms-houses.

—DOROTHEA DIX (1802–1887), TIRELESS ADVOCATE
FOR PEOPLE WITH SERIOUS MENTAL ILLNESS

Introduction

A POLICE OFFICER ESCORTS EARL, fifty years old, to my office. Earl was yelling bizarre proclamations on the street and scaring people. He cannot explain why he's meeting with me and insists that the police overreacted. He is planning to take a bus to the capitol because he believes that his participation in the next presidential campaign will prevent children from getting sexually abused. He explains that someone has ordered him to kill anyone who prevents him from getting on the next available bus. He is not able to provide the name of any family member or friend. He never gets to a bus. Instead, he is involuntarily taken to a hospital emergency department. Hours later, the hospital releases him to the streets without treatment.

This is just one of countless examples that demonstrate the broken system. The mental health system across the United States is a mess. The duration of inpatient psychiatric courses has dramatically declined over recent decades. The number of inpatient beds has plummeted. Criminalization of the mentally ill population has worsened. The consequences of these failures are evident in the astronomically high rates of readmission to emergency settings of undertreated or untreated seriously mentally ill patients. In an ideal world, one tragedy due to serious mental illness would be enough to trigger the legislative changes that would improve the broken system. One tragedy should be enough to sound alarms, but we do not reside in an ideal world.

The emergency psychiatric setting is in a unique position to illuminate examples of our broken mental health system because it is at the intersection of all types of therapeutic mental health treatment and the lack of treatment. We can learn a lot about the system from emergency psychiatry because it entails a variety of situations and problems. The work is dramatic and vibrant. In addition to cited research, this book is my perspective on the mental health system, which has been shaped by my work roles. My perspective is a narrow lens in the context of the whole system. I appreciate that this differs from others' perspectives.

I appeal for a reformation of the Massachusetts and United States mental health systems. The dysfunctional aspects of this system are too abysmal for me to take on alone. For concerned citizens who are interested in improving the mental health system, this book is a tiny introductory feat compared to all that needs to be done. The greatest expression of passion for a subject is teaching it to others and asking for legislative reform. A goal of this book is to persuade and motivate readers to advocate with legislators by requesting improvements in the system. I hope to inspire readers to persuade legislators to make positive changes that would improve the system.

This book can serve as a source of validation and comfort for family members and friends of seriously mentally ill people. Many of these loved ones feel outraged about the broken mental health system. It is my hope that this book lessens their sense of despair and isolation.

There is a shortage of psychiatrists in the United States.[2] Perhaps the dysfunctional aspects of the system deter medical students from choosing this specialty. Or perhaps the stigma associated with psychiatry, as may be perceived by other medical specialties, deters them. Unfortunately, some people value the management of mental illness less than they value the management of other types of illnesses. I particularly sensed stigma when I worked on an inpatient unit that was part of a large multidisciplinary hospital. Occasionally, when I consulted about patients with medical doctors who were not psychiatrists, the doctors conveyed an attitude of superiority over the psychiatrists. The stigma might explain why mental health insurance reimbursement rates are usually lower than reimbursement rates in other specialties, which in turn may be another reason for the shortage of psychiatrists. Most, if not all, new medical doctors want to be paid sufficiently for their work.

Commonly used terms should accurately reflect the relationship between professionals providing mental health services and service recipients. Doing this gives psychiatry and its recipients the respect that they deserve. In this book, I refer to the people whom I help as *patients* to reflect my work and to reduce stigma. Any other label (e.g., *client*) would indicate that they have the capacity to direct the course of their treatment independently. Although most emergency cases involve patients who voluntarily seek treatment, some patients are too sick to understand that they need help. When I authorize involuntary transportation to hospitals for these patients, they are unable to choose treatment rationally.

* * *

Most clinical cases in emergency psychiatry involve high-functioning patients. I do not officially specialize in any type of clinical case. Therefore, the cases assigned to me are largely random, based on how my hours of employment coincide with times that patients are ready to be evaluated. I am most passionate about working on complicated cases that involve the most impaired patients. Some of them are not able to initiate treatment or formulate their treatment plans. These cases often involve psychosis.

Depression and anxiety are common disorders in psychiatry but often don't present with as much devastation as psychosis does. Although depression can accompany psychosis, this book does not present any case of depression. This book also does not present any case of generalized anxiety disorder.

I am more passionate about helping patients who need government assistance than patients with a higher capacity for independence. The Massachusetts Department of Mental Health (DMH) funds facilities and services for many of these low-functioning patients. When I use the term *inpatient unit,* I am referring to an inpatient psychiatric unit that is non-state-operated, unless I indicate otherwise (e.g., *inpatient medical unit, DMH inpatient*).

I am aware of rare instances of early childhood psychosis, which warrants scientific consideration in the fight against schizophrenia. However, schizophrenia is far more likely to begin in late adolescence or early adulthood. For this reason, this book does not focus on the child mental health system.

The use of illicit drugs or alcohol by patients can mask mental illness and distort clinicians' ability to diagnose mental illness accurately. For this reason, the clinical cases in this book involve extremely minimal to no use of illicit drugs or alcohol.

According to scores of scholarly articles examining possible etiologies of schizophrenia, trauma and environmental events are not likely culprits in the onset of the disease. This book does not examine the possible etiologies of schizophrenia and bipolar disorder. When helping a patient who is in crisis, determining the cause of his mental illness is not the highest priority. It is not necessary to obtain an extensive history of a patient's childhood development and traumatic experiences. With each case lasting only about three hours, there's simply not enough time for this. Clinical emergency work is more focused on the current and most recent functioning of patients. A few patients believe that trauma induced their psychosis, but I have not found a pattern of association between trauma and psychosis.

My professional role is that of a full-time mobile emergency psychiatric clinician in Massachusetts. This entails my direct observation of a wide range of mental disorders that manifest in how patients verbally, nonverbally, cognitively, and behaviorally present. When patients appear unreliable in their ability to report information, or their mental impairments interfere with their ability to report accurately, I try to seek out their family members or friends for their input. These observations of psychiatric dysfunction are used to recommend and implement a variety of treatment options. Unlike stationary emergency psychiatric clinicians, who remain in hospital emergency settings, a hospital does not employ me.

I evaluate patients in the following settings:

+ personal homes

+ DMH residential programs

+ day treatment programs

+ rest homes

+ sidewalk benches

+ homeless shelters

+ doctors' outpatient offices

+ psychotherapists' offices

+ respite units

+ city hall

+ holding cells of police stations

+ inpatient medical units

+ hospital emergency departments

+ my office

The emergency services interview that I conduct provides a tiny snapshot of a patient's life. The interview usually lasts anywhere from twenty to ninety minutes, which is much longer than the time each patient spends in the emergency department talking to a hospital emergency medical doctor or a psychiatrist employed by the same hospital. Regardless of the location, the expected brevity of the emergency interview usually warrants a review of available clinical records about the patient. Recent records from triage nurses, psychiatrists, psychotherapists, and other emergency services clinicians are especially useful.

Ultimately, the emergency clinician is expected to collaborate with patients in formulating and executing treatment plans. I critically think through various treatment options and then use my best judgment to choose and apply the safest outcomes for patients. For instance, I give recommendations about how to decrease insomnia or how to improve communication skills during conflicts with others; encourage patients to advocate for themselves when requesting better mental health treatment; provide lists of supportive and educational websites that focus on mental illness and lists of in-person support groups; recommend that patients be admitted to inpatient units; recommend that patients follow up with their already established outpatient treatment providers; suggest that they remain in their DMH residential programs or continue attending their outpatient psychotherapy and psychopharmacological appointments.

Toward the middle of 2018, I learned about DMH's intention to replace the Community-based Flexible Supports (CBFS) model of care with Adult Community Clinical Services (ACCS) effective July 1, 2018. The case vignettes of this book are based on the CBFS model. CBFS program staff members are referred to as *rehabilitative outreach workers* or *outreach workers* in this book. ACCS is new and in effect at the time of book publication.

The CBFS and ACCS models are similar in many ways. Both programs entail a wide range of rehabilitative outreach services that are designed to provide extra support and supervision for mentally ill people outside of locked inpatient and unlocked crisis units. Recipients typically reside in their apartments with supportive outreach in the form of visits from staff members. These programs are expected to help mentally ill people manage their symptoms and maintain daily living skills. They can assist people with medication management, financial responsibilities, occupational pursuits, and medical illnesses. Group residential programs fall within the realm of both these models. Staff members provide close supervision and support to residents, which can include the administration of medication to residents. ACCS implements greater clinical staffing and integration of specialties than CBFS implemented.

I sometimes refer patients to new psychotherapists and psychiatrists or advanced psychiatric nurse practitioners. I occasionally refer patients to intensive group therapy programs. I often refer patients to substance-dependence programs. I frequently facilitate admission to Community Crisis Stabilization units, referred to as *crisis units*. Crisis units are described in the following chapter.

I also encourage patients to follow up with the Program of Assertive Community Treatment (PACT) programs to which they belong. These programs are also for DMH recipients. PACT recipients are offered a multidisciplinary array of psychiatric rehabilitative services designed to prevent crisis and hospitalization. The patients are given the opportunity to obtain direct services from psychiatrists, nurses, master-level clinicians, vocational specialists, addiction specialists, housing specialists, and peer specialists. They can receive medication management, crisis intervention, and social skills training; get help with coordinating medical and psychiatric appointments; learn how to manage and decrease psychiatric symptoms; and get help with the basic tasks of daily living. These patients are not ACCS recipients. To avoid duplication of services and state funding, it's not possible for patients to receive both services.

I determine whether patients are dangerous to themselves or others. I authorize and implement the involuntary transportation to hospital emergency departments of patients who are in danger due to mental illness, according to Commonwealth of Massachusetts General Laws, Part 1, Title XVII, Chapter 123, Section 12(a). This is referred to as *Section 12* in this book.

Massachusetts legislators granted me the privilege of authorizing Section 12s toward the end of 2010 because I am a licensed, independent clinical social worker. Although this authorization allows the receiving hospital to prevent the patient from leaving for three business days, a patient can be discharged to his resources, or lack thereof, before this expiration. I explore the suspected and apparent reasons for this in this book. In the 1990s, Section 12 expired in ten days. In 2000, this expiration changed to four days. In 2004, the expiration changed to three days.

For the criteria of Section 12 to be met in any case, one or more of the following three states must apply:

+ The patient is at imminent risk of engaging in serious self-harm.

+ The patient is at imminent risk of engaging in major harm to another person.

+ The patient is at imminent risk of sustaining physical damage or injury, or the patient's judgment is so impaired that she or he is not able to protect herself or himself from basic harm in the community, and reasonable contingencies that would provide this patient with protection are not available outside of a secured setting.

The last of these prongs typically pertains to profoundly psychotic patients.

Section 12 cannot be authorized when illicit drugs or alcohol induce the dangerous symptom(s). During the interview process, I rule out alternative causes of symptoms that appear psychiatric on the surface. Substance-dependence is common in emergency mental health. It is important to consider the timing in which the illicit drug or alcohol was used. I often educate patients who are dependent on illicit drugs or alcohol on the fact that diagnosing mental illness during rampant use of these substances is close to impossible. This is because the substances can mask mental problems. If a patient has been using heroin daily for the last two years, was functioning well during extended periods of sobriety without psychotherapy or medication, and is now reporting anxiety for the first time, I would primarily diagnose him with opioid-dependence. It would then be appropriate for the patient to undergo detoxification before considering long-term mental health services.

I diagnose each patient toward the end of each case. I use my observations of patients to diagnose them using the *Diagnostic and Statistical Manual of Mental Disorders-Fifth Edition* (DSM-5). This manual defines all mental illness. Psychiatry is not as straightforward as other medical specialties. There's no harm in diagnosing someone using the DSM-5 in such a short timeframe. Correctly diagnosing a patient in the emergency setting is not always possible. Of course, I try to diagnose someone accurately. However, safety trumps diagnosis in emergency psychiatry.[3]

This doesn't mean that diagnosing the patient isn't important. It is, but it is not the most important part of the assessment. The most important goals of emergency psychiatric services are to promote and protect the safety of patients and surrounding parties and to reduce danger. If a patient presents with only scant signs of depression (e.g., depressed mood with no other sign of depression) but expresses a strong intention to complete suicide with a specific plan and available means, I would arrange for inpatient hospitalization. After I've ensured that the patient is safe, I would diagnose him with depression—unspecified, rather than with major depression, which includes many other signs of depression (e.g., inability to feel joy, disturbed sleep, and low motivation to attend to routine tasks).

Another reason diagnosing is not the most important part of my job is that medication can be used to stabilize a variety of disorders. For example, antipsychotic medication can be used to treat mood disorders. Occasionally, choosing a diagnosis is challenging because the symptoms don't neatly fall into any diagnostic category. Other times, the diagnosis is clear.

To reduce redundancy and prevent distraction from the main purpose of this book, I do not describe all the therapeutic interventions that I use with patients. For instance, I am empathic and supportive toward patients and their family members or friends in actual practice more than this book reveals.

Regardless of the disorder I present, confidentiality is paramount. To protect the confidentiality of all patients whom I refer to and describe in this book, I have changed all their first names and omitted their last names. I've also changed all identifying details and have not identified locations.

I have compressed some details of clinical events described in this book and altered the chronological order of some events. Although part of the dialogue is accurate, it was impossible to convey with total accuracy all dialogue between myself, patients, other professionals, and family members or friends of these patients. In other words, I have not reconstructed every conversation verbatim. All case vignettes that I present are based on real clinical events and true clinical con-versations. I do not delve into patients' family histories, childhood developmental histories, environmental precipitants, or histories of trauma when presenting case vignettes.

One factor that has contributed to the decrease in length of stays on inpatient units and the elimination of inpatient beds over the last several decades is the lack of adequate reimbursement to hospitals by health insurance companies—private or public. Advocating with health insurance companies to obtain authorization for levels of care is a critical piece of emergency psychiatry, but I do not describe my experience with private or state-operated health insurance companies. Although I do not intend to criticize any of these plans, I have noticed an array of inconsistencies in their willingness to authorize the most financially costly level of care—inpatient. My presentations of clinical information when requesting authorization for inpatient treatment have led to various outcomes, from generous to criminal. Insurance companies agreed to pay for inpatient when patients could have been safely treated in outpatient settings. Or they refused to pay for inpatient when patients were not safe elsewhere. A detailed examination of how health insurance companies contribute to the broken system is beyond the scope of this book.

* * *

I am especially passionate about helping people who are the most dysfunctional due to serious mental illness and who demand more attention than others. I'm concerned about people who are at risk of seriously harming others or themselves due to their psychosis. The dramatic impact that my dedication has on these patients' lives demonstrates this passion. Helping psychotic patients—with or without mood instability—is invigorating. Whenever psychotic patients ask me to help them improve the quality of their lives, they're usually genuine. Whenever they present themselves to emergency psychiatry reluctantly or involuntarily, the lack of insight into their psychosis startles me.

While sharing with readers my passion for helping the seriously mentally ill population, I also hope to educate readers about what it's like to work in my profession. Readers who have never done this work can get a unique microscopic view of emergency psychiatric services. This landscape cannot be captured in any classroom, for the classroom doesn't provide the opportunity to witness inequity. My fascination with the psychotic population relates to how grossly the mental health system underserves them. Neglect of this population motivates me to help them with this book. My employment is not enough.

Long after leaving the classroom, I became alarmed at the extremely high rates of readmission to the inpatient units where I worked. These units were part of either freestanding or general hospitals. The patients were quickly readmitted to inpatient care because they did not sustain gains in mental functioning after they were discharged, or because no progress was made. They often returned because they were discharged too soon. When treatment was not sufficient the first time around, they expectedly relapsed.

Likewise, in emergency psychiatry, it's a rare week when I meet a patient for the first time. I'm shocked at the extremely high rates of readmission to the emergency psychiatric setting. They return because they have not sustained psychiatric gains that were achieved since I last met with them, because they have not made a psychiatric improvement, or because they have been discharged from inpatient units too soon.

When I am limited in my ability to help patients because of overly restrictive laws or the absence of laws, this motivates me to act abundantly on patients' behalf and to learn about the reasons for such outrageous rates of readmission. The alarm triggers in me a desire to discover what about the inpatient and outpatient settings contributes to these readmission rates. I do my best to reduce readmission through my dedication and a tendency to develop myself professionally.

The system is especially ineffective at helping psychotic people who lack insight into their psychosis. The broken mental health system sparks outrage in me and others who care about its recipients. Using clinical cases, I aim to inform readers about the flaws in the system and to identify barriers to accessing proper treatment.

Among the countless patients with delusions—medicated or unmedicated—who I interview, seeing a patient who has insight into being delusional is rare. I'm surprised that this is not part of the DSM-5 criteria for schizophrenia. In fact, I can recall only one emergency case involving decent insight into delusional thinking. I have no problem taking a patient-centered and patient-directed treatment planning approach with those who are well enough to understand their mental illness and their need for treatment to lessen its effects. However, this approach is deficient for the patients who lack insight into their mental illness. It unrealistically expects them to seek treatment independently when they don't understand that they need treatment.

First, I give readers a historical perspective to help them understand why the current mental health system is broken. For instance, I describe how the shortage of inpatient beds affects care.

One chapter focuses on people who pretend to be ill in emergency settings; I am amazed at the prevalence of this problem. These malingerers, who often use illicit drugs or alcohol, take up limited beds needed by seriously mentally ill people and drain other resources.

I devote another chapter to borderline personality disorder because I am stunned at the extent of damage it inflicts. Although it is the most researched personality disorder,[4] its prolific nature prompts me to question why it remains classified as a personality disorder rather than as a serious mental disorder.

Most of the case vignettes involve psychosis. Readers can learn about clinically premature discharges of patients from hospitals and the legislative barriers to meeting the needs of the psychotic population, especially patients with poor insight.

Finally, I offer solutions to reform the broken mental health system.

CHAPTER 2

Snapshot

ALLOW ME TO DESCRIBE a specific case as an example of performing an interview and how patients may respond. It's meant to illustrate the lack of security and confinement in mobile emergency cases. It shows what is at stake in many interviews. This patient easily could have pulled a gun on me if he were carrying one. And if police officers had not responded as quickly as they did to my authorization of Section 12, or if the patient intended to follow through with his homicidal and suicidal plans, lives easily could have been lost.

I'm working for an agency with a crisis unit when a clinician on that unit calls me. She says that something seems off kilter with Greg, thirty-two years old, who was admitted earlier in the week. She explains that in an individual session with him about thirty minutes ago, he was more guarded than usual. She asked him if he was suicidal, and he hesitated and couldn't provide her with a clear answer.

After reviewing the latest emergency record about Greg, I introduce myself to him. "Hi. I'm Lynn from emergency services. I want to get to know you a bit to figure out how to best help you."

Greg appears well-groomed and is wearing his jacket. He is carrying a large bag, which I assume contains his personal belongings. He stares flatly at me, asking, "What is this about? Why do I have to talk to you?"

"Your clinician said you are having a harder time than usual. She's concerned about you and thought I should talk to you."

Reluctantly, he follows my lead to sit down in my office but leaves his jacket on. He says, "I've just got to get out of here. I thought you all could help me, but I feel too cooped up in here."

I ask him some background questions about recent stressors, his mood, his ability to sleep, and whether he has recently used any illicit drug or alcohol. I ask about the purpose of his prescribed medication. I ask for the main reason he was admitted to the crisis unit and what he was hoping to get from the unit. He answers all these questions as I empathize with him. He takes off his jacket. I ask him, in a non-leading way, if he has ever thought about killing himself.

"Of course, I have! I want to now!"

Otherwise, he's calm. His affect varies from depressed to flat to angry.

I ask him if he has a suicidal plan in mind.

"I'm going to find a gun. I have to. I can't live like this anymore."

"Do you have a gun on you?"

"No."

"Do you own a gun?"

He doesn't answer me, avoiding eye contact.

"Greg, the only way that I can help you is by getting to know you. This is why I'm asking these questions."

"I can find one. No problem. I know people."

"Have you had any thoughts about wanting to harm anyone else seriously?"

"Hell, yeah. The first people I see out there have to die."

"Anyone at random or someone you know?"

"Anyone."

"Have you lately or today heard any voice that may not have sounded real?"

"I have to go." He puts on his jacket and stands up.

I'm not going to press for an answer. I remember reading the record that showed he didn't have psychosis when he was admitted to this unit. "I'm trying to help you. Is there something I can do to make you more comfortable? I am very concerned about you wanting to leave without help. Can I get you a snack or some water?"

He remains silent, straps his bag over his shoulder, and walks out of my office.

I quickly retrieve a Section 12 document and fill it out, noting specifically his homicidal and suicidal ideation. I sign it and fax it to the police. I call the police to tell them about what I just faxed to them. The police dispatcher asks me to describe Greg's appearance. About five minutes later, a police officer calls me and asks me to meet him outside. He wants me to ride along with him in his car to help identify Greg. I briskly walk outside and get in the officer's car.

Within ten minutes, we locate Greg on a sidewalk just a few blocks away. We find several police officers putting away their guns as they surround him. Greg's hands are up over his head. His bag is on the ground, getting searched by an officer. I never learn whether they find a weapon in there. Nevertheless, we are lucky. I offer to call an ambulance to take Greg to a hospital emergency department. The police have already done this, and he is on his way to containment. The story demonstrates why this work is important.

All residents of Massachusetts can access mobile emergency teams and crisis units. When the mobile emergency service model was created, the state was divided geographically so that each catchment area would have a mobile emergency services team with crisis unit beds.

A crisis unit is an ideal solution for someone who does not qualify for inpatient treatment yet would not be safe to remain home, on the streets, at a homeless shelter, or anywhere else outside of the hospital. Although the crisis unit is staffed continuously, it is significantly less supervised and structured than an inpatient unit. It cannot provide close and constant supervision of any patient. There is no locked door. Thus, any patient can easily leave.

A crisis unit also cannot manage a patient's physical withdrawal symptoms from stopping the use of any prescribed controlled substance, illicit drug, or alcohol. Instead, formal detoxification units are designed to manage this need.

Despite these shortcomings, the greatest benefit of the crisis unit is how quickly a patient can access psychiatric medication prescribed by a psychiatrist or advanced nurse practitioner. A patient who is admitted to the crisis unit can begin to take psychiatric medication or have her medication adjusted. Staff members administer all medication, which adds a layer of supervision. This ensures the safety of any patient who is suicidal and plans to overdose on prescribed medication. Generally, I can admit a patient to a crisis unit if she is physically able to take care of her basic grooming. A patient who is organized enough to execute such simple tasks is likely to be safe on this unit. Crisis units lack the ability to include locked doors and contain danger. They also lack the degree of supervision available on inpatient units.

* * *

The main purpose of any inpatient unit is containment of danger involving the substantial risk that a patient will do serious harm to herself or another person or is unable to care for herself adequately. The unit's role is to prevent the advancement of danger daily, using supervision and therapeutic techniques issued by psychiatrists, advanced nurse practitioners, nurses, social workers, mental health counselors, and occupational therapists. At first, supervision of patients is continuous and close, and then it typically tapers down as the risk of danger abates. Although the police can restrain someone who becomes physically out of control, legal standards do not allow mental health professionals to restrain any patient outside of the hospital. On an inpatient unit or hospital emergency department, danger can be abated by medication intended to sedate and reduce anxiety. A patient can access new medication and have medication adjusted much more quickly on an inpatient unit or hospital emergency department than on a crisis unit. This is a primary consideration when deciding that the crisis unit is not enough to ensure safety.

The lack of capacity to secure and contain danger outside of the hospital is precisely the reason that I hesitate to admit anyone to the crisis unit who is rapidly pacing, highly restless, or too impulsive. The crisis unit is simply not secure enough for a person in this condition. I have learned to examine the degree of agitation when I have difficulty deciding whether a patient with psychosis could be safe on the crisis unit. I once worked on an inpatient unit with a nurse who taught me that when deciding whether a patient needs to be restrained, the patient's deteriorating ability to listen to others is telling. If the patient can no longer listen, her self-control is dissipating.

I usually do not admit to the crisis unit any patient who's disoriented to person, time, or place. The exception is if she had previously been admitted to the same unit frequently enough to feel comfortable with the unit and its immediate surroundings due to familiarity. I would not admit anyone who's too agitated or whose psychosis is interfering with her ability to form a basic sentence. This type of patient can be unpredictable. I do not admit anyone who has a suicidal plan of hanging. One of the most lethal suicide attempts is hanging. Death can occur and often does occur within fifteen minutes. Throughout my experience as an inpatient social worker, I witnessed three suicide attempts involving hanging and am aware of two deaths on inpatient units from suicide by hanging. Even inpatient units are not always safe.

In the zeal to impeccably protect the patient's civil liberties and rights, an increasing number of troubled and psychotic patients are what I choose to term dying with their rights on.

—Darold A. Treffert, M.D.,[5] Director, Winnebago Mental Health Institute (retired); Executive Director of Inpatient and Outpatient Services, Fond du Lac County Mental Health Center (retired); Clinical Professor of Psychiatry, School of Medicine and Public Health, University of Wisconsin – Madison (retired); Research Director, Treffert Center, Agnesian HealthCare; Award recipient, Lifetime Achievement, Envision Greater Fond du Lac; Award recipient, 2017 Badger of the Year, Wisconsin Alumni Association, University of Wisconsin; Award recipient, 2006 Torrey Advocacy Commendation, Treatment Advocacy Center; Member, Fellow, and former Officer, American Association of Psychiatric Administrators, American Psychiatric Association, and American College of Psychiatrists

CHAPTER 3

Tribute to Farron

W HEN HOSPITAL AND AGENCY administrators and legislators state that mentally ill people are no more likely to become violent than those in the general population, it is akin to a meteorology professor telling his students that most hurricanes don't cause much damage. If I were a meteorology student, I would not be properly educated. Tropical cyclones, more commonly referred to as hurricanes, are rated from categories one to five. Category five storms cause the most damage to life and infrastructure, and category one storms cause the least damage. From 1851 to 2006, a total of two hundred seventy-nine hurricanes struck the mainland of the United States. Only twenty-one, or approximately 8 percent of these, were rated as category four or five.[6] From 1851 to 2014, Florida was hit by a total of thirty-seven category three or higher hurricanes,[7] while only twelve or fewer of these were category four or five.[8] In 2005, Hurricane Katrina, ranging from category four to five, was one of the deadliest hurricanes ever recorded in the United States. More than 1,800 people died because of this monster. The government faced over $100 billion worth of structural damage.[9]

As a meteorology student, I would expect to be informed about the possible devastation by category four and five hurricanes, despite their low prevalence, before learning about category one, two, and three hurricanes. The most destructive hurricanes should be prioritized. An instructor who glosses over category four and five hurricanes because they are less common is neglecting to teach how communities can prepare for the possibility of such devastation and prevent loss of life and money.

Likewise, while the prevalence of schizophrenia in the entire mentally ill population is slight, its effects can be devastating. Until November 2017, the National Institute of Mental Health (NIMH) estimated that 1.1 percent of the adult population had schizophrenia.[10] Toward the beginning of 2018, NIMH remarked that just .3 percent of the population in any given year had schizophrenia.[11] From 2016 to 2018, there was no advancement in how schizophrenia was treated. No cure for schizophrenia banished it from existence. Therefore, the statistical drop in the prevalence of schizophrenia that NIMH reported was astounding. According to the Treatment Advocacy Center, NIMH's drop in prevalence to .3 percent indicated that it failed to account for two million schizophrenic people.[12] The federal government is expected to exercise *parens patriae*—Latin for "parent of the country"—for the most psychotic population. The government should have an ethical, legal, and moral obligation to care for its people. It is stunning to realize that the NIMH refused to acknowledge the existence of up to two million schizophrenic people. Later in the same month, NIMH changed the prevalence statistic again, this time stating that less than 1 percent of the population had schizophrenia.[13]

While I do not know the details of Farron Barksdale's care in Alabama, I doubt that a crisis unit outside of an inpatient setting would have been enough to prevent him from killing two police officers on January 2, 2004. I interviewed Mary Barksdale before she died, and she told me about her son Farron. I then interviewed Phillip Barksdale, who told me about his brother Farron.

Farron's ability to care for other people and animals was admirable. His humor was remarkable. Phillip said that Farron cycled through varying degrees of psychosis. Farron trusted Phillip and their mother sometimes. Farron was suspicious of everyone at other times. Mary said the government did nothing to ensure that Farron took his professionally recommended medication. When she attempted to secure inpatient commitment for him, the state-appointed judge who heard her testimony refused to grant it because he believed that doing so would have been a waste of money. The judge was also upholding the law and concerned about Farron's civil liberties.

While Mary was at her place of employment, Farron was visiting her home. He called 911 asking for help from the Federal Bureau of Investigation (FBI) because he believed that aliens were attacking him. He told the 911 dispatcher that he wouldn't be able to know the difference between the fake police and the real police. Two police officers, Sergeant Larry W. Russell and Officer Tony Mims,[14] arrived at his mother's home. Farron killed both of them in her driveway using a rifle. Farron had never been violent before this tragedy.

Farron was unaware of his psychosis during this tragic incident. He was not alone. In Ohio, one hundred twenty-two schizophrenic patients who were violent were compared with one hundred eleven schizophrenic patients who were not violent. The violent patients had significantly less insight into their psychosis than the nonviolent ones.[15] Researchers studied sixty-three schizophrenic patients who were receiving inpatient care in Spain and found that lack of insight into psychosis most predicted violence.[16]

At the time of this tragic incident, Farron was suffering from schizophrenia and had not used any illicit drug for approximately two years. His toxicology screen immediately following the incident was completely negative, and he had not consumed any alcohol that day. Although he had never become dependent on alcohol and had never abused it days in a row, he occasionally drank alcohol. He did this to help him get to sleep whenever his auditory hallucinations kept him awake for days.

Despite inpatient mental health professionals' recommendations that he take medication outside of the hospital, Farron was unmedicated during this tragic event because he was not aware of his psychosis. The judges, inpatient units, and outpatient teams who knew him allowed this status to go on—not due to any bad intention but due to policies and laws. They did this by not involuntarily admitting him to inpatient units often enough, by discharging him from inpatient units prematurely, and by not ensuring that he took his medication. It's reasonable to assume that they put too much emphasis on Farron's civil liberties and did not sufficiently consider the liberties of others. These officers' liberties vanished along with their lives. The public and law enforcement personnel are at risk of harm when seriously mentally ill people are not adequately treated. In this case, an overemphasis on Farron's rights was a disservice to the officers, and they paid for it with their lives.

Following this tragic day, Farron was given the antipsychotic medication Haldol while he was jailed for three years and seven months awaiting trial. This is an extraordinarily long time to spend in a place designed for criminals. Was Farron truly a criminal? According to the legal standards set forth by Alabama—yes. According to Mary, Phillip, and me—no.

Farron then spent three months on an inpatient psychiatric unit to obtain a determination of whether he was competent to participate in his trial. There, a state psychiatrist declared that he was competent. For an unknown reason, this psychiatrist changed his diagnosis from paranoid schizophrenia to psychosis—not otherwise specified, even though countless previous psychiatrists had diagnosed him with paranoid schizophrenia. According to Mary, Farron's psychiatric medication was discontinued, despite evidence showing that this medication helped him. The reason for this decision is also unknown.

After competency was determined, the hospital psychiatrist no longer saw any reason for Farron to receive further inpatient care. He returned to jail, where he stayed for six more months. During this time, his psychosis worsened because he was unmedicated. His lawyers asked him if he wanted to accept a plea bargain. Farron sensed that regardless of the direction he took, he would never reside outside of a secured setting—prison or inpatient—again. He replied to the lawyers in the affirmative because he wanted to spare his family the ordeal of a trial that would have lasted for several weeks. Farron agreed to a guilty plea bargain while his family didn't have the authority to intercept. The final trial lasted just one day, and the jury and judge found him guilty. The judge sentenced him to life in prison without the possibility of parole.

After the trial, Farron's psychiatrist in prison ordered medication to decrease his psychosis. This medication came with a warning about its use in excessive environmental heat. Excessive exposure to heat could result in a negative reaction to the medication. Farron was placed in a cell with no air conditioning or circulation while the outside temperature rose to one hundred eight degrees. This was the cause of his death. Mary successfully sued the state for maltreatment of Farron by the prison system.

Farron was unstable and not competent when he killed the two police officers. If he had been court-ordered to take antipsychotic medication for treatment of his schizophrenia, he probably would not have killed them. Following this deadly incident, the ideal legal and psychiatric systems would have allowed Farron to serve his sentence on a locked inpatient psychiatric unit rather than in a jail or prison. He would have been protected with the correct diagnosis and consistently prescribed antipsychotic medication. No one would have allowed him to agree to a guilty plea bargain. He would have not been found guilty because of insanity. Perhaps if inpatient criteria were not as restrictive as they are, or if more inpatient beds were available, Farron would have received adequate treatment to maintain a stable life. Three lives unnecessarily ended due to schizophrenia that was left therapeutically unmanaged because of the notion that civil liberties trump safety.

CHAPTER 4

Roots

WHEN EXAMINING THE DETAILS of Farron's life, it's obvious that our mental health system is broken. He revolved through inpatient units just as repeatedly as many of the patients I encounter. Many patients on my inpatient caseload often got readmitted quickly after their discharges, sometimes within two months. At times, patients were discharged prematurely under pressure from mental health insurance plans. Sometimes, it seemed as if they were released too soon just because they didn't want to be there.

When I send a patient to the hospital emergency department and the patient is released on the same day, rather than moved to an inpatient unit as I expect—the system is broken. When a patient waits two weeks for an inpatient unit to accept her without receiving adequate treatment at a hospital emergency department—the system is failing. Although psychiatric consultations can occur in hospital emergency departments, they cannot mimic the comprehensive interdisciplinary treatment of inpatient units. Non-psychiatric physicians are vastly limited in their capacity to provide these patients with psychiatric care. Many of them lack sufficient training in psychiatry. All of them lack adequate time to act like psychiatrists for these patients while attending to the array of medical demands in the rest of the emergency department.

When the Department of Mental Health (DMH) closes the case of a person with schizophrenia who refuses to engage in treatment because she does not recognize that she is ill—the system is not working properly. When a patient believes that if she drinks any water, she will be tortured, and as a result dies from dehydration after refusing to engage with rehabilitative outreach workers—the system is not functioning as it should. When someone who refuses to take her antipsychotic medication for almost a year kills someone else because she believes that her victim was planning to kill her first—the system is broken. When a person jumps off the roof of a ten-story building in response to commanding hallucinations after not taking any of her psychiatric medication for months—the system is inadequate.

The goal of the mental health system is to provide comprehensive care to mentally ill people. This system includes an array of interdependent and interacting groups, organizations, law enforcement agencies, hospitals, and private practitioners that combine to form a whole. The mental health system includes crisis units and staff-supervised residential programs. More specific levels of care designed to help mentally ill people include DMH-funded or private inpatient units, Adult Community Clinical Services, and Program of Assertive Community Treatment (PACT) teams. The system also includes courts and, unfortunately, an increasing number of jail and prison beds. It includes professionals such as administrators, psychiatrists, psychologists, nurses, social workers, master-level emergency clinicians, occupational therapists, residential counselors, vocational rehabilitation specialists, housing specialists, primary care physicians, coaches, judges, licensed mental health counselors, teachers, professors, advanced nurse practitioners who can prescribe medication, mental health insurance clinicians, state and federal legislators advocating for or opposing the passage of bills, and police officers.

Case managers and peer specialists are also part of the system. Case managers facilitate and support patients' access to psychiatric, housing, vocational, social, and educational services that are intended to improve their overall quality of life. Case managers refer patients to such services and resources based on individual needs and preferences as well as broker community resources. They coordinate treatment services, update treatment providers (e.g., psychotherapists, social workers) on individual progress or concerns, advocate with these providers for improved care for patients, and provide support to the family members and friends of mentally ill people.

Peer specialists are not clinically trained. Their main role is to provide support to patients. Peer specialists socialize with patients; ensure that staff members have enough paper, pens, and other office supplies; and engage in other menial tasks requiring no clinical skill. I've recently seen an increase in the use of peer specialists by mental health agencies. Meanwhile, I've also seen the mental health system increasingly neglect patients who are most psychiatrically impaired. The Transformation Center supports the advancement of peer specialists. Its Certified Peer Specialist Training Application includes the following prerequisite: no college education is required with a "history of psychiatric diagnosis, or experience with emotional distress or trauma resulting in significant life disruption."[17] The peer specialist role is a relatively new addition to the system.

* * *

An overemphasis on seriously mentally ill people's civil liberties didn't always exist in the United States. Exploring the past can help us understand how the mental health system evolved into its current configuration. Beginning in 1752 in the United States, insane patients were contained inhumanely at the Pennsylvania Hospital. The most agitated and violent of these patients were shackled to immobile structures for days and left to sit in their bodily excrements. In the 1800s, after witnessing the suffering of large numbers of mentally ill people in jails, homeless shelters, and on the streets, Dorothea Dix wanted to help alleviate that suffering. She observed the deplorable physical and mental conditions in which mentally ill people were housed in various institutions that were not designed to care for them. She was also appalled at the treatment of patients in asylums, which were designed to care for the mentally ill—and this further motivated her to work for change.

In 1833, Worcester State Hospital in central Massachusetts opened as the first government-funded psychiatric hospital. Dorothea lobbied legislators throughout the United States for the creation and advancement of state asylums that would treat mentally ill individuals in a humane and supportive manner. By the late 1880s, she had facilitated the opening of countless state psychiatric hospitals throughout the country. Asylums were intended to offer protection from the misfortunes that these individuals were especially prone to, including victimization, crime, and poverty.

Just as state hospitals were growing in bed capacity and new state hospitals were opening, the political tide turned. The practices of lobotomies and electroconvulsive therapy grew toward the end of the 1930s. A lobotomy often resulted in decreased aggression and agitation. It's well known that the procedure fell out of use and favor long ago because it inflicted brain damage. Electroconvulsive therapy was initially used to treat psychosis, and currently, it is primarily used to treat severe depression. Plans to eliminate beds and hospitals, referred to as deinstitutionalization, took root in the 1940s. In 1954, the first antipsychotic medication, Thorazine, was created to reduce psychosis and agitation. The government aimed to minimize the financial cost of treating the mentally ill population, considering that institutional care was more expensive than outpatient care. Mental health professionals and government officials expected that lobotomies, electroconvulsive therapy, and medication would allow mentally ill patients to reside outside of hospitals by reducing their symptoms safely. As a result, vast numbers of seriously mentally ill patients were discharged, and outpatient treatment options were increased.

In the late 1950s, California led the United States in transferring patients from state hospitals to alternative settings such as unlocked residential programs. In 1955, there were an estimated 3.3 million seriously mentally ill adults in the United States.[18] Toward the end of the 1950s, there were only about 560,000 patients on inpatient psychiatric units throughout the country.[19] In 1967, California passed the Lanterman-Petris-Short Act, which grossly restricted the criteria for which people could be involuntarily admitted to inpatient units. Interestingly, California then became the first state to have an increase in homelessness, incarcerations, and violence.[20] An estimated 30 percent of the chronically homeless population has a serious mental illness.[21]

In 1963, during the John F. Kennedy Administration, Congress passed the Community Mental Health Services Act. In brief, its purpose was to cut financial costs for states by closing entire state-operated hospitals. Grants were provided to open outpatient mental health agencies instead. Federal administrators justified doing this by promoting their belief that with adequate supervision and support, most mentally ill people could successfully reside outside of hospitals. However, deinstitutionalization did not result in the great outcomes that it promised. Inadequately treated and untreated serious mental illness is highly correlated with homelessness, criminalization, and violence.

As the state beds emptied, homelessness, arrests, victimization, and violence rose among a portion of the patients who were discharged.

* * *

Let's suppose that a pendulum symbolizes the degree of secured confinement to protect seriously mentally ill patients from harm. The high number of inpatient beds in the 1950s represents a suspension of the pendulum's weight at one extreme, with no gravity to pull it downward. Toward the end of the 1950s, gravity began to pull the pendulum away from the end and toward the middle. The Massachusetts DMH was still overprotective to the extent that liberties were violated—some people were inappropriately hospitalized involuntarily, and others were held too long on inpatient units without foreseeable probability of discharge.

Despite a substantial increase in the overall United States population since the 1950s, there were only 77,000 patients on inpatient psychiatric units in the United States by the fall of 1996.[22] By 2006, there were approximately 40,000 mentally ill people in state hospitals.[23] The United States eliminated approximately 6,000 psychiatric hospital beds between 2010 and 2016.[24] By 2016, fewer than 38,000 state inpatient beds were available for 8.1 million seriously mentally ill people.[25] Gravity has allowed the pendulum to swing to the opposite end of the spectrum: the number of government-funded inpatient beds in the country has dropped by at least 96 percent since the 1950s.

Decades before the average inpatient length of stay shrank to approximately one week and the number of inpatient beds dropped to a critical low, the legendary psychiatrist Darold Treffert made this observation in 1973: when clinicians made psychiatric decisions, the rights of patients to be free were given priority over the rights of people closest to these patients to be protected from harmful actions caused by serious mental illness. He emphasized that the rights of both groups should be given equal consideration.[26]

Before the number of available inpatient beds further declined, psychiatrists in the 1970s cautioned their peers about overemphasizing the rights of their patients. According to Dr. Treffert, prioritizing a patient's autonomy can have disastrous results. For instance, a forty-nine-year-old woman in Wisconsin was admitted to an inpatient medical unit with anorexia. Although she did not have psychosis, her judgment was abysmal, as she continued to lose weight due to inadequate eating. She requested permission from the physician to leave the hospital against the advice of her family. The physician asked the court to allow for involuntary admission to a psychiatric unit. Overemphasizing her right to autonomy, the judge denied the request. Three weeks later, she died from starvation "with her rights on."[27]

The DMH's role as protector of the seriously mentally ill population declined as inpatient beds were eliminated. I do not wish to return to the inhumane treatment of the mentally ill population at Pennsylvania Hospital in 1753 or Worcester State Hospital in 1833. But in recent decades, the pendulum has swung too far in favor of keeping mentally ill people out of inpatient psychiatric hospitals. Since the 1970s, Massachusetts has closed ten psychiatric hospitals, leaving thousands of people to grapple with their mental illnesses in an insufficient outpatient system.[28] The population of Massachusetts as of April 1, 2010, was 6,547,629. As of July 1, 2016, the population was an estimated 6,811,779 (an increase of approximately 4 percent).[29] In 2010 in Massachusetts, there were a total of six hundred ninety-six state hospital beds. Since then, eighty-eight of these beds have been eliminated, leaving just six hundred eight state hospital beds by 2016 (a drop of over 12 percent).[30] The state's increase in population inevitably involved an increase in seriously mentally ill people. Nevertheless, the network of inpatient units and hospitals declined, resulting in an insufficient supply to meet the demand for inpatient psychiatric care.

The pendulum's swing has endangered lives. In 2016, the Spotlight Team of *The Boston Globe* wrote a series of articles titled "The Desperate and the Dead" exposing the dysfunctional mental health system in Massachusetts. In 2017, the Spotlight Team was a Pulitzer Prize Finalist in Local Reporting for the series.[31] The series pointed out that the elimination of inpatient beds increased police involvement with the seriously mentally ill population. *The Boston Globe* learned from the Boston Police Department that calls about emotionally distressed people increased from approximately 2,800 in 2008 to approximately 3,400 in 2014 (an increase of over 20 percent).[32] Without enough inpatient beds and an adequate outpatient system, seriously mentally ill people are inevitably abandoned. Without treatment, they are more likely to show poor judgment and act in ways warranting police involvement.

According to *The Boston Globe*, the outpatient mental health system of Massachusetts is shattered, especially for the most severely mentally ill people. The professionals who are expected to help them often end up neglecting them instead. Rather than getting needed treatment, extremely unstable people often interface in challenging ways with their families, police officers, prison staff members, courts, and homeless shelters.[33] The patients who suffer the most are those who are the most impaired and who are unaware that they are ill and need treatment. They are more likely to decline offers of treatment or to fail to initiate treatment than those who are aware of their illnesses.

The autonomy of patients should not *always* be paramount when clinicians plan for treatment or when patients decide they don't want any treatment. A former clinical supervisor once cautioned everyone in a staff meeting that Section 12s violate clients' rights and should be used sparingly. He emphasized that when deciding whether to authorize involuntary holds, clinicians should consider primarily if anyone will imminently die without them. In his view, unless serious injury or death is expected to occur immediately, a Section 12 is not warranted. Clinicians follow that instruction out of fear of being reprimanded. As a result, the agency develops a trend of hesitating to authorize Section 12s. Far from promoting a preventive attitude, this threshold for danger can have deadly consequences—not necessarily immediately, but eventually. As treatment is delayed, illnesses progress and brains deteriorate, making it harder for patients to recover.

Schizophrenia, in and of itself, is not a dangerous illness. There are many schizophrenic patients who don't need to be incarcerated, who can be managed safely in the community; however, there is a second part to that. When your delusion, your fixed delusion, tells you to kill people, and when your lack of insight doesn't allow you to cooperate with treatment, then schizophrenia becomes dangerous. In such a case, schizophrenia can be an extremely dangerous illness if left untreated.

—KENNETH CASIMIR, M.D., ASSOCIATE MEDICAL
DIRECTOR, WINNEBAGO MENTAL HEALTH INSTITUTE,
WISCONSIN DEPARTMENT OF HEALTH SERVICES

CHAPTER 5

Schizophrenia

The difference between serious mental illness and minor mental illness lies in the degree that the illness interferes with a person's ability to meet his routine and ordinary demands of life. In 2013, the federal Substance Abuse and Mental Health Services Administration (SAMHSA), a branch of the United States Department of Health and Human Services, estimated that 4.2 percent of the United States adult population had a serious mental illness.[34] In 2015, the National Institute of Mental Health (NIMH) estimated that 4 percent of the United States adult population had a serious mental illness.[35]

Deinstitutionalization served well the high-functioning people who had the mental capacity to seek outpatient support services voluntarily. They were capable of safely functioning using outpatient treatment to help them manage their symptoms. Before deinstitutionalization, some of them remained hospitalized for years while stable. Perhaps many of them recovered from psychosis or were not psychotic to begin with. Psychosis is a faulty sense of reality and is at the core of schizophrenia. There was no mechanism in place to push anyone to abide by outpatient treatment recommendations, but this high-functioning group didn't need it, anyway.

Deinstitutionalization did not appropriately serve the people whose disabilities interfered with their capacity to initiate outpatient treatment. This group largely involved seriously mentally ill people, particularly those with psychosis. Although a variety of serious mental illnesses can be debilitating, little surpasses the effects of losing one's connection to reality.

Serious mental illness *without* psychosis, including anxiety, depression, or mania, is more likely to be managed properly than serious mental illness *with* psychosis. Psychosis with awareness is more likely to be managed properly than psychosis without awareness. When a patient is unaware of his psychosis, the system often expects him to decide whether to seek treatment independently. Without awareness, it is too easy for him to avoid treatment.

Some readers may not be familiar with the specific signs of psychosis. I would like to prepare them for the clinical vignettes that are described in later chapters. Schizophrenia involves abnormal alterations of thinking, emotions, and behaviors. The core symptoms of schizophrenia include hallucinations, delusions, and disordered thinking. A hallucination is a perception that is not based in reality, and it can include any or all the main five senses—vision, smell, touch, hearing, and taste. A delusion is a false belief held despite contradictory evidence. Disordered thinking is thinking that is illogical. The thought process can be highly disorganized in schizophrenia. Subcategories of thought process and content in schizophrenia include derailment, illogicality, disorganization, echolalia, phonemic paraphasia, alogia, clanging, incoherence, and neologisms. In addition, motor behavior can be disorganized or abnormal.

Other symptoms of schizophrenia are more closely associated with emotions and behaviors. These include decreased verbalization, difficulty starting or maintaining behaviors, and flat or blunted facial expressions. Additional signs include decreased concentration or difficulty comprehending concepts. Although these symptoms can occur because hallucinations distract a patient, they also can be a function of cognitive deficit. Research shows that poor insight into mental illness often correlates with deficient cognition.[36]

Intrinsically, a person with minimal to no insight into his mental illness is cognitively disadvantaged. The person is less likely to understand the implications of his illness. He has difficulty understanding that proper psychiatric treatment would help him and that lack of treatment would be detrimental to his ability to function. It can be futile to use rationalization and reason to persuade someone battered with psychosis to accept treatment, especially if he is not taking his medication. The NIMH estimates that in any one-year period, 40 percent of schizophrenic adults have not undergone treatment.[37]

The most frequently recommended treatment for schizophrenia is antipsychotic medication, which can be prescribed by psychiatrists, physician's assistants, primary care physicians, or advanced nurse practitioners. Psychotherapy can teach and remind patients about healthy coping strategies for dealing with a range of problems, especially when schizophrenic patients are stable after acute episodes or between acute episodes. Psychosocial rehabilitation services can be extraordinarily helpful to schizophrenic patients.

Although scientists are uncertain about what causes this disease, most scientific evidence points to biological factors. There are clear anatomical differences between normal and schizophrenic brains, according to countless sources. Certain genes might raise a patient's risk of developing schizophrenia. Knowing that schizophrenia is biologically based enhances psychoeducation to patients and their families or friends.

Schizophrenia is a serious mental illness with no cure. In the wide range of psychiatric pathology that I encounter, it is the most devastating and virulent mental illness of all. Deinstitutionalization did not serve well schizophrenic people who lacked awareness of their psychosis.

CHAPTER 6

On the Fence

SOMETIMES IN EMERGENCY psychiatry, I evaluate
patients who do not qualify for inpatient treatment but are displaying
moderate chances of harming themselves or others, or of not being able
to attend to their basic needs adequately. At times I can predict that
a Section 12 (involuntary transfer to the hospital due to danger) or a
clash with law enforcement will occur soon. But foresight is not a solid
argument when deciding whether someone qualifies for Section 12 in
Massachusetts. There aren't always clear indicators that point me to
either side. When patients straddle the fence between Section 12 and
remaining safely in the community, I use my best judgment along
with my instincts.

Many schizophrenic patients do not meet inpatient criteria and
can reside outside of hospitals for years. The reasons vary widely. When
none of the Section 12 qualifications are met, treatment providers
can arrange for outpatient support services instead. Alternatively,
admission to crisis units could be enough to alleviate the main concerns. Although many patients on inpatient units show a reduction in

psychosis and increased mood stability because of treatment, many do not follow through with outpatient treatment recommendations. This often results in relapse and readmission to the hospital.

Cross-institutionalization has correlated with the large-scale elimination of inpatient beds. Often, lack of compliance with the outpatient recommendations made by inpatient teams leads to arrests[38] and incarcerations.[39] As of September 2016, researchers estimated that ten times more seriously mentally ill people were in jails and state prisons than in state psychiatric hospitals in the United States.[40] When needed mental health treatment is insufficient or missing, a patient's judgment declines. When judgment declines, the patient is more likely to commit a crime, intentionally or unintentionally, that leads to an arrest. During periods of instability, a patient experiences limited problem-solving ability or becomes impressionable. The woman who drowns out her distressing auditory hallucinations with alcohol becomes loud and disruptive at a supermarket, resulting in her arrest. An elderly woman's delusional beliefs interfere with her ability to keep up with rent payments, which renders her homeless. In a blizzard, she cannot find a place to rest her head aside from a building that she thought was abandoned. She is then arrested for trespassing.

Although he still lacks some insight into his psychosis, Mitchell, forty-five years old, has eventually come to realize that something is psychiatrically amiss. He has gradually figured this out after being transferred countless times among various units within the Massachusetts Department of Correction (DOC) and Department of Mental Health (DMH). He realized he was mentally ill when he was repeatedly arrested for assaulting others in response to commanding auditory hallucinations. He gathered that he was different from most people after he was involuntarily admitted to inpatient units more than thirty times in nine years.

I meet Mitchell in the office on the same day that he is released from prison. He tells me that a DOC staff member has instructed him to be psychiatrically evaluated, but he offers no reason for this. The DOC never contacts me. His latest legal charge included using a knife to stab his friend in the leg. I read in the record that he was charged at least seven other times with assault and battery, which often resulted in strangers being injured without provocation. One of these assaults involved a police officer. The record also shows a variety of other charges, including armed robbery, petty theft, trespassing, and driving a car with a suspended license.

I communicate lots of reassurance that I intend to help him. After telling me about his latest stint in jail, Mitchell says that DOC staff members were expected to call the pharmacy to fill his prescription for psychiatric medication. When he went there to get it, the pharmacy staff knew nothing about this and had no medication to give him. He struggles to explain the purpose of the medication that he last took.

Without understanding the benefits of medication, a patient has a high risk of not complying with medication protocol. Without awareness of and insight into illness, a patient has a considerable risk of relapse. Some schizophrenic or bipolar-disordered people learn to take their psychiatric medication despite lacking insight into their psychosis. For instance, they may have figured out that there's a correlation between not taking psychiatric medication and being hospitalized.

Family members have pressed their loved ones to take medication, as seen in another case. Harry, forty-four years old, and his parents tell me about the financial arrangement involving bribery between them. His parents initiated it years ago out of desperation because all other attempts at persuading him to take his prescribed antipsychotic medication had failed. The parents regularly pay their son under the condition that he take all his medication. They pay him in cash, housing, and food. When I ask Harry what the medication is for, he cannot provide a logical answer. Yet, it is obvious to me that he has psychosis.

Regardless of the measures taken that contribute to medication adherence, taking needed medication is usually healthier than not taking it. I wonder how Mitchell would pay for the medication, if it were available, considering he has no income. He explains that his Medicaid benefits could cover some of its cost. I reassure him by saying that if there's a bed available for him on the crisis unit, he could receive new psychiatric medication quickly.

I want to admit him to the crisis unit because I know that his psychosis will likely worsen without any supervision or support. He has no money, no phone, no family, and no home. Mitchell has no outpatient psychiatrist, no advanced nurse practitioner, no primary care physician, no psychotherapist, and no supportive outreach worker. He is not involved with DMH.

In a somewhat guarded manner, Mitchell tells me about his history of having commanding auditory hallucinations telling him to kill random strangers. He reveals that he stabbed his friend in the leg because someone ordered him to do it. He can't describe who this was and appears to realize that this was a hallucination. He goes on to say that his hallucinations commanded him to seriously injure random people. He doesn't target anyone whom he wants to harm. He cannot identify any means of how he'd harm anyone. He expresses no intention to harm anyone else.

I ask if he has ever killed anyone. Mitchell is unable or unwilling to answer this. I avoid pressing for more information. I tell him that I'm on his side and won't judge him. This facilitates his revelation that he heard "Joseph" instruct him to kill three cats. He followed through with this. Tears well up in his eyes. I tell him that he was sick when he did this.

He tells me about his history of having commanding auditory hallucinations telling him to kill himself. He hasn't been suicidal recently, but he attempted suicide twice long ago, by hanging himself and overdosing on medication. He's not suicidal now. He cannot describe his mood after I ask him about his mood. He often smiles inappropriately.

He accepts my recommendation of crisis unit admission and allows me to make a few phone calls to the DOC and the pharmacy to track down his medication. He waits for the follow-through of this in a general waiting area just outside of the office, out of my view.

I call the DOC, and someone tells me that Risperidone and Cogentin were called into a pharmacy. I call this pharmacy, which is part of a large outpatient clinic, and ask for the whereabouts of the medication. The pharmacy staff member tells me that whenever a jail sends a prescription, the prescription is trashed if it is for a patient who has not previously registered with the clinic. Even though Mitchell has never registered with this clinic, this practice of discarding prescriptions is negligent. I ask to talk to a supervisor to inquire about the clinic's justification for doing this, but I am given only the option of leaving a voicemail for the supervisor. The DOC is not able to authorize a new prescription for this medication, even after I explain that the pharmacy had discarded the original order.

I plan to update Mitchell about this. I also expect to tell him that a bed is available for him on the crisis unit and that he will be admitted shortly. But when I go to the waiting area, he's gone.

A couple of years go by, and again I evaluate Mitchell in the office after he refers himself at the suggestion of a family member. This time, he says he had been living with a relative who had asked him to leave because the home was too crowded. He was uncomfortable sleeping at the loud and chaotic homeless shelter. Instead, he has been sleeping in abandoned buildings, in stairwells, or outside over the last three days.

I notice in the record that about two weeks ago, he was psychiatrically evaluated at a hospital emergency department every day for a week. Excessive waiting periods for hospital emergency department patients result in lost revenue for hospitals.[41] Hospital revenue is based more on the number of patient admissions than the patients' length of stays. Insurance reimbursements to hospitals do not increase throughout length of stays. When patients wait at hospital emergency departments excessively for inpatient beds, typically referred to as boarding, this prevents new patients from getting admitted. Imagine walking into a restaurant, hungry for dinner, without making a previous reservation. As you wait and increasingly become impatient, you notice that some seated guests are lingering long after they've finished eating, and just chatting. They don't pay the restaurant for the time they spend; they just pay for their food and drinks. The restaurant would rather increase its revenue with a higher turnover of customers.

When medical doctors prematurely release patients from hospitals, the decision is likely related to administrative pressures aiming to increase revenue. During the week that Mitchell was confined to the hospital emergency department, mobile emergency staff members conducted inpatient bed searches, to no avail. Every inpatient unit in the state and a few inpatient units in surrounding states declined to accept him for admission, likely due to his history of violence against others. I suspect that the inpatient units did not want the potential legal risk that could accompany staff members or other patients getting injured by an aggressive or agitated patient. Likely related to administrative pressure, the hospital emergency physician was unwilling to continue waiting for a bed to become available and discharged him to the streets with no outpatient follow-up.

Remarkably, Mitchell tells me that he knows that physically assaulting others would interfere with his ability to get help. He knows the system. Even though he recently experienced auditory hallucinations instructing him to assault others, he has learned to control himself. He has told himself repeatedly that these were not real voices. Previously, he felt as though a demon possessed him or as if a puppeteer controlled him.

Today, he requests new psychiatric medication since he ran out of it again without any refill. He tells me that the medication helped to "calm the voices" and reduced their intensity. I am impressed when he tells me that despite having no means of transportation, he started researching mental illness at the public library. The crisis unit admits him.

The crisis unit course is short, usually lasting less than a week. There is a high chance that Mitchell will interface with police officers again. They will either authorize a Section 12 or refer him to mobile emergency psychiatry.

Most of the cases that I manage with police officers involve psychotic patients. Officers refer cases to me, and I require their assistance in executing involuntary transfers of agitated or aggressive patients to hospital emergency departments. I assess patients in holding cells immediately following their arrests.

A police officer calls me for advice about someone on the police department's radar who resides in her own apartment. This person excessively calls the police, complaining that her neighbors are stealing her belongings and physically assaulting her. The police officer tells me that she has been making such calls several times per week for the last couple of weeks and has gone as far as inappropriately calling 911. The police officer says that they investigated these complaints and found no evidence that they were valid.

We head off together to this patient's apartment. A clinical assessment done in a patient's residence is the purest type of assessment. There are great benefits to evaluating someone in her natural environment. It is impossible to capture exactly how someone lives when you see her in an office. At a patient's home, I see the garbage that hasn't been removed for weeks. I readily observe prescription pill bottles that have been picked up from the pharmacy months ago but not touched since then.

Sara, forty-one years old, lets us in without any hesitation. She does not appear underweight. I don't smell anything foul. It appears that she has an excellent ability to attend to her hygiene and grooming. I see no clutter. Her belongings are neatly organized and clean.

Before I question her about whether she's suicidal or homicidal, she blurts out, "I'm not suicidal. I'm not homicidal. I don't need to be sectioned." By using the word "sectioned," she means that she does not wish for a professional to authorize a Section 12 for her. Her knowledge of these terms indicates that this is not the first time she has been psychiatrically evaluated. Perhaps she was involuntarily transported to a hospital in the past. She reveals in an unhurried manner that this happened when police "made me go to the hospital because they said I was hearing voices. I really wasn't."

Sara tells me that she has indeed been trying to persuade the police to arrest her neighbors for physically assaulting her last week and stealing her belongings. Wearing a sleeveless shirt, she shows me her arms, pointing to what she believes are bruises. I don't see anything outstanding on her arms—nothing that resembles a bruise. She tells me that she knows neighbors have been stealing from her because whenever she returns home from errands or work, she notices that objects have been moved, and she has not moved them. While I know these are delusions, I do not dispute these reports. Doing so would be futile.

I ask her about her medical background. Sara tells me that years ago, a doctor injected a flu vaccine into her upper arm and it made her sick. She elaborates by saying that even though she was vaccinated only once, the effects remained in her for years thereafter. She says that this injection made her extremely energetic for fifteen minutes per night, usually around the same time. During these periods, she cleaned her apartment. She has been prescribed only a medication to control her blood pressure, and she admits she is not taking the medication because of her belief that this also made her restless. Her ex-boyfriend physically assaulted her years ago, resulting in the fracture of her jaw and nose. Despite how horrific this sounds, she does not show any sign of post-traumatic stress disorder (PTSD) and doesn't have any negative feeling toward him.

Sara's speech rate is fast, her thoughts seem to be racing, and she is speaking excessively. She describes her mood as frustrated, irritable, and anxious, which she attributes to the police not acquiescing to her requests to deal with her neighbors. She is not agitated. She has not been prescribed any psychiatric medication and does not have a psychiatrist or advanced nurse practitioner. Sara is not receiving rehabilitative outreach services. I am not startled because this is not an anomaly.

Although there is no cure for mental illness, medication typically plays a key role in alleviating its signs and symptoms. Nonadherence to antipsychotic medication substantially increases the risk that patients will experience the following behaviors or outcomes:

+ suicide

+ instability

- violence

- inpatient admission

- use of emergency services

- arrest

- victimization

- use of illicit drugs or alcohol[42]

When patients do not adhere to medication, we expect an increase in rates of criminalization, homelessness, and premature death.

Sara tells me that she has no positive social support. The only family member who remains in contact with her is her mother, whom she describes negatively.

I educate Sara about the benefits of the crisis unit and offer this to her. She declines to accept this, expressing her belief that it would not help her. All she wants is for the police to get rid of the neighbors who are causing trouble for her.

I offer to make a referral to an outpatient clinic for her. She declines this, too. She says that this would be useless because she doesn't have a mental illness. Although she undoubtedly would benefit from receiving DMH-related services outside of a locked setting, such as rehabilitative outreach services, it is impossible to connect her to this option if she doesn't want it. No DMH eligibility application can be accepted without the signature of the patient or her legal representative, such as a legal guardian or doctor-invoked health care proxy.

There are moments when I can predict disastrous human costs due to the dysfunctional system but have no legal ability to prevent them from happening. Without treatment, Sara will probably continue to contact the police inappropriately and excessively. A Section 12 cannot be authorized just because I predict that the police department's resources will be burdened. There's no doubt that she is at risk of being assaulted by her neighbors due to her intrusiveness and the false accusations she makes about them, but I cannot authorize a Section 12 for this, either.

Sara tells me that she volunteers in the cafeteria of a nursing home, arranging flowers to put on tables and helping residents grow flowers. Her delusions are not interfering with her ability to attend to her basic biological needs. Her refrigerator is well stocked with nutritious food. She has been sleeping well lately. She is coherent. She accurately tells me the current month, date, season, her date of birth, and the town we are in. I wish her luck and say goodbye.

*There has probably never been a worse place
and worse time to have a severe mental
illness than now in the United States.*

—ALLEN FRANCES, M.D., PROFESSOR EMERITUS OF
GENERAL PSYCHIATRY, DUKE UNIVERSITY SCHOOL OF
MEDICINE; FORMER CHAIR, DEPARTMENT OF PSYCHIATRY,
DUKE UNIVERSITY SCHOOL OF MEDICINE; FORMER
CHAIR, *DIAGNOSTIC AND STATISTICAL MANUAL OF
MENTAL DISORDERS-FOURTH EDITION* TASK FORCE;
AUTHOR, *SAVING NORMAL: AN INSIDER'S REVOLT
AGAINST OUT-OF-CONTROL PSYCHIATRIC DIAGNOSIS,
DSM-5, BIG PHARMA, AND THE MEDICALIZATION OF
ORDINARY LIFE;* AUTHOR, *TWILIGHT OF AMERICAN
SANITY: A PSYCHIATRIST ANALYZES THE AGE OF TRUMP*

CHAPTER 7

Borderline Personality Disorder

Borderline personality disorder is common on inpatient and crisis units, and in emergency settings. Would the borderline personality-disordered population have been better served if this disorder were classified as a serious mental illness rather than just a personality disorder in the *Diagnostic and Statistical Manual of Mental Disorders-Fourth Edition*? Despite the misleading label, borderline personality disorder is a serious mental illness. People with this disorder are easily dysregulated emotionally and have difficulty soothing themselves using internal resources. Difficulty in regulating their emotions often leads them to act impulsively. Superficial self-injurious behaviors, such as cutting, are common. They tend to have intensely unstable relationships involving idealization and devaluation of others. Thought distortions are common. They can be overly sensitive to signs of social rejection. Although environmental factors might play a role in whether someone develops the disorder, research studies show that 60 percent of the risk of developing this disorder is related to genetic predisposition.[43]

The following characteristics of borderline personality-disordered people that I've observed in clinical settings are not apparent in all patients. However, they are the most common and outstanding characteristics that I have noticed on both inpatient and emergency settings.

+ Suicidal gestures. These fall between wanting to kill themselves and making suicide attempts. A suicidal gesture can include holding a knife close to one's wrist. I think of the teen who often ties clothing around his neck in the presence of residential staff members—and does so just loosely enough to avoid losing consciousness, but tightly enough to cause concern.

+ Intentional superficial self-injury. A man's arms are scarred with nerve damage from self-induced cutting. Borderline personality-disordered people tend to intentionally cut their wrists or arms superficially with no intention to die.[44] Rather, their goal is to provide relief from emotional distress.[45] This relief is often short-lived, which leads to further self-mutilation. They are often readmitted to inpatient or crisis units.

+ Accidental death. For example, a man overdoses on pills forty-five times while passively suicidal. He accidentally dies from his forty-sixth overdose, passively suicidal again.

+ Suicide attempts with a high probability of rescue—in front of others. I recall a woman who hanged herself on an inpatient unit. Staff members quickly interrupted her attempt.

✦ Inability to identify any *new* precipitant that contributes to their worsened mental functioning. For example, a young adult reports having a conflict with his loved ones again.

✦ Passive suicidal ideation without any suicidal plan at baseline (usual functioning). For example, every night at bedtime, a man prays that he will never wake up.

✦ Intense wish to be admitted to inpatient units when they don't qualify for this level of care. A significant number of them appear desperate to enter. It's more important than with other patients to divert these patients away from inpatient and not enable this desire.

An estimated 75 percent of borderline personality-disordered people who attempt suicide do so in nonlethal ways at least once. A higher percentage of this group engages in self-injurious behavior, especially while hospitalized.[46] This is the reason many experts recommend against granting these patients inpatient admission, especially in response to self-injurious behavior.[47] Inpatient treatment for this population could be inefficacious,[48] as self-injurious behavior on inpatient settings is common.[49]

Offering admittance to the crisis unit can sometimes be used as a compromise when patients are inappropriately pressing for inpatient admission. Crisis units do not provide the extent of supervision, support, and structure that inpatient units do. Nevertheless, they can provide just enough comfort that patients need.

CHAPTER 8

No Intention to Die

Many sources indicate that 10 percent of borderline personality-disordered people die from suicide.[50] Other sources estimate that the rate of suicide completion by this population is 8 to 10 percent.[51] It is common for them to have suicidal thoughts and make many suicide attempts.[52] Roughly 60 to 70 percent of them make suicide attempts.[53] The most common method of suicide attempts among this population is overdosing on pills, and the act is commonly triggered by interpersonal conflicts.[54]

The main difference between a suicidal gesture and a suicide attempt is that a suicide attempt involves at least some intention to die, and a suicidal gesture involves no intention to die. The person who engages in a suicidal gesture may think, "I couldn't care less if this kills me," while injecting a little more heroin than usual with other addicts and Narcan less than ten feet away. This is vastly different from someone climbing to the rooftop of a building that is 1,700 feet high and jumping off.

In Massachusetts, a patient needing long-term Department of Mental Health (DMH) inpatient care typically first enters an inpatient unit that is not state-operated. That is, unless the patient needs a forensic evaluation on a DMH inpatient unit for a determination of whether she is criminally responsible for a crime or not guilty due to serious mental illness. The unit holds the patient until a state bed becomes available. Many patients on my inpatient caseload who were waiting for entry to DMH inpatient units were borderline personality-disordered. Among those patients waiting for this type of transfer, this disorder was the second most common, behind illness involving psychosis.

It once struck me as odd that borderline personality disorder would be this common among patients waiting for DMH inpatient care. After all, this is a personality disorder, not a serious mental illness, according to the *Diagnostic and Statistical Manual of Mental Disorders-Fifth Edition* (DSM-5). These patients often were not depressed or manic. They typically were not psychotic. So why were they frequently getting admitted to the most intensive and restrictive level of inpatient care?

Borderline personality disorder is serious because it involves a high risk of accidental self-inflicted death. The danger lies in the frequency of suicide attempts or gestures, which can be unpredictable. If the person with the disorder doesn't get what she wants because of attempting suicide or engaging in suicidal gestures, she can "up the ante" and raise the level of lethality risk. The patient is most dangerous when she has recently increased the potential lethality of her self-injurious behavior.

I usually do not grant inpatient admission to a patient who desperately wants to be admitted to inpatient, hasn't recently engaged in serious self-injury, and doesn't have a suicidal plan. On the other hand, I ensure that a patient who swallows an object other than food or medication, such as a pen cap, is transferred to safe confinement.

Rebecca, forty-five years old, with borderline personality disorder, demands that I grant her an inpatient admission when she does not meet the criteria for it. Although passively suicidal, she functions safely. Lately, she has been sleeping and eating enough. She has neither harmed nor threatened to harm herself or anyone else recently. I try, to no avail, to redirect her to using healthy coping strategies. She continues to press me for an inpatient admission until she pours large handfuls of pills into her mouth, gradually swallowing them in my view. The result she wishes for materializes, and she is admitted.

What is so appealing to her about inpatient units that she would be willing to do just about anything to be admitted? Does she not have enough outpatient care and support? I'm not sure. Is functioning normally outside of inpatient units so anxiety-provoking that she feels compelled to sabotage herself? Perhaps. Even though personality disorders are, by formal definition, less problematic than major mental illnesses, the only mental illness that this patient presents is borderline personality disorder.

* * *

A counselor on the crisis unit reports to me that Maggie, thirty-seven years old, was admitted yesterday directly from a state-funded DMH inpatient unit. The counselor tells me that Maggie told her and other staff members that although she was suicidal and planned to overdose on her medication, she wanted to be discharged prematurely from the crisis unit. Reluctantly agreeing to remain on the unit, she consents to meet with me. She tells me that she is not having any active thoughts of suicide, but she was more suicidal just hours before meeting me. She says that she was contemplating a request for discharge so that she could attempt suicide by overdosing on her many bottles of medication. She wants to cut herself.

Maggie tells me that she's depressed and that the depression worsened hours ago. She tells me about the stressors in her life immediately before her latest psychiatric hospitalization. She still hates her residential situation. She continues to complain about her finances. None of these are new stressors.

The last time that she swallowed an object besides food was four days ago while on a DMH inpatient unit—she swallowed a hair band. She said that an inpatient medical admission wasn't needed because the problem was resolved at the hospital emergency department.

We discuss various coping strategies that Maggie could try to improve her mood and decrease her desire to cut herself or to swallow objects. She tells me that drawing has soothed her. I encourage her to try this again. She tells me that she doesn't want to kill herself because she doesn't want to hurt and abandon her sister and nephew.

I remind her about the benefits of dialectical behavioral therapy (DBT). DBT has long been considered the gold standard treatment for borderline personality-disordered people. Developed by psychologist Marsha Linehan, DBT teaches patients how to regulate their emotions and alter their thoughts about situational triggers in ways that prevent maladaptive behaviors, such as superficially cutting themselves. The main behavioral skills that DBT teaches include mindfulness, distress tolerance, interpersonal effectiveness, and emotion regulation.

Although patients can employ formal individual and group DBT sessions, they can easily access self-help workbooks both online and on paper from bookstores. Therefore, patients can't use many fair excuses for not learning and implementing these skills.

Maggie can't remember when she last tried to use DBT, but she believes it has been months since she worked on it. I encourage her to work on this and give her some paper sheets of exercises from this modality.

Maggie has just completed two lengthy courses on inpatient psychiatry. The clinical record shows that in the last two years, she has been admitted to inpatient psychiatric units thirteen separate times. Her arms bear permanent scarring from the many times that she has cut herself, and she occasionally has cut herself deeply. The last time she intentionally cut herself, which resulted in a superficial cut, was approximately ten weeks ago. Although she has never attempted to hang herself, she was admitted to critical care units of hospitals several times due to severely overdosing on pills. The last time she tried to kill herself, which was about eight months ago, her attempt involved pills. During this suicide attempt, she overdosed on forty Benadryl capsules. Today, she tells me that when she medically recovered from that attempt, she was disappointed that she was still alive.

I ask her if the thought of suicide brings her a sense of relief or fear. She tells me that she's afraid of death. This answer is less risky than saying she would be relieved. Except for someone who's very religious, such as a priest, fearing death is a protective factor.

Her baseline involves passive suicidal ideation with intermittent urges to superficially cut herself. She is functioning at her baseline today. I recommend that she remain on the crisis unit. She agrees to use the DBT handouts. She tells me that she will not attempt suicide and agrees to stay on the crisis unit. She agrees to talk with a staff member if her level of suicidal ideation increases.

I speak with the crisis unit staff members about this, and they agree to work with her plan to stay. Several hours later, they inform me that because Maggie threatened to elope from the unit to overdose on pills from a nearby pharmacy, she is at a hospital emergency department awaiting a psychiatric evaluation. These patients can be highly unpredictable.

* * *

When preparing to evaluate Barbara, thirty-five years old, I see in her clinical record that she has been admitted to the crisis unit and various inpatient units more than fifty times in the last ten years. Reasons for these admissions ranged from voicing suicidal ideation to attempting suicide. I agree to meet Barbara at her home with her rehabilitative outreach worker. The outreach worker refers her to me because she has expressed a desire to kill herself by drinking all her liquid cleaning supplies at home.

Barbara's apartment is immaculate and organized. I praise her for this. She tells me that she has many bottles of cleaning liquid, perhaps twenty of them. She tells me that she has been feeling hurt by various family members who've emotionally abused her. She doesn't report having experienced any new precipitant. She tells me that she's depressed but barely elaborates about this. She reports having mild insomnia lately. No psychosis is evident. She was severely abused both physically and sexually as a child, and she reports having flashbacks and nightmares daily relating to past trauma. Part of her baseline is to experience such signs of PTSD.

Her baseline also involves wanting to superficially harm herself and wishing she were dead. She has cut herself superficially and burned herself with lighters over one hundred times. Besides wanting to drink the cleaning supplies, she tells me that she wants to burn herself. She burned her leg with a lighter yesterday and earlier today before meeting me. Before yesterday, the last time she engaged in this behavior was three months ago. She tells me that she has also occasionally swallowed paper clips and staples. She couldn't be more specific about the frequency of harming herself because she has done this so many times that she has lost count.

She has engaged in almost-lethal suicide attempts in the past, including overdosing on her medication. Therefore, all her medication is locked in a box with a code known only by the visiting nurses. She has been taking these as prescribed. Barbara made another suicide attempt years ago by drinking liquid cleaning supplies until she lost consciousness. The last time she tried to kill herself was about eight months ago while she was on an inpatient unit. During this inpatient course, she swallowed three paper clips and attempted to hang herself with a sheet from her bed. On the same inpatient unit, she then attempted to swallow a pencil and attempted to strangle herself by tightly tying a shirt around her neck.

Today, Barbara expresses a sense of relief at the thought of suicide, and this expression itself increases her risk of suicide. She tells me that her positive feelings toward her two-year-old nephew wouldn't prevent her from killing herself because "he's so young that he'd forget I did anything." She believes that God and an afterlife exist. Although this lowers the risk of suicide, she is unsure if this belief would prevent her from killing herself.

Barbara's use of healthy coping skills appears highly limited. I remind her about the benefits of DBT work, which she dismisses. She tells me that she will not work on DBT because it never helped her in the past. She couldn't remember when she last worked on DBT material. I gently press for an estimated timeframe. She admits that she hasn't done any DBT work in the last five years.

She is most at risk of seriously harming herself by accident. I propose that she be admitted to the crisis unit, knowing that she won't have access to any cleaning supplies there. She agrees to this, and she is admitted to the unit. Several hours later the same day, she is discharged to her home at her request after meeting with the unit's clinician and promising not to kill herself at home.

* * *

The prevalence of suicide attempts and death by suicide probably contributed to the National Institute of Mental Health's (NIMH) conclusion that borderline personality disorder is a serious mental disorder.[55] If it were considered a major rather than a minor mental illness in the DSM-4 and DSM-5, it would induce a more sobering view of this disorder by mental health professionals, psychiatric and psychological researchers, stakeholders, and, most importantly, borderline personality-disordered people. Federal grants for research into how to treat this mental illness might be awarded to psychiatrists and psychologists more often if this disorder were viewed as more serious. Borderline personality disorder should be transferred out of the realm of personality disorders and receive formal classification as a serious mental illness.

What kind of "freedom" is it to be wandering the streets, severely mentally ill, deteriorating, and getting warmth from a steam grate or food from a garbage can? That's not freedom; that's abandonment.

—DAROLD A. TREFFERT, M.D.[56]

CHAPTER 9

Police

I'M AT A DEPARTMENT of Mental Health (DMH)-funded residential program and conclude that an involuntary transfer to the hospital via Section 12 is needed for Jessica, who is forty-two years old. Her delusion is that feces is in food, which prompts her to avoid eating. She cannot listen to staff members encouraging her to eat her lunch. She cannot concentrate and is highly distracted by her hallucinations instead. I cannot gather what exactly these involve because she is guarded. The staff members tell me that she has lost thirty-eight pounds in just six weeks. She emphasizes, "Feces is in there. They won't remove it!" She cannot elaborate on how she came to conclude this.

The ambulance crew asks us what her current medications are. Almost in unison, the residential staff members and I state that she has no prescribed medication because she has not wanted any for months. Despite our attempts to persuade her to cooperate with the ambulance crew, she won't budge. She yells, "I'm fine. I don't need to go to the hospital!" as she becomes restless before slumping on the couch.

Four police officers arrive to assist. I tell them why Jessica needs to go to the hospital. Two of them approach Jessica and introduce themselves, expressing an interest to help. Their attempts to persuade her to go to the hospital don't work. As the officer glances and points at me, he highlights, "They said you're delusional. There's no feces in your food. You have to go to the hospital." Jessica suddenly picks up a nearby ceramic vase and attempts to throw it at me. The officers quickly immobilize her using their arms. They handcuff her as she curses and screams.

If the officer had known that delusional patients often lack insight, perhaps he would not have chosen such a brutally honest approach. He might not have disputed her belief that the food is contaminated. Jessica's lack of insight is impenetrable. The officer is not part of a specialized Crisis Intervention Team (CIT).

CIT police officers have completed forty hours of mental health training. This teaches the officers how to verbally de-escalate potentially volatile encounters with mentally ill people. The main aim of the CIT is to help people avoid being arrested and instead access mental health treatment.

Traditional police training might increase the risk of fatalities with its push for rapid solutions.[57] This approach might not allow sufficient opportunity for officers to listen to people in crisis. If an officer's approach is too authoritarian, the person in crisis might react impulsively out of increased fear. Empathizing with him is more likely to result in more trust, less defensiveness, a decrease in fear, and a willingness to collaborate cooperatively.

The first CIT in the United States was formed in Memphis, Tennessee, in 1988 as a reaction to a tragedy in that city.[58] On

September 24, 1987, a relative of Joseph DeWayne Robinson called the Memphis police because Joseph, twenty-seven years old, was posing a danger to himself and others. It was believed that Joseph had paranoid schizophrenia. Police officers found him holding a large knife. He threatened to harm others seriously and cut himself. Failing to cooperate with the officers' demands to let go of the knife, the man charged the officers. Police officers believed their lives were in danger. A police officer shot Joseph repeatedly, killing him.[59] This event provoked outrage and generated a movement toward the CIT model.

Suicidal threats, regardless of whether psychosis is involved, often involve police confrontations. *The Boston Globe* reviewed police reports involving suicidal people in Massachusetts and the District Attorney's reports of fatal shootings. In 65 percent of the shootings involving apparent mental illness, the weapon was a sharp object, such as a knife. In 13 percent of the shootings, police shot people holding firearms. They found that 90 percent of the people who were shot by police did not drop their weapons when ordered to do so.[60] *The Boston Globe* found that many of these confrontations with police could have been prevented. For instance, some of these cases involved premature discharges from inpatient psychiatric units or a lack of enough support for mentally ill people.[61]

The faulty mental health system has forced law enforcement personnel to do the work that mental health professionals stopped doing. Law enforcement officers interact so frequently with people in psychiatric crisis that they can authorize Section 12s. For example, a young adult being prescribed antipsychotic medication refuses to take his medication and consequently threatens to seriously harm the family with whom he resides because he believes that they are plotting to kill him. His mother calls the mobile emergency services team to request that a clinician come to their home to evaluate him. But if he is not agreeable to this, no clinician can see him at home.

Moments later, he pulls a knife on his mother and threatens to harm her. She successfully persuades him to drop the knife and calls the police for help.

Familiarity with such cases is ingrained in officers. As expected, all police officers are required to have a basic knowledge of mental illness. But most officers are not part of CITs. They are not sufficiently trained in managing the breadth of mental illness that exists outside of secure settings. Most police departments in Massachusetts do not have CIT programs due to funding limits and shift coverage.

Many of the CIT programs that do exist in Massachusetts are limited, involving too few CIT-trained officers.[62] The Memphis CIT recommends that 20 to 25 percent of police officers become CIT-trained.[63] According to *The Boston Globe*, only about 20 percent of Massachusetts police departments provide major mental health crisis training to officers or obtain help from social workers for mental health cases.[64] Not nearly enough officers have gained the skills required to identify subtle signs of mental illness and to placate mentally ill people who might be at risk of becoming violent. Cooperation with treatment recommendations for this population is more likely to occur when police officers are proficient in managing interactions with these people.

CHAPTER 10

Deterioration

PSYCHIATRIC HOSPITALS were commonly referred to as asylums (defined as "that which protects") because they protected patients from the inherent harm of unsecured environments. One of the reasons that state hospitals emptied their beds was that, in some cases, people were involuntarily committed inappropriately. Massive numbers of people were discharged to their own resources because of increased concern by courts for their civil liberties. Fortunately, there are legal safeguards in place to prevent the violation of patients' civil rights from happening in modern times. But what are the consequences of out-of-control hypervigilance and unfounded fear about hospitalizing the mentally ill? Too many inpatient units close. Consequently, many people who are psychiatrically deteriorating and who need the protection and care of confinement are abandoned.

* * *

A police officer refers me to Becky, forty-one years old, who was arrested three times on the same day. I evaluate her in a holding cell at the police station. The short-term holding cell is always the step immediately after an arrest and prior to extensive jail, or prior to a person's release on paid bail—unless a police officer authorizes a Section 12 or emergency medical attention is needed. Becky doesn't understand why I am meeting with her; her only concern is not being late for her expected professional performance as a singer that night. This is one of her delusions. Although she does not desire any mental health treatment, I am concerned when I observe her intense eye contact and disordered thinking along with loud and rapid speech. She strings words together loosely and without logical connection.

Over the span of three years, I repeatedly documented Becky's symptoms in her clinical record for inpatient units to review. There is extensive documentation that she was unable to protect herself from basic harm due to untreated and profound psychosis. Later, I learned that Becky was stabbed to death on a sidewalk while presumably suffering from psychosis and without medication. Toward the end of her life, the government closed Becky's case due to her nonadherence with treatment. Did the DMH consider that she refused to accept treatment offered to her because she did not believe that she had a mental illness? Probably not.

I prepare to go to the police station to meet Dante, twenty-five years old. His record shows that he has a history of not complying with his antipsychotic medication and of experiencing auditory hallucinations commanding him to act dangerously. He had repeatedly called police with complaints about someone who attempted to kill him and who physically assaulted his mother. On this day, he became so enraged that he went to the police station and demanded the arrest of this alleged perpetrator. When he arrived, the police realized that he was probably delusional when they could not confirm the existence of the person about whom he was complaining. When the officers were unable to meet his demand to arrest this person, Dante refused to leave the police station.

When I introduce myself, his facial expression indicates bewilderment. He tells the police officer and me that he doesn't understand why I'm involved. After all, he just wants justice to be served.

I'm about to engage with someone who's paranoid. To increase the chance that he will view me as a credible professional, I show my work identification badge and say that I just want to get to know him a little because the police expressed some concerns and requested help. We sit near each other in a private area at the police station, and I note that Dante displays good hygiene.

He tells me that Ken punched him in the face approximately two weeks ago.

"That's horrible. How do you know him?" I ask.

"I don't. We never met until he targeted me." He clarifies that their first interaction was during this assault, which happened on a sidewalk.

He becomes guarded and barely says anything over the next few minutes. When patients are having difficulty revealing themselves, it can be helpful to ask open-ended questions and provide gentle commands, such as "Please tell me." I employ those techniques. He eventually expresses his belief that Ken is plotting to kill him.

I ask, "What makes you think this?"

"I get mail every day from him with clues. Like the other day, he sent me a photo of a dog that was killed. There was blood everywhere around the dog. It was lying down."

He also tells me that recently he has been experiencing increased auditory hallucinations, which have involved hearing people make condescending statements about him.

"Do these people tell you to do anything?"

He refuses or is unable to respond.

"When did you start feeling scared for your life?"

"I don't know. Two weeks ago?"

After Dante permits me to contact his mother, Carina, I ask the police officer to supervise him while I step away to call her.

Carina tells me that she fears for her safety at home and immediately recommends that he be admitted to an inpatient unit. "Just today, he threw a lamp across the room, shattering it into a million pieces," she says. She believes that he has become increasingly delusional, with more auditory hallucinations, over the past two months. She confirms that he has not been getting any unusual mail.

"What are some signs that he's been having auditory hallucinations?"

"When he doesn't know I'm around, I sometimes catch him talking to imaginary people. Yesterday, he punched his fist through a window, breaking it. He's been punching the walls every day." She again begs me to connect him with treatment and says, "This is not him."

I ask Carina whether Dante has ever physically assaulted her.

Carina says yes, Dante was arrested approximately ten months earlier for an assault that resulted in moderate injuries. She says he had pushed her, which made her fall to the floor. As she lay there, he kicked her in the stomach numerous times. She described herself as "lucky" because her begging him to stop hurting her somehow prompted him to stop long enough for her to reach the phone and call the police. She physically recovered from this incident. She tells me that he has been taking all his prescribed medications, including the ones for psychosis.

I rejoin Dante, who seems to be enjoying a snack and water that the police have given him. I ask him what his medications are being prescribed for.

"My anxiety. Voices."

We talk about how the PACT workers recently have been helping him. I ask him if he has ever physically assaulted anyone else.

"Nope. Never."

I offer the crisis unit to him, which he quickly refuses to consider; he is not interested in being admitted to an inpatient unit, either. I write up the Section 12 and arrange for the ambulance to arrive. After many attempts by the officers, ambulance crew, and me to persuade him to cooperate and his many threats to return home, he eventually cooperates with us. They transport him to a hospital emergency department. Later, I notify his PACT worker, including his psychiatrist, about the plan for an inpatient bed search.

A rehabilitative outreach worker drives Nicole, forty-three years old, to my office. Nicole is thin, has messy hair, and is casually dressed. I do some rapport building, including explaining my role, and she tells me that she filed a report with the police last week against people who have been harming her. I ask her to elaborate on this.

"They won't let me eat … They drug me, so I can't chew. I can't swallow any food because my throat closes from the drugs they give me."

Nicole can't explain how they managed to force her to ingest drugs. Eventually, with gentle prompting and reminders that I intend to help, she reveals that they injected her when she was asleep. While she slept, they stole her belongings. She goes on to report that they stole her personal identification card and money directly from her bank account. She doesn't know who they are, and she cannot state how they accessed her bank account. She is terrified of them.

Nicole has been evicted from numerous apartments. I suspect it could be at least partly attributed to psychosis because records indicate that property owners became fed up with her complaints about people breaking into her apartment. Since her latest eviction, her residential situation has been transitory. When a friend who had allowed her to stay there for a while told her that she had to leave, she slept outside. When the weather became unbearably cold, she climbed into an unlocked parked car on a rental car lot. She slept there and snuck out before workers arrived in the morning.

Nicole was admitted to and then discharged from the crisis unit within the same week about one week ago. When I ask why she was admitted, she identifies homelessness as the only reason. She expected the crisis unit to resolve her homelessness and didn't understand that she was admitted for other reasons. By health insurance standards, clinicians cannot use homelessness as the main reason to admit a person to the unit.

Suddenly, she tells me that she works closely with the President of the United States, who allowed her to take a leave of absence. Her thought process is disorganized, and she makes loose associations. "Phone." A few minutes later, "Gloves." The words are unrelated to any topic of conversation between us. Her eye contact is fierce. Her body movements are restless. She periodically stands up to pace. Without any apparent purpose, she loudly bangs her hand against the wall.

She acknowledges not having taken any of her prescribed medication for the last few weeks, and she is unable to give a specific timeframe. Her rehabilitative outreach worker believes it might have been months since she last took any medication.

She reports that it has been months since she last used any cocaine or alcohol. She has never had a problem with excessively using any substance.

Although she is not homicidal, she voices vague aggressive thoughts against the people who she believes have been harming her. According to her record, she physically pushed a stranger in a hospital parking lot about one year ago. At the time of this incident, she had recently used cocaine and was not taking any medication. The outreach worker tells me that she almost physically assaulted a member of his team earlier that day. I ask Nicole if this happened.

"He was taking their side! That is fucked up! They're supposed to be helping me!"

Her ability to sleep is questionable. She says that she has slept for only one hour in the last few days. The last time she ate anything was three days ago. The last time she drank any water was earlier that day. Curious about how she would account for the ability to swallow water, I point out, "Swallowing food cannot be done because of these people drugging you. How were you able to swallow water?"

"The drug doesn't stay in me all the time. It wears off after a while." She clarifies that she has been able to eat and drink during lapses of drug inducement.

I praise her for attending her latest outpatient appointments with her psychiatrist. Her outpatient psychiatrist is not available to talk to me, so I leave a voicemail message for her.

Nicole never acknowledges that she has psychosis and has had this for years. She tells me that she has never hallucinated. This may be true, but she does not believe that she is delusional. I ask her what the psychiatrist has been helping her with.

"Trauma." Nicole tells me that caregivers physically and sexually abused her as a child.

I inquire about any signs of post-traumatic stress disorder (PTSD). The only symptom that Nicole reports is flashbacks.

I state that she has been on the crisis unit more days than not over the last two months, while her outreach worker has become increasingly concerned about her ability to care for herself.

"Put me in there," Nicole says, referring to the crisis unit.

"I can't. This hasn't worked out. It seems you haven't been acting like your usual self these days. I believe a hospital could help you."

Nicole threatens to elope prematurely from our interview. Somehow, I manage to persuade her to remain. After ordering an ambulance, I persuade her to cooperate with ambulance staff members. They transport her to the hospital emergency department on Section 12.

The Crisis Intervention Team (CIT) police officers and I go to meet Kate, fifty-five years old, at her apartment. Kate's bedroom is connected to a common area shared by other patients in a rehabilitative outreach program. This common area includes a kitchen and lounge with tables, couches, and a television. In preparing to meet Kate, I review her record and talk with her rehabilitative outreach worker.

The court has appointed Kate a Rogers Monitor. A Rogers Monitor is someone the court appoints to ensure that an incapacitated patient is medicated in conformity with a court-approved treatment plan. The court can also grant an already established legal guardian additional authority—that is, Rogers authority. This can be authorized when a person is not capable of providing informed consent regarding being prescribed antipsychotic medication due to her mental illness.

Any person, facility, agency, or hospital can petition for Rogers authority, but an affidavit must be submitted to the court by a licensed physician, psychiatrist, or certified psychiatric nurse clinical specialist. The affidavit explains the clinical rationale for this request, along with a detailed listing of recommended antipsychotic medication. The court then approves a treatment plan, which specifies ranges of medication that the patient must adhere to. At a minimum, a judge must review the Rogers treatment plan annually. It can be reviewed more frequently, such as every ninety days or every six months.

Kate has a history of being prescribed a variety of antipsychotic medications. However, outside of inpatient units, she has been largely noncompliant with taking any prescribed medication. During one of these periods, she physically assaulted her roommate. Although the injuries she inflicted were minor, the incident prompted police involvement. Over the past twelve months, she has been briefly hospitalized on inpatient units four times. The staff members tell me that she's gotten better at covering up her psychosis. It's possible that employing this scheme allowed her to appear stable to the inpatient psychiatrists, and this led to quicker discharges. The outreach workers tell me that Kate has also refused to see any advanced nurse practitioners or psychiatrists for months.

The Rogers Monitor's foremost flaw is translucently clear. It is nearly impossible to enforce a Rogers Monitor outside of an inpatient setting. Imagine if someone engages with a rehabilitative outreach worker to receive packages of medication at her home and then she adamantly refuses to take any medication. No outreach worker has the authority or capacity to do anything to change this. Outside of hospital emergency and inpatient settings, no outpatient staff member in the mental health system has the authority to force a patient to take medication. As a result, patients are often left to act based on their own free will. There are no consequences for patients who refuse to take their medication as ordered by their Rogers Monitors. Rather than undergo psychiatric evaluations ordered by courts, they are left to deteriorate.

Although Kate usually refused to take any medication offered to her in the last year, there was a brief period when she did take it. This lasted for a mere month immediately following her last inpatient stay. Today, she is not functioning at her baseline. Since she started refusing to accept her medication again, she has been increasingly agitated and delusional. This has manifested in her accusing staff members of contaminating her food. About one month ago, she physically assaulted a roommate again. And again, the injuries she inflicted were minor, but police had to get involved.

Kate is thin and well-groomed, and she is still wearing her pajamas in the late afternoon. She is smart. She completed some college. Her cat appears well cared for and nourished. She prides herself on regularly cleaning her bedroom and common area. After praising her for these strengths, I ask about her ability to eat lately.

"I have to throw out a lot of it. It all goes bad." She elaborates by stating that recently she has felt the need to do this daily. Moments later, she tells me that she has been eating well. When I point out the discrepancy, she becomes verbally abusive toward me. She bangs her hand hard on the table and yells profanities at me.

After I help to de-escalate her behavior, she blatantly states, "I'm not mentally ill." She cannot tell me why her last psychiatric medication was prescribed. The last time that Kate was hospitalized on an inpatient unit was approximately three months ago. When I ask her about the reason for this, her only reply is, "Because my mother wanted me there." This is interesting because her mother has been deceased for years. She describes her mood as "fine." This contradicts her affect, which portrays anger.

"Does the food spoil fast?" I ask curiously to gain clarification.

Rather than answering my question, she talks about something irrelevant. Does she lack the capacity to listen? I rephrase my question.

"God knows what they put in there. I can't trust them to handle my food." In between her replies to my questions, she continuously whispers or says things inaudibly. Her lips move to create words as dictated by her brain, but I don't hear anything coming out of her mouth.

I ask her if she has ever heard any voice that seemed odd.

She tells me this has never happened.

"How do you know that stuff is going into your food that shouldn't be there?"

"My mother tells me."

I recommend inpatient hospitalization. Although she disagrees with this, she physically cooperates and doesn't need to be restrained by the police officers. I suspect that the presence of the officers is a core reason for her compliance. As I'm writing up the Section 12, I hear her occasionally speaking loudly in a nearby room. The outreach workers report to me that their supervisors intend to ask the next inpatient team to hold Kate long enough for them to transfer her to a DMH-funded residential program, which would provide more supervision and support than she's receiving now. She was residing in a group residential program until about two years ago when she transitioned to her current living situation.

Clinically premature discharges of patients to less restrictive levels of care—or no level of care—are commonplace. The DMH-funded residential programs discharge some of their residents to largely unsupervised apartments. Although they tout improvement in patient functioning as the main reason, I wonder if it is partially fiscally motivated. Or it might be due to a lack of sufficient community services to meet the clinical demands outside of hospitals. Regardless, it follows the mantra that mentally ill people should reside in the least restrictive and least professionally supervised setting possible. But psychotic deterioration sometimes follows.

I see in her record that Kate has a legal guardian who is an attorney. She did not have a family member or friend available or willing to pursue legal guardianship for her. I place a call to this guardian to update her on my clinical determination for Kate. I try calling both phone numbers listed for her brother, to no avail. When I call the first one, the phone rings for about a minute before I hang up. The second phone number is wrong. No other family member is listed on her record.

I go to meet a nurse and Lily, thirty-five years old, at an agency designed to alleviate homelessness by providing medical, psychiatric, and substance-dependence services to homeless people. The nurse reports to me that a bystander contacted this agency to express concern about Lily. The bystander had observed her sleeping outside and yelling bizarre statements to no one in particular. Some concerned citizens found Lily sitting in a road where cars easily could have struck her.

Lily's appearance is unkempt. Her long blonde hair is in a tousled bun. She has a cloth bag with a ragged handle. She is wearing loose-fitting pants, moccasins, and a blouse. There are random stains on her bag, blouse, pants, and shoes. She presents no problem with illicit drugs or alcohol. She tells me that she intentionally became homeless two years ago because a spirit she refers to as "Crystal" ordered her to do it. She says, "Crystal doesn't want me to get hurt. She said it's okay." More recently, she realized that she'd be safer in stable housing. It's possible that she concluded this because she was assaulted, or her personal belongings were stolen. An estimated 25 percent of mentally ill people are victimized with thefts or assaults each year.[65] Schizophrenic adults are more likely than their peers without schizophrenia to be victims of violence.[66]

There are few records about Lily available to me. Just about six months ago, she migrated to Massachusetts from Maine "because Crystal told me to," she explains. Unable to report having any financial income, she reveals that she has a total of $1.25, which she spreads out before us on the table. She expresses her belief that all her family members are dead. She is unable to name any friend.

After empathizing with her and expressing my desire to help her, I ask, "What are you hoping to get from emergency services?"

Lily wants a safe home of her own, food, water, and money. "If I stay inactive, Crystal will find me a home. She didn't allow me to have a home."

I ask for clarification. Her sense of humor remains intact, and she is very pleasant and easily engageable. Lily explains that Crystal has been talking to her through trees, plants, the cracks in the ground outside, and "there are animals that she chose." She tells me that she knows how to identify these animals. She occasionally laughs for no apparent reason. She expresses her belief that certain animals were born with telekinesis. An animal shelter employed her when she first arrived in Massachusetts. Lily identified special animals with this power to customers who wanted to adopt animals. Although she no longer has this job, she sometimes delivers animals that she believes have been "chosen" for animal shelters because "they need the extra protection."

Lily has never been suicidal. She has never intentionally injured herself, assaulted anyone, or been homicidal. Nevertheless, she demonstrates an inability to protect herself from basic harm. She cannot independently attend to her basic biological needs. She is not meeting the ordinary demands of life. She is not functioning at her baseline. She was a student at Dartmouth College when she was stable. She couldn't meet the academic demands there due to the onset and progression of schizophrenia, and she either subsequently withdrew or was administratively removed. She can't tell me which one of these occurred.

Lily has no outpatient treatment provider and no prescribed psychiatric medication. She doesn't believe that she has a mental illness. Thus, I cannot refer her to any outpatient mental health services. She doesn't want any outpatient treatment. Rather, she just wants shelter, food, and water. She thanks me for granting her admission to the crisis unit. To her, it's a relief to be given these things. To me, there are opportunities for the crisis unit to protect her from harm and enhance her ability to care for herself. It's also a chance for staff members to persuade her to accept treatment.

Approximately two months later, another nurse from the same homeless outreach team that initially referred Lily escorts her to my office. Lily has just been discharged *today* from an inpatient unit where she'd stayed for approximately eight days. They gave her a taxicab voucher to go directly to this agency, without any specific recommendation.

A stranger had reported Lily to the police because Lily tried giving this stranger a dead dog. For unknown reasons that incident did not result in a hospitalization. Shortly after that, police officers found her walking into a flow of fast-moving cars, which prompted drivers to swerve to avoid striking her. She was carrying dead birds and a dead dog in her bag. I see in the record that over the last five months, she was discharged four times from hospital emergency departments to homeless shelters without outpatient care.

Today, she is less tidy in appearance than she was when I last saw her. She is wearing a hospital gown. She is malodorous, which I didn't previously find. She is more delusional, more disorganized, and more agitated as compared with my previous interview with her. Her bizarre and nonsensical statements have increased in frequency. She is unable to answer my question about the reason for this latest inpatient admission.

"I will pray for your recovery," Lily softly whispers in my direction, even though I had not disclosed any problem. She requests safe housing, food, water, clothing, and a shower. When I tell her that I am very limited in my ability to provide her with these things directly, she stands up and walks away. The nurse and I persuade her to sit back down when she says in a loud voice, "I don't know why I'm here then!" The nurse gives Lily a cup of water and a snack.

Lily still has no outpatient psychiatric provider and no medication. The nurse tells me that she was discharged from inpatient without any prescription medication. She is not known to the Massachusetts DMH. Did the last inpatient social worker recommend this to her? I will never know. Except for inpatient care, mentally ill people receive DMH services only voluntarily. If it were recommended, Lily probably declined.

Lily doesn't respond to my questions about whether she's suicidal or if she has been sleeping enough lately. She states that she is not hallucinating, but this is not accurate. Unexpectedly, her eyes wander beyond me and then to the right of me for no apparent reason as I express my intention to help her by getting to know her. She might be experiencing tactile or visual hallucinations. I don't suspect that she has used any illicit drug or alcohol since leaving the hospital earlier today.

She tells me, "Whatever errors you made, you can heal. Follow the path of the stones and sand. I will pray for your recovery. I see the suffering in your eyes." She whispers and mouths something inaudibly when I don't verbally respond.

I ask her if she has any money with her, recalling the scant amount she previously showed me.

"You betrayed me! You stole money from me!" she yells, followed by an inappropriate smile.

I try to reassure her about my intentions to help her and tell her that I never betrayed her.

She wipes the wall a couple of times with her hand, unable to explain why she's doing this. She believes that she has special powers that no one else possesses, referring to animals that only she can save.

Just as before, Lily is at high risk of victimization. She is unable to protect herself from basic harm. She cannot meet ordinary demands of life. She is unable to attend to her basic biological needs.

The crisis unit didn't stabilize her. This unit wouldn't be enough for her at this time because she does not want to take any medication, which cannot be forced upon anyone there. Lily agrees with my recommendation that she be readmitted to an inpatient unit, but not for the same reasons I have in mind. She doesn't understand the reason for this recommendation because she doesn't believe that she has psychosis. To Lily, the only benefits of inpatient care are food, water, housing, and a shower. The presence of police is not warranted, as she cooperates with ambulance staff members, albeit superficially. She is transported to the hospital emergency department on Section 12.

Regardless of whether patients are agreeable to my inpatient recommendation, I typically authorize Section 12s for them and ensure that they get to the hospital by ambulance. Let's imagine that a patient, whom I'll refer to as Janine, says she's willing to be admitted to an inpatient unit because she's suicidal with a plan to hang herself. A taxicab is called to take her to the hospital. At a red light, she decides that she no longer wants to go to the hospital, so she exits the cab. Then she kills herself.

Or Janine agrees to get into the ambulance, and a Section 12 is not given to the ambulance workers transporting her to the hospital. They arrive at the hospital parking lot. Ambulance staff members unbuckle her from the stretcher, and Janine runs away from the ambulance and hospital altogether, still suicidal. The staff members now have no legal grounds to stop her from fleeing and are not allowed to contact the police for assistance in bringing her to the hospital because there is no Section 12 in place. The Section 12 ensures that she gets to the hospital for treatment and protects me from liability.

Lily apparently needs to be committed to an inpatient unit under Massachusetts General Laws, Part 1, Title XVII, Chapter 123, Sections 7 and 8. When a patient asks to be discharged from an inpatient unit, but the psychiatrist believes that her discharge would be unsafe, the psychiatrist can submit a petition to the court pursuant to Section 7. If the judge determines that the only safe option for the patient is for her to remain involuntarily on the inpatient unit for an extended period, the request for Section 7 authorization is granted, and the hospital can hold her. This means that she can be involuntarily held on the inpatient unit for up to six months. If the inpatient unit wants to keep her beyond the expiration of Section 7, the psychiatrist would be required to submit another Section 7 petition to the court. If the judge approves it, the patient could be involuntarily held on the inpatient unit for up to one year.

If the inpatient psychiatrist convinces the judge that the involuntary administration of antipsychotic medication is needed, the judge grants the request for a Section 8b and its treatment plan. If the judge approves the Section 8b request, the patient will receive antipsychotic medication, regardless of whether she wants it. The psychiatrist orders the medication, and the nurses are permitted to forcibly administer medication to the patient.

Unfortunately, there are many instances of inpatient units discharging patients after the courts grant Section 7s and 8s and months prior to their expirations. I suspect that loss of revenue combined with patients pressing for release might prompt premature discharges. You may recall the analogy I gave between restaurants and hospitals earlier when I provided a possible reason for hospital emergency departments prematurely discharging patients. Hospital revenue increases with every admission, and insurance reimbursement doesn't increase with increased length of stays. This process is true for both emergency departments and inpatient units.

About a year ago, Lily might have been faced with the chance of being involuntarily held on inpatient for weeks. She alluded to this by stating that the only reason she took psychiatric medication on an inpatient unit in Maine was to avoid being taken before a judge who would have decided whether to order forced administration of medication. Although she avoided this by taking medication prescribed to her, she immediately stopped taking it after being discharged.

Before 1970, state governments were less protective of patients' civil liberties than currently. In previous decades, the criteria for qualifying for inpatient psychiatry were overly vague.[67] Since then, inpatient criteria have become highly narrow, and the number of inpatient beds has declined. Now, governments are overprotective of patients' civil liberties to the detriment of their well-being.

If Lily continues to spend most of her days on the streets without any psychiatric treatment, social support, or supervision, she will likely continue to pose a danger to herself because of an inability to care for herself. Lily exemplifies the reason that *parens patriae* is necessary. Massachusetts and all other states have a legal and moral obligation to protect people who are unable to protect themselves from harm. With no social support, Lily has only the system to protect her. When the outpatient system is not enough to protect her, she needs the protection of an inpatient unit.

* * *

Due to the excessive elimination of inpatient beds, patients who are not able to meet the ordinary demands of life due to severe mood instability, psychosis, or both are often left to fend for themselves. There is not enough inpatient care available to meet all their needs. Mental illness can interfere with a person's ability to perform the basic tasks of daily living, including eating, bathing, and managing finances. Mental illness can also interfere with a person's ability to relate safely with her neighbors or to avoid engaging in destructive behaviors that put neighbors at risk of being harmed. This can result in repeated evictions from independent apartments. Psychotic patients who lack awareness of their psychosis sometimes present to emergency psychiatry complaining primarily of homelessness while not understanding that their psychosis contributed to becoming homeless.

I believe that we as a society have an obligation to treat those who need help the most, the least among us, before we move on to others. If there were unlimited resources, sure, help everyone. But it is clearly the untreated seriously ill who are most likely to become homeless, hospitalized, incarcerated, and cost more. The consequences of leaving the seriously ill untreated are more horrific than leaving the less ill untreated.

—DJ JAFFE, AUTHOR, *INSANE CONSEQUENCES: HOW THE MENTAL HEALTH INDUSTRY FAILS THE MENTALLY ILL*; EXECUTIVE DIRECTOR, MENTAL ILLNESS POLICY ORG.; TIRELESS ADVOCATE FOR PEOPLE WITH SERIOUS MENTAL ILLNESS

CHAPTER 11

Three Hots and a Cot

MALINGERING PATIENTS burden an already broken mental health system. They do this by abusing professionals, wasting taxpayer funds, occupying precious and limited inpatient bed space, and depleting health care resources. Malingerers pretend to be acutely mentally ill to qualify for hospitalization or the crisis unit. They lie about what they are feeling and thinking and how they have behaved most recently, all to give the appearance of illness. They intentionally exaggerate and feign symptoms. Feigning mental illness is a lot easier than feigning other types of illnesses, whose reported symptoms are often confirmed through lab work. Verbal interviews are the most common means that clinicians use to determine whether patients have mental illness. Patients can easily manage verbal misrepresentation, while they are highly unlikely to alter lab work results. They would likely find the latter too daunting to try.

The experience of past inpatient courses can lure malingering patients into requesting this setting again. I know this because I am familiar with the comforting amenities that are offered to patients there. Inpatient units provide beds with sheets and pillows, three square meals a day, snacks, supportive attention, and the opportunity to socialize with other patients (and learn from them how to improve malingering skills). Patients can engage in artwork, watch television, meditate, play board games, and read novels. Of course, this is more comfortable than trying to find an abandoned building to sleep in because the homeless shelter is full.

In graduate school, the possibility never crossed my mind that patients could lie about their mental states. At the beginning of my emergency work, when I was gullible, it was more difficult for me to decipher the condition of patients who lied abundantly in interviews. The realization that lying patients had fooled me while I was working on inpatient units eventually crystallized years later.

I now consider the following behaviors in patients when I suspect malingering:

+ suddenly voicing suicidal ideations upon notice of discharge from formal overnight treatment programs

+ using many consecutive, closely timed, formal overnight treatment programs, especially involving presentations of quasi-dangerous statements

+ losing the ability to stay where they were residing immediately before seeing me

+ showing a chronic pattern of not following through with outpatient referrals or taking medication as ordered by inpatient or crisis units

+ vaguely describing depression or anxiety

+ listing symptoms in a rehearsed fashion as if common diagnoses were just searched on the internet

+ inconsistently reporting information—for example, when a patient's behavior or affect belies his report

While the last of these signs can be an enigma, it's certainly not the most telling. Acting skills can come into play; a patient can feign crying.

If someone is homeless, there are appropriate resources other than hospitalization that he can use to alleviate or resolve homelessness. Hospitals are expensive institutions designed to provide medical and psychiatric care. They are not hotels or motels. Hospitals are not expected to provide respite. Granting someone an inpatient bed when he doesn't clinically qualify for one does not help him because it enables his audacity, and it renders a bed unavailable to someone who truly needs one.

Not all malingerers use illicit drugs or alcohol. However, most malingering patients whom I interview have substance-use or substance-dependence problems. I hesitate to diagnose mental illness when someone is regularly using illicit drugs or alcohol because these substances usually mask any mental illness. The presence of substance-misuse convolutes efforts to assess mental illness or lack of illness accurately. Along with Section 12 law, this is the reason I have never written on any Section 12 form that the patient was under the influence of any substance.

The reasons vary as to why patients want formal overnight care. The secondary gains that malingerers seek when requesting admission to inpatient or crisis units are sometimes mysterious. Other times, they are evident. A patient, perhaps accidentally, may reveal to me that reducing loneliness is a factor in his decision to seek inpatient services. Or a peer of the patient may have recently threatened to kill him because he owes a large sum of money from an illicit drug sale, and now wants to hide from this peer on an inpatient unit. Perhaps a patient has run out of places to sleep and eat and has exhausted the scant social support system he has left. A patient could be avoiding a warrant for his arrest or trying to build a disability case to obtain financial benefits from the government due to "illness."

How prevalent is malingering in emergency psychiatry? Few research studies have been conducted to examine this problem. Existing studies demonstrate a 13 percent rate of malingering in psychiatric patients in urban emergency settings, and a 10 to 12 percent rate of patients on inpatient psychiatric units falsely report being suicidal.[68] I suspect that the true malingering rate is much higher than these studies claim. These studies don't consider the suspicion of malingering.

I tracked one hundred cases in a row assigned to me to see what percentage of patients were malingering. Assignments are largely random, as no clinician specializes in any type of case. An astounding 25 percent of these one hundred cases involved either my strong suspicion of malingering or evidence of it. This didn't include the patients who were so proficient at acting and lying that I could not see or suspect it.

✳ ✳ ✳

Ivan, twenty-three years old, arrives at my office. He has a backpack over his shoulder, and he is wearing jeans and a T-shirt. I ask him what he's looking for.

With a frown and somewhat avoidant eye contact, he tells me that his sister died of pancreatic cancer within the last two months and that he needs a place "to get my head together." He asks for admission to the crisis unit.

I explain that he would need to be interviewed to see if he qualifies for that. I convey my condolences.

"I'm really depressed about this. We were really close. I couldn't go to the funeral because I was in jail. Not that my family would've allowed me to go either way."

He tells me that he has been homeless and staying in a local homeless shelter since his wife kicked him out last year. He tells me that it has been four months since he last used any heroin or cocaine. He has never had a problem with alcohol.

His social support system is insufficient. He says that he and his wife are trying to reconcile and resume their marriage if he can demonstrate sustained sobriety from using heroin and cocaine. Meanwhile, she has full custody of their child. His hope to reunite with his child is his primary motivation to work on sustaining his sobriety.

We go through routine questions. He has been incarcerated for a variety of legal offenses relating to his drug addiction. Charges include larceny, theft, assault and battery, and armed robbery. He reports that he was administratively discharged from a halfway house recently due to relapsing with cocaine.

He is goal-oriented and expresses a motivation to resolve his homelessness by saying that he's on various waiting lists for residential programs for people who are recovering from drug addiction. The combination of an overabundance of substance-misusers and a shortage of residential treatment programs usually means that patients must endure long waits to be accepted into programs. They usually fill out applications, go to interviews, have treatment providers forward clinical material, and then sometimes wait for weeks before placement.

Homeless individuals struggling with illicit drugs or alcohol often sleep in transient settings. They "couch surf." They convince family members to take them in until they overstay their welcomes. They sleep with other addicts in abandoned buildings and hallways.

I ask Ivan to describe his depression.

"I don't know. Just sad. Not wanting to do anything." He pauses before continuing. "I get panic attacks, too." He tells me that these involve an inability to catch his breath, increased heart rate, trembling, and "racing thoughts." The last panic attack occurred yesterday. The last one before that was two days ago.

I ask him how long each of these attacks lasted.

"I don't know. Like two hours?"

I ask him if there were any triggers immediately preceding these episodes.

"No."

I am suspicious. Panic attacks typically last no longer than fifteen minutes. Unpleasant situations or encounters typically trigger them.

Ivan tells me that he has impulsively overdosed on heroin three to four times in the past while not caring if he lived. He tells me that otherwise, he has never tried to kill himself. Right now, he is passively suicidal without any plan to kill himself. Out of context, he blurts out, "I can't go back out there. If I do, I'll just use again." He is referring to using illicit drugs.

I propose that we part ways for a few minutes to allow me a chance to review his records. Looking at these, I notice that over the last four months, he has been admitted to the crisis unit four separate times. I also notice that I evaluated him approximately two years ago. What was my impression of him then? As I review my old notes, I catch the word "pancreatic." I read, "Sister died of pancreatic cancer three months ago."

Interesting. Is it possible that he lost two sisters to pancreatic cancer? I see that other emergency clinicians also referred to this death. If he had traveled much among inpatient units in another area of Massachusetts or in another state, I would have a much more arduous time figuring out if he were malingering due to lack of access to records from afar.

I rejoin Ivan. I ask him if he has other siblings.

"Yeah, I do, but they want nothing to do with me," he says.

I ask him if he ever had another sister who died of pancreatic cancer.

"Nope."

I point out the inconsistency in the timeframe that I found and refer to the record showing that this sister died approximately two years ago.

His eyes widen. He says, "There must've been a mistake. That's not true."

Typically, when giving disappointing news to a patient, it's important to consider the chance of violence erupting. Ivan has a history of violence relating to illicit drug purchases. Many research studies show that violence in the substance-dependent or substance-misusing population is more common than in the rest of the population. With coworkers present, I inform him that he cannot be granted admission to the crisis unit, and we ask him to leave. He curses at me and walks away. I did the right thing after I tried to give him the benefit of the doubt. He demonstrated that his report could not be trusted as reliable. I move on, knowing that more malingerers will appear.

Winston, twenty-seven years old, arrives in the office with a couple of bags of personal belongings. He tells me that he attempted to get help at a hospital emergency department without success. "They told me to come here," he says. "I feel unsafe. I have PTSD, depression, anxiety, ADHD."

He was hospitalized on an inpatient unit about a month ago. Thereafter, he didn't follow through with attending the intake appointment scheduled by the inpatient social worker to begin psychotherapy and psychopharmacology.

Winston is in early remission from having stopped using heroin and hasn't had any luck in securing placement at a sober residential program since becoming homeless. Just like many other homeless patients struggling to remain sober, his residential situations have been turbulent and fleeting, leading him to rest his head anywhere that he can find. He refuses to consider staying at a local shelter because he's "paranoid" there. Malingerers use the word "paranoid" because they've learned from peers or on the internet that a common feature of psychosis is paranoia.

Winston was discharged from the crisis unit just yesterday. I review records from this course, which show that he told a clinician there that he expressed fear that a drug dealer could be looking for him to kill him since Winston wasn't able to pay the expected amount of money in exchange for illicit drugs. I mentally pocket this and ask him why he went to the hospital yesterday.

"I was feeling suicidal. I feel better but not great." He tells me that he has not been suicidal since then.

According to the record, he was not suicidal while on the crisis unit yesterday. I delve into what his suicidal thinking involved at the hospital yesterday.

He reveals that yesterday he wished to die without having any suicidal plan and without having any intention to die. He tells me that his positive feeling toward his father is a reason not to kill himself. He reports having many future goals. He wants to stay sober, find employment again in construction, and resolve his lack of housing. His most prolonged period of sobriety outside of a formal program was four months, which ended about a year and a half ago.

I ask him to describe his anxiety.

"Racing thoughts. My heart pounds like it's going to come out of my chest."

I ask him to describe his depression.

"Sad. I'm tired of living this way. I have nowhere to go. It's hell trying to find food—" he pauses for a couple seconds and then finishes the sentence "—when I'm hungry. I want to get on the right path, but it's hard without anywhere to stay."

I empathize with him and ask him to describe what he means by feeling "unsafe."

"I'm afraid someone could hurt me. I could hurt myself." He tells me that the only safe place he can think of is the crisis unit.

I ask if he has ever attempted suicide.

He tells me that as a teenager, he overdosed on a bottle of aspirin. He says that he attempted suicide just one other time, about three months ago, by overdosing on pills. This is inconsistent with the record, which shows that he told another clinician just last week that he has never attempted suicide.

I remind him that he has been admitted to the crisis unit countless times over the last several months. Each of these courses was lengthy. This inclination upholds the belief that he had plenty opportunity to stabilize. I remind him that he started taking a new prescription psychiatric medication during his last crisis unit stay. Thus, he probably wouldn't benefit from accessing more medication.

"Well, then, I'll just go to the hospital and tell them I'm suicidal."

I tell him he is free to do that.

"If you're not going to help me, call me an ambulance."

I do not fulfill his request. He knows how to order one for himself. With coworkers present, I ask him to leave. He refuses to do so and asks for an ambulance again. I call the police for assistance, and they escort him out. As they are doing this, he tells them that he is suicidal.

On the following day, another clinician told me that she has found in the record the following revelation about Winston. During the hospital emergency course that immediately followed my interview with him, he told the nurse that he overdosed on heroin and pills. Despite no existing evidence of this, he was admitted to an inpatient psychiatric unit that same day.

* * *

Some malingerers lose track of their stories and forget what they said to previous clinicians. Or their drug intoxication interferes with their memory and ability to provide clear stories. When malingering is evident, it facilitates the decision to decline a patient's request for inpatient or crisis unit admission.

As with any skill, practice results in proficiency; the malingerers' practice at fabricating symptoms renders them experts. A few malingering patients who are well known to the emergency services team are evaluated with astonishing frequency. They have been admitted to virtually all inpatient units in Massachusetts. They offer no opportunity to be found out. They present no holes in their stories.

They can metaphorically tie my hands, obliging me to grant them what they want. A malingering patient might accidentally inflict serious harm on himself or someone else to qualify for formal and overnight levels of care. If I suspect that this might happen because there is a history of doing this or because he says that he'll do this, I cannot do anything to stop the cycle.

The prevalence of malingering is high enough that clinicians become proficient in managing them—and confident that the patients probably will not kill themselves or anyone else. When malingering patients are turned away and not granted inpatient or crisis unit admission, they don't kill themselves. Instead, they find other mobile-based or hospital-based emergency clinicians who will admit them, unless they resume the use of illicit drugs or alcohol.

Often, my reason for suspecting malingering is instinctual. But suspicion is not enough reason to show patients the exit door, and so they take inpatient beds from those who truly need them. The hospital emergency departments smoothly move malingering patients to inpatient units. Three hot meals per day and a bed are granted. Meanwhile, some patients who need to be transferred to inpatient units are instead discharged to their homes, the streets, family members' homes, or homeless shelters.

CHAPTER 12

Tribute to Amy

WHEN TRAGEDY STRIKES and lives are lost due to untreated serious mental illness, apparently it is easier for the government to blame the person with serious mental illness than to consider that the person refused to accept treatment because she didn't understand that she was ill. The federal government promotes the recovery model and its mindset that recovery is person-centered. The SAMHSA, a branch of the federal government that oversees mental health treatment, touts the belief that mentally ill people should be the primary decision-makers about their treatment. To them, recovery means that mental health service recipients, including many patients on inpatient units, are expected to self-direct their treatment plans, or lack thereof, regardless of their capacity to do so.[69] The recovery model drives administration of mental health programs. This prioritizes the recipients who know that they are mentally ill with the assumption that all mentally ill people know that they are ill.

A meta-analysis of 8,994 schizophrenic people from twenty countries was recently conducted to determine recovery rates. Researchers defined recovery as involving at least two years of substantial abatement or total elimination of clinical symptoms; two years of significant improvements in educational, occupational, and social functioning; or two years of both markers. They found that the annual median recovery rate for schizophrenia is 1.4 percent[70] and that the recovery rate has not increased in recent decades. Indeed, recovery involving both elimination of clinical symptoms and improved functioning is an unrealistic goal for many schizophrenic people.

The recovery model and person-centered approach to treatment marginalize seriously mentally ill people who lack the capacity to initiate treatment. Robert "Joe" Bruce of Maine, the father of William Bruce, has told his story to the *Wall Street Journal*. I interviewed him as well. "The recovery model works only for people after they stabilize, not for psychotic and untreated people," says Joe. I don't recommend a complete elimination of the recovery model. However, some mentally ill people remain incapable of directing their treatment plans because they're severely psychotic. The recovery model, with its person-centered approach to treatment, abandons people who don't understand that they are mentally ill and subsequently refuse to accept any treatment. The recovery model is inappropriately overemphasized in the United States. This apparently stems from the influence of organizations that are dominated by peer specialists.

Joe watched his son, William, display psychosis for the first time in his early twenties. They were in a department store that had security cameras. William expressed his belief to Joe that people were specifically targeting him negatively through the security cameras. Joe became nervous about the obsession with surveillance that William displayed. William whispered to Joe his belief that they were tracking his every move. He pressed for his father to allow them to leave the store with, "We gotta get out of here," before they embarked on another department store.

William's paranoid delusional thinking increased in frequency. Clinicians recommended psychiatric treatment, but he declined to accept this. He did not believe that he had a mental illness despite evidence to the contrary. In 2005, William had psychosis when he was involuntarily sent to an inpatient unit because of threatening two men with a loaded assault rifle. Upon release from the unit, he stopped taking his psychiatric medication, and his psychosis subsequently worsened. He inappropriately walked into random houses. In another incident, he placed his mother, Amy Bruce, in a headlock.

In early 2006, believing that his father had disobeyed instructions from the Central Intelligence Agency, William punched Joe in the face. Shortly after that, William was involuntarily hospitalized at a state hospital. A court ordered him to stay there involuntarily until April 2006. Diagnosed with paranoid schizophrenia, William was urged to take antipsychotic medication. But he disagreed and refused to do so. Joe explained that although the state system has been improved since then, in 2006 it was designed to make it nearly impossible to allow for the forcible administering of medication despite the involuntary status. Rather than apply to the court for permission to forcibly administer medication to him, the psychiatrist allowed him to remain unmedicated on the inpatient unit. Less than a month before the expiration of the court-ordered commitment, the psychiatrist who was treating William didn't believe that he met the restrictive criteria that would have allowed for an extension of the order. Instead of petitioning the court for an extension of the commitment, the inpatient psychiatrist actively planned to discharge him.

According to Joe, an "advocate" funded by state and federal governments coached William on how to act and what to say to the psychiatrist. The "advocate's" goal was to get William released as quickly as possible. Accordingly, the "advocate" told William that he had the right to refuse treatment. The "advocate" neglected to consider the rights of William's family. With the encouragement of this "advocate," and despite the psychiatrist's reservations, William was discharged in April 2006. As expected, he continued to decline to participate in any psychiatric treatment thereafter. As a result, Joe found William pacing outside of their house and speaking incoherently.

On June 20, 2006, William was unmedicated and did not believe that he had a mental illness. While not under the influence of any illicit drug, alcohol, or both, William struck his mother on the head with a hatchet, killing her. Amy was forty-seven years old. Joe found his wife's bloody body in their house when he returned from work. William was not there. Joe called 911. William was found, arrested, and charged with murder.

Interpersonal violence inflicted by seriously mentally ill people is usually directed at people they already know—especially family members—and occurs in the privacy of their homes.[71] Eventually, William reported to a psychologist that the pope had ordered him to kill his mother because of her involvement with al-Qaeda and Saddam Hussein. Finally, in 2007, a judge concluded that William was not criminally responsible for the death of his mother due to his schizophrenia. Faced with the threat of being forcibly administered antipsychotic medication, William agreed to take Abilify. This resulted in a reduction of his psychosis.[72]

The US mental health system is set up for people who are well enough to walk in and say, "I need help." If you are not well enough to walk in and say, "I need help," you're in trouble.

—DORIS A. FULLER, CHIEF OF RESEARCH AND PUBLIC AFFAIRS, TREATMENT ADVOCACY CENTER (RETIRED); TIRELESS ADVOCATE FOR PEOPLE WITH SERIOUS MENTAL ILLNESS

CHAPTER 13

Bipolar Disorder, with or without Psychosis

CLINICAL CASES INVOLVING bipolar disorder will soon be displayed. Some readers may not know much about the disorder. Their understanding of the cases would likely be enhanced with a basic familiarity of the disorder. Bipolar disorder involves alternating episodes of depression and mania or episodes of concurrent depression and mania. It can also involve a person experiencing hypomania instead of mania. It has been estimated that 2.2 percent of the adult population has severe bipolar disorder.[73]

For the criteria of bipolar disorder to be met, the mania or hypomania must last for at least a week.

Signs of mania include:

+ feeling elated or overly giddy

+ having excessive energy

+ not needing to sleep and being awake for days in a row

+ pressured, impulsive, or excessive speech

+ easily feeling irritable

+ displaying mild grandiosity

+ engaging in reckless behaviors

Signs of depression include:

+ suicidal thinking

+ anhedonia (inability to feel pleasure)

+ decreased energy

+ decreased volition

+ decreased concentration

+ excessive sleep or moderate to severe insomnia

+ decreased appetite or excessive food consumption

+ feeling sad or hopeless

Bipolar disorder can also include psychosis. The NIMH estimates that 51 percent of bipolar-disordered people are not receiving any treatment.[74]

The most recommended treatment for bipolar disorder, with or without psychosis, is mood-stabilizing medication, antipsychotic medication, or both. Especially after a patient with bipolar disorder has stabilized from an acute episode, psychotherapy can teach and remind him of healthy coping strategies to deal with a wide range of problems.

CHAPTER 14

Revolving Door

WHILE THE INPATIENT COURSE lengths have declined since deinstitutionalization, the rate of readmission to inpatient units has increased.[75] The revolving door in the mental health system refers to the rapid cycling of admissions to and discharges from inpatient units and hospital emergency departments, jails, and prisons. It is common to see psychotic patients cycle through hospital emergency departments five times in less than two months before they are moved to inpatient units.

According to Dr. Treffert, deinstitutionalization occurred for the economic benefit of the states rather than for the best interest of the patients.[76] Hospitals are financially reimbursed for patients' care primarily by health insurance companies. Managed care companies, regardless of whether they are government-funded or private, regularly obtain clinical information from inpatient social workers, nurse case managers, or psychiatrists about patients' progress, treatment plan, and reasons for qualifying for inpatient. As they impose restrictive clinical criteria, they can completely stop payment to the hospitals, which presses the psychiatrists to order discharges.

The Treatment Advocacy Center recently examined the rate of readmission to state-funded inpatient units, excluding forensic patients, in the United States. They found that in forty-five states and the District of Columbia, patients with the shortest inpatient courses were almost "three times more likely to be readmitted within thirty days or one hundred and eighty days of discharge than patients" with the longest inpatient courses.[77] In this study, eleven states had a median inpatient course length of fourteen days or less, with 10.8 percent of patients hospitalized again within thirty days of discharge and 22 percent rehospitalized within one hundred eighty days. Nine states had a median inpatient course length of at least four months, with 2.8 percent of patients rehospitalized within thirty days of discharge and 7.9 percent rehospitalized within one hundred eighty days.[78]

Whenever *parens patriae* is not adequately applied, state governments are going against their own interests. Although the states see the short-term financial benefits to prematurely discharging patients from inpatient units, they lose in the long term when these same patients become even sicker. When their brains ultimately deteriorate to a point where their dangerous actions render them unable to reside safely outside of the hospital, they require more financial resources from the government than the amount that was originally saved. They require lengthier inpatient stays than they previously needed. Or they are permanently placed in Medicaid-funded nursing facilities. Some seriously mentally ill people do not ever recover.

A slight percentage of seriously mentally ill people need the protection and care of an inpatient unit not just for five months, but for years.

One's baseline can require years of inpatient care and protection. Over the span of five years, I arrange several involuntary transfers of Marcia, thirty-five years old, to the hospital. She has profound psychosis at her baseline. She doesn't *recover* after each of the four discharges from the Department of Mental Health (DMH) inpatient unit. Due to her inability to care for her own needs, she is a constant danger to herself.

I go to the apartment of Kendra, thirty-two years old, with a nurse from her primary care physician's office, because Kendra has stopped eating. She has stopped eating because she believes that people have been poisoning her food. She covers the heating vents because she believes that poisonous gas is coming out of them. She continuously keeps the water running because she believes that poisonous gas is coming out of her faucets and that running the water blocks the gas. As we stand in water, several inches deep because she flooded her apartment, she tells me that she is not mentally ill. Why would she consider taking any medication?

I call the police because she's unwilling to go to the hospital. When the officers arrive, Kendra attempts to assault them, and they handcuff her. An ambulance transports her to the hospital emergency department on Section 12. The emergency medical doctor calls me and says that Kendra is well-groomed, speaking intelligibly, not suicidal, not homicidal, and is being discharged back to her home. The doctor disregards everything that I report. Would she be moved to inpatient if I were a psychiatrist or the medical director of an agency? Would she be moved to inpatient if a family member were to advocate for her? Weeks later, she is evicted from her apartment with nowhere to sleep but the streets.

Earlier in the week, Carl, thirty-three years old, was discharged from Bridgewater State Hospital, which is managed by the Massachusetts DOC. He was admitted to that hospital because, while he was incarcerated, he was eating his feces and cutting himself to remove from his body what he believed was the devil. When I evaluate him on the state-funded respite unit, he yells about his fear of the devil.

He tells me that he was sentenced to prison because he pointed a loaded gun at a stranger. I ask what made him do this. He says that the devil told him to do it. He doesn't believe that he is mentally ill.

Although I determine that he is safe to remain in respite, another clinician arranged for his transfer to the hospital emergency department about a week later because he threatened to kill staff members.

The inpatient psychiatrist of a patient with psychosis lost the battle with the patient's lawyer when the psychiatrist tried to contain the patient for further involuntary treatment. Within twenty-four hours of the patient's immediate discharge, police officers found her sitting disoriented on the yellow lines in the middle of a road. The police transported her to another hospital. Because the former patient still had her hospital bracelet on, the emergency psychiatrist at the hospital knew which hospital she had been discharged from and called me. The new psychiatrist was astonished that the hospital had lost this legal battle and released the patient.

When patients need to be admitted to inpatient units, it is possible to avoid involving the hospital emergency department. I can arrange for the direct transfer of patients from my office to inpatient units. Of course, these patients are calm, cooperative, physically healthy, and free of agitation.

Frequently, transfer to the hospital emergency department cannot be avoided. A patient qualifying for a Section 12 is required to go to the hospital if she is at high risk of elopement or becoming violent, if she is acting violently, if she is severely agitated, or if I cannot continuously supervise her. It is required that a patient be continuously supervised immediately following the authorization of a Section 12—that is, if she doesn't elope. Toward the beginning of any inpatient course, staff members will continuously monitor her. After close and constant supervision are applied, the psychiatrist can order less frequent supervision of the patient.

Hospital emergency departments seem pressed to discharge their patients as quickly as possible. Therefore, if a patient is waiting "too long" for an inpatient bed, the hospital staff will attempt to discharge her as quickly as possible. Too often, after I send patients there on Section 12s, emergency departments discharge the patients to their homes or the streets.

I authorize a Section 12 for a patient who caused a fire at her home due to her psychosis. Not even twelve hours pass before she's home again. I authorize a Section 12 for a patient who has not consumed food or water for days because she believes that her food and water have been contaminated. The inpatient bed search for her is halted when I learn that she's home less than a day later.

There's a pattern regarding which patients are less likely to be transferred to inpatient immediately following Section 12 authorization and those who are likely to wait longer than other patients for inpatient admission. The following clinical factors accompanying

Section 12s are strongly associated with hospital emergency medical doctors discharging patients to anywhere other than inpatient units:

+ The patients do not want to be helped and are overtly psychotic.

+ The patients are violent.

+ The patients have no health insurance and cannot privately pay for services.

Emergency doctors want to avoid long length of stays. Many, if not all, of the doctors know that inpatient units prefer to get easily reimbursed and decline to accept patients without insurance. Therefore, if doctors can draw cases against imminent danger, they will quickly discharge the patients to their homes or the streets. If doctors recognize that the uninsured patients are too sick to be released and are imminently dangerous, the patients will likely wait excessively for inpatient units to accept them.

A study of ten hospital emergency departments in Massachusetts compared the length of stays of patients with various types of health insurance and patients without health insurance. The patients who had no health insurance had the longest total emergency department length of stays, on average.[79] Inpatient units typically decline to accept patients for whom they cannot get reimbursed. These units prefer to get reimbursed easily rather than lose money or scramble to help the patients apply for government-operated health insurance.

The patients who likely will need to be transferred to state-funded inpatient units from inpatient units are also likely to wait excessively long at hospital emergency departments—if they are not prematurely discharged to unsecured settings. If professionals on inpatient units determine that patients need DMH inpatient, they will submit applications to DMH. If DMH agrees that patients need extensive DMH inpatient treatment, the patients will languish for weeks or months before DMH beds become available. Inpatient units are quick to decline entry for these patients because they prefer shorter inpatient courses.

Mental health professionals discriminate against mentally ill people. Inpatient units do not want to accept certain patients for admission. When faced with the request to have patients with these challenges admitted to their inpatient units, admissions departments sometimes claim that they are full and don't have any bed availability. Or they claim that their units are "too acute" and wouldn't be able to manage the needs of the patients if they were to admit new patients. In other words, they state that their current patients are too difficult to manage and taking on other challenging cases would be too overwhelming.

For years, I regularly had the responsibility to conduct inpatient bed searches, and even now I still occasionally conduct searches. Therefore, I know that many of these claims are false. I witness the discrepancy in the length of stays in hospital emergency departments between patients with these factors and all other patients. The patients who have the traits listed above inevitably wait longer than other patients for inpatient placement. Other times, inpatient units flatly state that they cannot accept the patients because of their aggression.

When I was an inpatient social worker, administrators and psychiatrists persuaded me to facilitate discharges as quickly as possible. This goal dominated my every action. I suspect this goal remains at the forefront of inpatient care because the revolving door of emergency psychiatry seems to revolve faster than ever before. It's well known that the increase in managed care-driven health insurance has contributed to the increasingly shorter length of stays on inpatient units. A patient with borderline personality disorder on my inpatient caseload attempted to hang herself. On the same day that she did this, I tried to obtain authorization from her privately managed health insurance company for her continued stay. This managed care company refused to cover the cost of the rest of her stay. Perhaps the insurance clinician minimized the seriousness of the suicide attempt due to the patient's diagnosis of borderline personality disorder.

* * *

A CIT police officer escorts Owen, twenty-nine years old, to my office. The officer explains that a psychotherapist's office called the police to have Owen removed from the premises because he was verbally aggressive, disruptive, and refused to leave. He had gone there to attempt to participate in an initial intake appointment for psychotherapy and medication.

Owen appears thin and highly disheveled. Stains and holes mar his attire. The hair on his head and face is long, shiny, and matted. Even though the weather is warm, he wears three jackets. I give him a water bottle.

I cannot understand what message he's attempting to convey because he rambles quickly with a disorganized thought process for about five minutes. Suddenly, Owen slows down and displays enough coherency for me to determine what he might want or need. He tells me that a hospital emergency department referred him to this intake appointment. Besides telling me that he could benefit from some psychotherapy for his mania, he reports having no other concern and desires no other mental health treatment. He tells me that he has been residing with his mother for the last week since he was administratively removed from a homeless shelter.

He says, "Don't be alarmed. I've always talked this fast." He takes off his jackets, revealing a tank top. I look down and notice he's wearing only one shoe. I ask him where his other shoe is.

Instead of answering, he removes his shoe, saying, "My feet need to be aired out." He's wearing socks, but they are filthy and have holes.

As he rapidly reveals a wide range of stories, his hand gestures are animated. He fervently reports in detail his thoughts and feelings about airport policies, the library employee who asked him to leave, why he doesn't believe holidays should exist, and how the opioid epidemic can be resolved. He ridicules me while engaging in intense eye contact. "You really should learn how to write faster. You and your fancy degree. Where did you go to school? Or did you even go to school? Did you make it past kindergarten?"

His thoughts are disjointed. He jumps from one topic to another without any logical order. I sense that if I don't interrupt him, he might continuously talk for several hours, which we don't have to spare. Whenever I try to interrupt him by gently explaining that we don't have much time, he doesn't allow me to continue talking.

His facial expressions are expansive. He occasionally stands up from his seat for no reason other than to abruptly rearrange his clothes. When he sits down again, he plays with the water bottle for what seems like twenty minutes. He crushes it, throws it up in the air, and tries to catch it.

When he finally stops talking, I get into some routine questions, making sure they are closed-ended. In response to my question about any past trauma, he tells me that two peers physically assaulted him about two weeks ago. He refuses to elaborate on this. His history of arrests is mostly limited to trespassing. He refuses to disclose the details surrounding these incidents. He has not recently used any illicit drug or alcohol. He cannot describe his mood today or recently.

In response to my suggestion that perhaps psychotherapy wouldn't be enough to help him, he says, "I have everything under control. All I need to do to get stable is exercise." He tells me that running is what has kept him most stable.

I contact the psychotherapy office, and a staff member tells me that Owen refused to cooperate with the required intake documentation and became belligerent.

I call his mom, Martha. Input from patients' family members can be helpful when attempting to decide if Section 12 is needed. They often know signs of instability, what has helped the most, and what has not helped. Martha tells me that Owen has been functioning at the level I see today for the last four years, during which time she has been trying to get him help, to no avail. "They keep on discharging him with nothing. They keep telling me he can't be helped unless he wants to be helped. He can go for weeks without sleeping. He has not even a cent to his name!"

I ask her if he was recently discharged from an inpatient unit or hospital emergency department. Martha tells me about her experience with the revolving door among law enforcement, hospitals, and her home. "The police usually bring him to the hospital. They call me, and I beg them to keep him. But instead, they just let him go. It's the same thing over and over again, and I'm sick of it." The last time he was inpatient hospitalized for bipolar disorder was four years ago. During this inpatient course, he was held involuntarily for several weeks because the hospital won a court hearing. It was only then that he received psychiatric medication. Martha says, "He was diagnosed with bipolar and has been unmedicated for the last four years."

I tell his mother about my intention to arrange for his hospitalization. She is relieved, and she agrees with this plan but cautions, "He knows what to say to get out. They always believe him." He knows to tell them that he's not suicidal, not homicidal, and not hearing any voices. Some patients who are intelligent have learned to cover up their symptoms of psychosis or mood instability.

When deciding if Section 12 is needed, qualifying criteria for inpatient treatment are considered. Whether or not the patient wants inpatient treatment is not a criterion. Owen is clearly unable to meet the ordinary demands of life, adequately attend to his basic biological needs, maintain normal relationships, and communicate normally.

I formulate a plan to gauge if Owen would be willing to go to the hospital. I try to find him, but he is gone. His whereabouts are unknown. I fax the Section 12, with his mother's address on it, to the police. Hours later, the police tell me that they never found him.

* * *

A week later, I am walking in the hallway just outside my office when I happen to see Owen. He is speaking in a loud tone of voice and arguing with a staff member. I'm not sure what this is about or what brings him here. Concerned that he's not in the hospital, I gently approach them. Seeing him again doesn't surprise me. This type of situation happens with alarming frequency.

He immediately remembers me as we smile at each other. Luckily, I am available to work on another case, so I ask Owen what he's looking for.

This time, Owen is walking barefoot. "Is this the intake office for the outpatient department? I need to find this."

I check and find that he has no appointment in the present agency. I report this to him.

He seems to accept this, despite being unable to explain why he believed he had an appointment today. He still appears disoriented to the situation as he demands that I give him socks, shoes, a new apartment, and employment.

I tell him that I cannot directly provide those things. Believing there is a moderate chance that he'll prematurely elope again, I quickly latch on to anything that could persuade him to allow me to interview him. I attempt to reassure him about my intention to help him by offering to help him investigate when and where his next outpatient appointment will be, or if he even has one scheduled. Engaging patients by finding common ground helps to build rapport.

We sit down together in my office. He is thin. His appearance is still bizarre and disheveled. He is more malodorous than he was last week. He tells me that he's still residing with his mother. "You have no fucking permission to talk to her!" he shouts.

I recall how invaluable the information was that she gave me last week. I emphasize that his mother knows him much better than I do. Thus, it's important to get her perspective. "People closest to you might be able to observe things about you before you can."

"Just don't!" He either quickly forgets about or is no longer concerned with any outpatient appointment because he reveals that he was in a hospital emergency department yesterday. He provides me with a dubious explanation for this.

Owen's eye contact is intense. He is excessively talking again, rapidly bouncing from topic to topic in a disorganized fashion. The content of his speech is not transparent. Following his train of thought feels impossible. I attempt to interrupt him numerous times, to no avail, and he quickly interrupts me at every such attempt. His affect ranges from inappropriately laughing to angry. He is erratic and animated with restless body movements. He says loudly, "What kind of fucking establishment are you running here? You're a joke."

I try to appease him by explaining my role, expressing concern for him, and offering to help him.

"You are writing all lies about me, so you can do a Section 12. Not happening!"

I stop writing. "I'm just trying to help you." In the brief silence, I take the opportunity to ask him if he has used any illicit drug or alcohol. Owen tells me he has not, which I believe. From my experience with interviewing innumerable patients with substance-dependence, sound organizational ability seems to increase the probability of accessing illicit drugs. Owen is grossly disorganized. He then immediately begins to express different opinions about how the opioid epidemic can be curtailed.

I ask him about his mood. He either cannot describe it or is unable to listen to me because he instead expresses his belief that I should not be employed and that I am useless to him. Not allowing this to curtail the progression of the interview, I ask him what he was hoping to get by coming to this agency today. He asks me to help him make a new outpatient appointment for psychotherapy.

The chance is quite high that Owen will leave the interview without the help he needs. For this reason, I withhold my suspicion that psychotherapy would not be enough to stabilize him right now. I don't want him to get so angered or disappointed that he leaves. Besides, many patients who are without treatment providers are expected to wait weeks before intake appointments become available. Agencies often require that patients meet with psychotherapists before psychiatrists or advanced nurse practitioners can see them. This means that patients sometimes must wait months before they have access to psychiatric medication.

Owen tells me that he has no medication and is not being prescribed any because all he needs is psychotherapy. I gently express my reservations about concluding with just an intake appointment for psychotherapy, telling him, "I'm not sure that would be enough." I know it would not be enough.

He insists that psychotherapy and adhering to his running regime would be enough. I ask him if he has been running recently. He laughs loudly, saying, "Oh, yeah! I don't have any shoes!"

I notice in the clinical record that he has not been able to follow through with any outpatient referral made by any emergency clinician in months. I offer him water and tell him that I would like a brief break so that I can consult with colleagues for advice. We agree to part briefly, and he accepts the water.

I ask a colleague to watch him while I fill out the Section 12 form out of his view, suspecting that he would likely elope if he sees me writing it. I fax the Section 12 to the police. Almost whispering so that he won't hear me, I call the police and ask for their assistance. I also call an ambulance.

When I go to check on Owen, he is nowhere in sight. My colleague tells me that he bolted. Only the police would've had the ability to prevent him from leaving with Section 12 already authorized.

I contact his mother to let her know that he left while I was writing up the Section 12 and to ask her where he might be going. Martha gives me a suspected address. I complete a new Section 12 form with this address, fax it to the police, and tell them why I'm sending the second one. I cancel the ambulance request.

I call Martha again, this time to update her more thoroughly and obtain background information. She is unaware that he was at any hospital yesterday. "Maybe the police brought him there again? They found him the day after you saw him last week and brought him to the hospital. Again, they didn't hold him. I can't have him staying here unless he gets the help he needs. My neighbors tell me that they see him ranting aloud while alone on my porch all the time. He was … No, he *is* still a very smart guy who started college. He has nothing now. No job. No money. No one cares for him beside me. Please help him."

Hours later, I obtain confirmation from the police that they found him and took him to a hospital emergency department.

✳ ✳ ✳

About a month later, I reevaluate Owen in my office. This time, two police officers escort him. The officers tell me that they found him lying down in a roadway, and when Owen refused to get up and engage with them, they almost arrested him. Once they suspected that he had a mental illness, they tried to persuade him to go voluntarily to the hospital emergency department, but he was unwilling to do this. They came to the mobile emergency services team instead. The police officers leave Owen with me.

Owen's chief demands of me include an apartment, money, food, and a photocopy of the entire *Diagnostic and Statistical Manual of Mental Disorders-Fifth Edition* (DSM-5). His rapid speech, restless body movements, inability to listen and concentrate, verboseness, and expansive affect are like what I previously witnessed. His outer physical appearance is like his appearance the previous times I saw him. However, I observe a more intensified level of torment radiating from his thinking and behaviors. He appears more out of touch with reality than ever before. He is mindlessly repeating my words, a behavior called echolalia.

His agitation increases as I write. He then demands that I read to him everything I write. He says that I'm writing lies about him.

I stop writing. In a brief silence that interrupts his talkativeness, I ask if he hears any voice that may not sound real. He says, "No!"

Fifteen minutes later, he voicelessly utters words for a couple of seconds. This is the first time I see him do this.

He vehemently lists his many reasons for believing that I should never have been granted a college degree. He is barely able to carry on a normal conversation. I don't believe that calling his mother is immediately necessary. I'm already convinced that he needs to be involuntarily transported to the hospital on Section 12.

I tell him that I must use the restroom. Out of his view, I fill out the Section 12 form, fax it to the police, and ask them for assistance. I arrange for ambulance transportation, alerting them that this patient is agitated and that police are on their way.

Normally, only two police officers come to the office for Section 12s, but they are familiar with Owen's potential for high levels of agitation and elopement from treatment settings. With the assistance of four police officers and the ambulance crew, he reluctantly cooperates without becoming physically combative. As he is being rolled out on the stretcher, he loudly derides me with lots of profanity.

I call Martha and tell her where Owen is. She tells me that shortly after I evaluated him a month ago, he was admitted to an inpatient psychiatric unit, where he began taking a mood-stabilizing medication. Within seven days, he was discharged to her home with a paper prescription for this medication. Finding the right medication or mix of medications to relieve psychosis can take weeks or even months. Martha goes on, "I doubt he did anything with this," referring to the prescription for the medication that he started taking on the inpatient unit.

Too often, I've heard frustrated family members express outrage because their seriously mentally ill loved ones are released from inpatient units too early. It's common to hear from family members that their loved ones came out just as sick as they were before being hospitalized. This seems especially true for patients who don't fully understand that they need professional help.

The problem of the criminalization of the mentally ill continues for a number of reasons, chiefly that the money saved by deinstitutionalization did not follow the patients into the community. Politicians were more interested in the pocketbook of the system than the patients within it. It costs money to provide GOOD community psychiatric services, but without the dollars, we pay the costs in so many other ways.

—DAROLD A. TREFFERT, M.D.

CHAPTER 15

Dangerously Unaware

THERE IS A LINK BETWEEN violence, untreated serious mental illness, and a lack of awareness of one's own illness. In one study of fifty-eight male schizophrenic patients on an inpatient unit, researchers saw an inverse relationship between the presence of antipsychotic medication in patients' blood levels (indicating whether they were taking it) and a tendency toward violence.[80] Another study of three hundred forty-eight patients on an inpatient psychiatric unit of a Virginia state hospital found that patients who refused to comply with their prescribed medication were more likely to engage in assaultive behaviors than those who took medication.[81]

One hundred thirty-three schizophrenic patients were studied on an outpatient basis. In this study, ninety-four patients were not medication compliant.[82] Seventeen of them were markedly violent. Twenty-four of them threatened to impose violence against others. One predictor of violence is when patients are insufficiently treated with medication.

* * *

Agitation during psychotic presentations is often a risk factor for dangerous behaviors. I never learned this from any publication or seminar. I also didn't learn this in school. Over time, I noticed a correlation between moderate to severe agitation and Section 12s. When symptoms of bipolar disorder or schizophrenia intensify in someone, often in an acute stage of illness progression, agitation can arise. Agitation involves accelerated and abnormal physical movements and verbalizations such as pacing, yelling, screaming, throwing and breaking objects, or assaultive behavior directed at oneself or others.[83]

Dementia or delirium can cause agitation and psychosis. Alcohol or illicit drugs can cause agitation and psychosis. Brain injuries, infections, and thyroid disease are other causes of agitation and psychosis.[84] For this reason, inpatient units often require, as a prerequisite for admittance, that a hospital emergency department medically clear a patient. Hospitals must determine if psychosis is neurological, medical, or substance-induced.

Chemical or mechanical restraint is required if severe agitation appears imminent and efforts at de-escalation are failing, or if it escalates to physical assault, self-injury, or property destruction. This is best managed in a hospital setting due to the readily available resources. In the hospital emergency setting, a patient's arms and legs can be immobilized—preventing further danger—by forcibly giving medication, providing physical restraints, or utilizing both tools. I don't carry around any means of restraint, and I don't have the authority to physically restrain anyone.

* * *

Drew, forty-five years old, is escorted to my office by a police officer. Besides wearing a pair of pants, shoes, and a ripped shirt, Drew is only carrying a phone charger. His clothes are filthy, and he emits a foul odor. His presence is loud and intrusive. It's difficult to follow what he is saying because he is jabbering. He is disorganized and hyperverbal. I can barely verbalize any intention to help him because he often interrupts me with nonsensical statements.

Despite being well known to the Department of Mental Health (DMH) and many of the local inpatient units, he has been without any psychiatric medication for months. To top it off, he was evicted from his apartment earlier in the week. As expected, this was not his first home eviction. He can't explain the reason for the eviction in any organized way. He has been charged with an extensive list of criminal offenses, including an assault that inflicted serious injuries upon a psychiatrist on an inpatient unit, kidnapping of a child, rape, possession of an unlicensed firearm, and stabbing a peer with a knife.

A little less than two hours ago, Drew was released from a hospital emergency department. The physician immediately released him to his resources after police officers escorted him there on Section 12. The clinician at the hospital wrote that if Drew returns within the next few days, they will pursue inpatient for him. I immediate ask myself: If they knew he could not safely function outside of a secured setting, why did they release him? Inpatient units are likely to decline to accept for admission any patient with Drew's potential for violence. Knowing this, they likely didn't want him to remain in the hospital emergency department for any extended length of time.

Drew has never displayed a risk of suicide. When talking with me, he affirmatively denies that he has ever thought about seriously harming anyone else and denies being homicidal lately. Did the hospital staff members consider the possibility that Drew was not a fully reliable reporter of information?

After I give him lots of reassurance, support, and empathy (a snack seems to help, too), he eventually tells me that his purpose in coming here is to get housing. He does not want any mental health treatment.

I inquire, "Before the police brought you to the hospital, where were you resting your head?"

"The police didn't bring me there. My fellow Marines did. They monitor my every move. They saw that Operation DP wasn't going so well. They had to intervene."

"What's Operation DP?"

"I can't tell you. I'm a Major on a mission ordered by the CIA."

"What did they order you to do?"

"I can't tell you."

This is the most coherent thing I hear from him. He can no longer listen to me and yells, "If you cannot get me a room for the night, I can leave!"

I sense within the first ten minutes of interacting with him that he probably needs to return to the hospital. Later, I'm certain of it. I sign the Section 12 form and contact the police. It takes four police officers, two ambulance staff members, and me to execute the Section 12. As they restrain him on the stretcher, he yells at me some of the most profane words I've ever heard. They transport him to the same hospital emergency department he was released from earlier that day.

Hours later, a nurse from the hospital calls me, saying, "The doctor wants to know what you believe changed since we last released him. You didn't think that the doctor would do the same thing if you sent him here? The doctor's planning on releasing him again."

I respond, "Nothing has changed since he was last released from there. He should never have been released."

Occasionally, when I call nurses at hospital emergency departments to give them notice about patients they can expect to see on Section

12s that I authorize, they challenge my decisions. They even tell me that I should have obtained their permission to send patients there.

Hospital emergency departments might prefer that patients who require restraints be discharged sooner than patients who do not need restraints. Why? The use of emergency restraints burdens hospital resources. If a medical doctor orders the use of restraints, the physical strength and mobility of additional staff members are required to enforce the order safely. Additional hospital workers are then expected to observe the restrained patient closely and continuously. There can be an emotional burden on staff members, too. Usually, they first try verbal de-escalation techniques. They might offer the distressed patient choices, clearly set limits, and provide empathy, to no avail. They might be further stressed later when they process the use of restraints by talking with the patient, and when they discuss the incident with other staff members. Then, there are additional documentation requirements for all involved parties. All these tasks take staff members away from attending to other patients.

The use of restraints for psychiatric patients in hospital emergency departments results in these patients spending more time there than if restraints are not used. In one study involving more than 1,000 psychiatric patients in the emergency setting, the use of restraints was compared with the length of stays. Researchers found that patients who needed restraints spent an additional 4.2 hours there.[85]

Javier, fifty-six years old, spent years at various DMH inpatient units for profound psychosis and being at risk of seriously harming others. Then he was prematurely placed in a nursing home. This residence discharged him to a hospital emergency department because he was too violent. While at the hospital, all nursing homes and inpatient units in Massachusetts and surrounding states refused to admit him.

When I evaluate him at the hospital, two security guards constantly supervise him because he has choked one of the nurses in response to a delusion. He doesn't believe that he has a mental illness. He has a Rogers Monitor, but instead of accepting his antipsychotic medication, he throws it across the room, along with the television and the food tray. His potential for violence is a barrier to getting him released from the emergency department and admitted to an inpatient unit. Imagine that you are a patient with hypertension needing an inpatient medical bed, but inpatient units refuse to accept you for admission because your blood pressure is too high. Despite the fact that violence is part of Javier's mental illness, doors remain shut for him.

Another barrier to admission to an inpatient unit is the prospective challenge of discharge planning, which would render him stuck on any inpatient unit for months. When patients use the inpatient hospital setting for extended periods, hospital revenue decreases.[86] This is one of the reasons that inpatient length of stays are too short and patients are prematurely discharged.

Because there is no place for Javier to go safely, he waits in this emergency department for almost two-and-a-half months until an inpatient unit, perhaps with an unusually low census, accepts him for admission. Psychiatric patients in hospital emergency departments wait more than three times longer for inpatient psychiatric beds than medical patients wait for inpatient medical beds.[87] When patients use the hospital emergency setting for extended periods, hospital revenue decreases.[88] In interviews with members of the Massachusetts College of Emergency Physicians, *The Boston Globe* found that, due partly to the shortage of inpatient beds, the length of time that patients wait in hospital emergency departments for placement has drastically escalated over the last several years. From 2011 to 2016, the prevalence of psychiatric patients in emergency departments awaiting inpatient treatment rose 23 percent, and the length of time they spent there increased by approximately 20 percent. Among these patients waiting for inpatient beds, those with a history of violence waited longer than those without such a history had to wait.[89]

The Crisis Intervention Team (CIT) police officer meets me at the homeless shelter as I prepare to evaluate Jon, forty-four years old. He recently displayed increased persecutory delusions to his rehabilitative outreach worker. The rehabilitative outreach worker tells me that he knows that Jon barely slept last night because he and other staff members received a myriad of profane voicemails from him. The shelter staff members, though not clinically trained, tell me that he tends to be intrusive with his peers, and they fear that this could escalate to violence. I keep in mind that Jon has inflicted moderate physical injuries on people within the last six months, according to the clinical record.

According to the Treatment Advocacy Center, seriously mentally ill people commit an estimated 29 percent of family homicides. They perpetrate an estimated 7 percent of all homicides and cause an estimated 20 percent of all law enforcement officer deaths. An estimated 50 percent of all mass homicides—that is, homicides involving at least four victims at approximately the same time and place—are related to serious mental illness.[90]

They find me a private room in which to meet Jon. I'm grateful that this room has a window so that workers can see us. I sit closest to the door, as I always do, to enable a quick exit if needed.

After a few seconds of rapport building, he tells me that his only problem is a lack of income. He expresses confidence in his ability to secure an apartment if he could only find the money for this.

Jon has refused to attend most of his outpatient appointments since his last inpatient discharge. I see in his clinical record that he was appointed a Rogers Monitor. This is useless outside of a locked inpatient setting. Jon was discharged from an inpatient psychiatric unit approximately three months ago, and his next injection of the antipsychotic medication Prolixin was due about two weeks ago. When patients are known to have a pattern of not complying with their antipsychotic medication, psychiatrists or nurse practitioners can prescribe injectable medication. Once injected, this form of medication stays in the body for weeks. Jon refused to accept his last scheduled injection, and most recently, he refused to take all psychiatric pills outside of inpatient settings.

There are sound reasons for professionals to tackle the problem of medication noncompliance, even when the patients don't perceive this as problematic. Longer periods of untreated psychosis are associated with increased severity of symptoms, poor prognosis, increased risk of suicide, increased biological resistance to medication when it is taken later, and increased risk of relapse with hospitalization.[91] Jon's chronic refusal of medication now poses consequences that burden the system.

I count sixteen inpatient admissions in Jon's clinical record, and these were just in the last four years. I read in his record that for years, he has engaged in a repetitive pattern of not complying with his pre-scribed medication and outpatient appointments following inpatient discharges. Although this is his baseline, it is not safe. When I was an inpatient social worker, I saw many patients who cooperated with taking prescribed medication, only to stop taking it immediately after discharge. I knew this because they were soon readmitted. Some of them learned that cooperating on inpatient could lead to faster discharges.

Occasionally, family members desperately called me with reports of the patients' quick deterioration due to nonadherence with treatment.

I learn from Jon's rehabilitative outreach worker that over the last several months, he was evicted from one apartment because he physically assaulted numerous neighbors, and shortly after that, he was evicted from another apartment for the same behavior.

Jon's psychosis is interfering with his ability to provide details about the circumstances of these evictions. I attempt to find out what made him assaultive.

"They were all working with the FBI and trying to kill me!" He stares at me intensely.

I ask for elaboration. He either can't elaborate about this or refuses to do so, perhaps because of suspicion. I let him vent more about his lack of money and housing.

The rehabilitative outreach worker tries to join us. Jon doesn't allow it. "Do I need to get a gun to shoot you?" He doesn't have immediate access to a gun.

Referring to the outreach worker, I ask, "What's going on between you two?"

"He is putting thoughts into my head!"

I ask Jon if the outreach worker is part of the FBI, too. He glares at me without answering, shaking his head.

I want to divert him to the crisis unit, but he threatened to assault a staff member there about a month ago. Even if this assault didn't happen, would he cooperate enough to benefit from this unit effectively? When patients become highly agitated or violent on crisis units, its staff members lack the authority to mechanically restrain patients.

Jon stands up from his chair and rapidly paces. I open the door and attempt to reassure him of my intentions to help.

He is quickly tiring of me. I tell him that it's important for me to get to know him better so that I can try to help him.

He sits down while glaring at me. I ask him about his ability to sleep.

It appears that he cannot listen to me. With an angry demeanor, he again expresses his suspicion about the FBI.

I ask what the current month is. He answers incorrectly.

I ask him what his prescribed medications are for. He immediately reveals a lack of insight when he says, "For my depression."

I ask him if he has ever physically harmed anyone else. He tells me he has never done so.

I offer the crisis unit. He immediately declines.

It's clear that Jon needs to be involuntarily hospitalized on inpatient psychiatry. I intentionally work on the Section 12 form out of his view. The risk of violence or elopement will likely increase if he learns that he will be forced to do something that he doesn't want to do. The police officer calls an ambulance and more officers to the scene. As they arrive, I brace myself for the possibility of combativeness. The presence of uniforms and guns is enough. Jon knows there's no use in fighting, so he gets on the ambulance stretcher without incident.

I meet a police officer at Antonio's independent apartment, where he resides alone. Antonio, sixty-two years old, is talking with his nurse from a home-care agency. The police officer and nurse are unaware of any history of violence that he has inflicted upon others. The nurse explains that she has been helping him to manage his medication daily. This doesn't mean that she administers his medications to him. Rather, she ensures that the correct dosages are available to him. She has been setting them up in plastic pill containers. She doesn't have much else to report.

The nurse also monitors Antonio's medical issues. His outpatient psychiatrist prescribes antipsychotic medication. The nurse says that he has been adhering to taking these medications. I see in his record that he's eligible to receive DMH services. Nevertheless, he cannot identify anyone or any service at DMH. Therefore, it seems that he is not receiving any direct help from DMH.

Alternatively, the police officer has plenty to report to me. The police department has received many complaints about Antonio from his neighbors throughout the last year. They told police officers that Antonio knocked on their doors and offered containers of insects. When they didn't respond, he smeared dead insects on their doors. When they responded to his knocks, he attempted to give them the containers, sometimes forcibly. He violated countless formal orders to stay away from these neighbors, and this led to arrests. I notice that Antonio has more than ten containers of insects in his home, some of which aren't covered.

I express to Antonio my intention to help him. Antonio appears thin as his worn pants fall from his waist before he pulls them up again. I smell a foul odor, which worsens as I get closer to him. He wears a thick beard, and the hair on his head appears shiny. I assume he hasn't washed it lately.

We engage in routine rapport building and questioning. Although I suspect that he needs help, he says, "I don't need any help with anything." He relays no understanding of the purpose of this meeting. As I've seen many times with other patients, Antonio demonstrates no awareness of being in crisis. If police officers were not involved, he probably would not have initiated contact with emergency psychiatry.

I ask him if he has ever heard any strange voice that didn't sound real, which is one of the simple ways of asking about hallucinations. In any disorder involving psychosis, auditory hallucinations are far more common than any other hallucination.

He tells me he never has, but later he says that his neighbors asked him for the insects. We start discussing his insect deliveries to neighbors. Although he acknowledges engaging in these deliveries, he denies many of the police officer's allegations. For instance, he denies that he smeared dead insects on anyone's door.

I allude to the accusation that he tried to force neighbors to accept these deliveries. He tells me that the neighbors lied about him.

I ask him to explain the purpose of delivering insects to the neighbors. He tells me that doing this minimized the effects of the poisonous toxins in their homes. He was just trying to help them. He tries to reassure us by saying, "I'm fine."

I ask him what his medications are for, besides the ones for medical issues. He tells me that they're intended to help him think better.

I ask him to elaborate. He cannot.

I briefly step away to talk with his sister and his psychiatrist. Although they don't have much more information to provide, they know him better than I do. They tell me that these behaviors have increased in frequency recently, and they recommend an inpatient psychiatric admission. His sister tells me that although she resides nearby, she has been limited in her ability to supervise him because she is the primary caregiver for her physically and mentally disabled child.

I emphasize to Antonio that it concerns the police and his nurse as well as his psychiatrist and sister that he's not behaving like his usual self. He remains silent when asked about this, offering no input.

I suggest that he allow us to arrange a checkup at the hospital. He's not willing to do this. Why would he? He doesn't see that anything abnormal is going on.

When Antonio becomes preoccupied with watching television, I quietly share with the police and nurse my intention to authorize a Section 12. I order an ambulance as I complete the form. Meanwhile, the officer requests that more police officers arrive for backup.

The ambulance staff members arrive. Two ambulance staff members, the nurse, the police officer, and I tell Antonio that he has to go to the hospital. He expresses his intention to remain home and asks us all to leave. Typically, seeing uniforms, especially those of police officers, is enough to gain a patient's cooperation. I wonder if Antonio could be convinced to cooperate if we scale back the alarm in our tone and message. I tell him that I talked with his sister and psychiatrist, who are both requesting this, and remind him that they know him much better than I do.

"There's nothing wrong with me. I'll be fine. Leave," he says in a flat tone of voice.

Another twenty minutes pass and the additional police officers have not arrived. We spend this time attempting to persuade him to accept the ambulance ride.

Antonio then raises his voice and demands that we leave. I attempt to reassure him that we are trying to help him.

With angry affect, he abruptly stands up, raises his arm, forms a fist, and charges toward me. The police officer intercepts Antonio, and he and the ambulance crew restrain him. They handcuff him as he lies on the floor on his stomach. He is taken to the hospital emergency department. The additional officers do not arrive.

Aside from the purpose of containment, Antonio is taken to the hospital emergency department to rule out the possibility of other sources of mental dysfunction, which is a common prerequisite for inpatient admittance. This is especially necessary for elderly patients, who are more prone to neurological problems, such as dementia. Except in people with Lewy body dementia, dementia doesn't typically manifest itself with hallucinations. In the realm of neurology, a more common mental sign of dementia is paranoia. Considering that the onset of dementia is usually late in life, I don't often see dementia because nursing homes have psychiatric teams.

Hours after I have written my report and obtained health insurance authorization in preparation for Antonio's pending inpatient admission, I get a call from a nurse at the hospital emergency department. She asks why I sent Antonio there. She doesn't sound like the same nurse whom I notified earlier that Antonio would be transported there. I explain why he was sent there on Section 12 even though the reason is on the formal documentation that I already faxed to the hospital. It's possible that she never saw it, so I mention that I faxed it. The nurse tells me that Antonio is demanding to go home. She adds that the doctor is not sure if he qualifies for Section 12. I emphasize the concerns brought up by the sources of collateral information. I ask that she pass these on to the doctor and read the documentation that I faxed to the hospital.

I move on to another case on the same day. After I complete it, I learn that the hospital discharged Antonio to his home.

A brilliant psychiatrist on inpatient said to a patient with psychosis, "The more you refuse to take medications, the more likely you are to become resistant to medications if you take them later." Research shows that in schizophrenic patients, each psychotic relapse makes other relapses more likely to occur.[92] Schizophrenic patients who use their prescribed antipsychotic medication are at lower risk of relapsing and needing hospitalization than those who are noncompliant with their medications.[93] The use of antipsychotic medication early in the course of schizophrenia could reduce the probability of symptoms presenting later, perhaps because this medication protects the brain from deterioration.[94] Researchers have found that upon psychotic relapses following first psychotic episodes, the period that it took to regain stability after treatment was resumed lengthened with each sequential relapse.[95]

One two-year study examined six hundred sixty-one people, with an average age of twenty-two, who were being treated for their first episodes of psychosis over eighteen months at the Early Psychosis Prevention and Intervention Centre. The ability to secure occupational pursuits and independent living was referred to as functional remission. The reduction or elimination of symptoms was referred to as symptomatic remission. Functional and symptomatic outcomes were measured after the patients engaged in treatment for up to eighteen months. Two-thirds of them were not fully compliant with their medication. Substance-use disorders were found in 61 percent of them. Improvements in functional and symptomatic outcomes were associated with longer engagement in treatment. After eighteen months, participants who adhered to their medication were twice as likely to display symptom remission. A history of engaging in a suicide attempt or not complying with medication was associated with a lack of symptomatic remission. The researchers concluded that intervention to treat psychosis should occur early to prevent an increase in symptoms.[96]

The Program of Assertive Community Treatment (PACT) refers Adam, twenty-eight years old, to me because staff members believe he's not functioning at his baseline. He was last released from an inpatient unit about three weeks ago. He reports being homicidal toward police officers, but he does not identify any officer or location. He does not report any homicidal plan. He's having difficulty listening to me.

Instead of answering my question about compliance with his medication, he is preoccupied with thoughts of violence. I learn from a PACT staff member that Adam has been noncompliant with taking his antipsychotic medication since his last inpatient discharge. During this last inpatient course, he received an injection of a long-acting medication. Since then, he refused to accept the follow-up order of this medication on an outpatient basis. Instead of answering my question about his ability to sleep, he voices delusional thought content.

Adam's delusions are religious, sexual, grandiose, and paranoid. He is restless and mildly agitated. He demonstrates no understanding of why I'm meeting with him, despite my attempts to explain my role and to elicit his consideration of why PACT staff members are concerned. He is disoriented to time and situation. He's unwilling to go anywhere except back to his apartment.

I know that he qualifies for Section 12. Expecting that the police will ask me if he possesses any weapon, I ask Adam about this. He tells me that he has no weapon with him. I contact police and warn them that he is homicidal toward them. Four police officers arrive with the ambulance. Despite mocking me in a loud tone of voice, Adam allows the ambulance staff members to buckle him onto the stretcher. Again, I believe that the presence of uniforms and guns helps to prevent violence or elopement.

Approximately one month later, I meet with Adam again. This time, he rapidly propels himself from his hospital bed to the hallway, all the while talking nonsensically to no one in particular. His urine toxic screen is negative for every illicit drug. His blood alcohol level is zero.

Adam's record shows that he has a history of inflicting moderate to serious physical injuries upon other people in attacks driven by delusional thinking. At least once, he was charged with seriously injuring a police officer. He was then deemed not guilty by reason of insanity (NGRI) due to his psychosis at the time of inflicting these injuries. Instead of a prison sentence, he spent ten months on a DMH inpatient unit. The unit then discharged him to a continuously staffed group residential program. There, he physically assaulted a staff member because he believed that this staff member was plotting to kill him.

Inpatient treatment was tried again. Because of this assault, he was not allowed to return to this residential program upon discharge from inpatient. Then he was admitted to a respite program. Respite units are not alternatives to crisis units or hospitals. Instead, they house people who are typically eligible for DMH services and homeless. Fortunately, staff members there administer all medications. Otherwise, these units do not provide much professional supervision for their recipients.

Months later, Adam moved into a new apartment with the assistance of rehabilitative outreach services. While living in this apartment, he physically assaulted numerous residents in the same building. After being evicted because of these assaults, his care was transferred to PACT. PACT has been monitoring him for almost a year.

I talk with his PACT clinician to inquire about what has happened since he was last hospitalized. Unsurprisingly, he was kept at the hospital for just one week after I met with him previously. He is the most impaired patient I have evaluated in at least a year. Recovery in this short timeframe seems unlikely. The clinician tells me that Adam was last released from an inpatient unit approximately three weeks ago, and that soon after, he was evicted from an apartment because of property destruction and an inability to pay rent.

No one from PACT has known his whereabouts until now. Immediately before Adam's discharge, his inpatient social worker provided petty cash to help transport him to the PACT office. Meanwhile, a PACT staff member retrieved his medication from a pharmacy, expecting him to arrive at their office to obtain it. He never showed up. PACT couldn't contact Adam's only next of kin, his sister, without his permission.

I talk with his PACT psychiatrist. Just about four months ago, Adam was discharged from an inpatient course that lasted a little more than three months. During this course, the inpatient psychiatric team won a court hearing when they pursued Section 7 and 8b. The hospital's execution of Section 8b enabled nurses to administer antipsychotic medication to him forcibly. Shortly thereafter, an application for DMH inpatient care, probably filled out by the social worker and signed by the psychiatrist, was submitted to the government. Considering his vast disability, I cannot imagine DMH *not* accepting him. But instead of being discharged to a DMH inpatient unit, Adam was prematurely discharged to his apartment.

This is certainly not the only time that an inpatient unit prematurely discharged someone to his home before the expiration of Section 7. It happens too often. Family members and treatment providers repeatedly tell me that successful court hearings on inpatient units precede premature discharges.

The Boston Globe found that in 2012, Tu Nguyen was released from an inpatient unit in Massachusetts, even though the court had authorized the unit to keep him there involuntarily for up to six months on Section 7. Against the recommendation of his family, Tu was released to his home only twenty-three days after this court order, despite having assaulted a psychiatrist there. Three weeks later, he stabbed his neighbor to death.[97]

What is Adam capable of?

"Be good," Adam says before I have the chance to introduce myself.

"Thanks. I will." I redirect him to a private and less noisy area. I inquire, "What brought you here?"

Adam's appearance is tousled. He doesn't report any concern. He does not report any precipitant. He does not sit still even for a second.

Apparently, he's incapable of this. Whenever I begin talking, he interrupts me. "God chose me to save the world. If it dances everything for me everything is open." He voices neologisms—newly created words—in a disorganized train of thought. "In plittering on our way setting searching often dinchton the whale was a beautiful whale."

I attempt to redirect him to my questions, saying that I can help him by learning about him.

He uses words without associations. "Jump. There's a rifle called the humanizer. Stretch. Crintal that head. I know when a woman is hot for me because I smell it on her. I'm a Ph.D. chemist."

I ask him orienting questions. I inquire if he knows the time of day, the year, the current location, and who he is. He displays disorientation. He stares at me and yells, "What did the devil say to you? You are writing to frame me!"

He cannot answer my questions about suicidal and homicidal tendencies. His psychosis interferes with his ability to report with any semblance of logic. It's impossible to gather how or if he has been sleeping lately. He cannot describe his mood. His affect ranges from anxious to flat to angry. He has no ability to concentrate. He is unable to listen to me despite my attempts to engage him.

This startling presentation is the result of months without taking any antipsychotic medication except when he was on inpatient units. He probably won't receive his next scheduled injection of long-acting antipsychotic medication soon. He will probably wait more than a week at the hospital emergency department before an inpatient unit accepts him for admission. The mental health system discriminates against patients that it perceives to be too tough to manage. Inpatient units discriminate against those patients with the potential for violence by not admitting them even when they have available beds. It's both tragic and ironic that the patients who most need inpatient admission are discriminated against and not prioritized.

I express my concerns about Adam with the hospital emergency medical doctor. I recommend that he be held until an inpatient bed is found. The doctor agrees with me and orders an oral dosage of Haldol for Adam. Adam readily accepts this from the nurse without any fight. He's all too familiar with this scenario.

Physical restraints should be used only as a last resort after attempts at verbal de-escalation fail to promote safety. Chemical restraints used to manage severe agitation or aggression typically involve antipsychotic or benzodiazepine medication. Intramuscular injection of medication enables quicker effectiveness than oral dosing. But intramuscular injection increases the risk of injury to professionals because they must manually immobilize the patients to inject the medication. The risk of injury is greater whenever patients physically resist being medicated. Therefore, staff should first try noninvasive and less intrusive means of decreasing agitation or aggression.

Widespread scientific research shows that early treatment of psychosis can prevent worsening of psychosis later. The system has failed to prevent worsening psychosis in Adam. Approximately one week later, the PACT clinician informs me that Adam was not admitted to an inpatient unit since I last evaluated him. Instead, he was discharged from the hospital emergency department to his resources. The extent of Adam's resources is scant. He has insufficient social support, no income, no home, no medication, no employment, and no means of transportation. His mental incapacity renders him dangerous. He lacks the ability to protect himself from basic harm. He cannot meet ordinary demands of life. He is unable to attend to his basic biological needs. He has psychosis, is gravely disabled, and nowhere in sight. Rehospitalization is inevitable.

✳ ✳ ✳

Gary walks into my office on his own and requests to be readmitted to the crisis unit. Earlier today, he was admitted there and then discharged, even though he didn't want to leave. He was discharged because he verbally abused a staff member and kicked over a chair, almost hitting another staff member. According to reports from workers, these incidents were not instigated. They happened without Gary being provoked in any way.

I offer to help Gary and explain to him that he probably won't be allowed to be readmitted on the same day. I suggest there might be other treatment options that he could access. Gary's hygiene is poor, his clothes are dirty, and he's malodorous. A dirty backpack is strapped over his shoulder. He glares at me. He hasn't slept in the last few days. He tells me that he has been eating adequately, but his clothes are falling off his thin body. Although Gary is eligible to receive state-funded services, he has no outpatient treatment provider. He is restless and easily irritable. He denies recently using any illicit drug or alcohol.

He tells me that his compliance with prescribed psychiatric medications has been good. When I ask him for the names of these medications, he cannot recall them. He removes prescription bottles from his backpack and shows them to me. I inspect the bottles and note that he has Olanzapine and Quetiapine, which are antipsychotic medications. I easily figure out that he has not been taking these recently. A crisis unit psychiatrist ordered the medications, and a staff member from that unit filled the prescriptions long ago, but many pills remain in each bottle.

He tells me that he has been staying at a homeless shelter recently but won't stay any longer because the noise bothered him. He adds that he resisted the urge to punch people in their faces at the shelter. He tersely expresses his belief that if he returns, he will physically assault someone. He has inflicted moderate injuries upon other people within the last six months. He refuses or is unable to speak about these incidents.

He has no family member or friend with whom he can temporarily reside. I ask him about his relationship with his aunt, who is not his legal guardian, although she is listed on his record. He tells me that he is all alone in the world with no social support. He has a legal guardian, an attorney, with a Rogers Monitor.

Gary attempted suicide by hanging years ago. About a year later, he attempted suicide again by cutting his wrist. He's not suicidal today.

Eventually, he reveals having auditory hallucinations commanding him to kill others. When I ask him for specifics, he either refuses or is unable to elaborate.

I subtly suggest that an inpatient hospitalization could be helpful. To sell this idea, I don't mention the benefit of restarting medications, considering that he's probably not in favor of medication. Rather, I refer to the extra support, a safe roof over his head, and the meals that he could get from a hospitalization.

Without apparently pondering his options, he responds with a lack of interest in this. I plead with him to consider hospitalization because his stays on the crisis unit haven't worked out lately. He won't budge.

I ask him about the incidents that led to his discharge from the crisis unit earlier today. He tells me that a staff member "told me that I'm nothing," which prompted him to become physically aggressive. "I'm sorry," he says. He promises not to harm anyone if admitted to the crisis unit.

I tell him that I will call the crisis unit to see if they could readmit him. As I'm preparing to call the crisis unit, I look at his record. Today's crisis unit course was the fifth one in less than two months. Most of these courses lasted less than three days. I see in the record something that prompts my decision to authorize a Section 12 for Gary. Yesterday, another mobile emergency clinician authorized a

Section 12 for him. Shortly after he was transported to a hospital emergency department, he was released to his resources. Beyond the extensive listing of Gary's inpatient hospitalizations, including consecutive years on a DMH inpatient unit, the clinician who sent him to the hospital yesterday noted something that strikes me as telling. When this clinician talked with Gary's health insurance company to get a pending inpatient admission authorized, she was told that eight days ago, the insurer authorized his inpatient stay through next week. Despite the insurance company believing that Gary should be on an inpatient unit for at least two weeks, the unit prematurely discharged him to the crisis unit.

I complete a Section 12 and fax it to the police. I call the police and ask that they come to assist. I order an ambulance. By the time police arrive, Gary is missing. Nevertheless, I give the Section 12 to them. The officers tell me they know him well because police officers have issued several Section 12s for him in the last couple of weeks.

I am astonished when Gary returns to my office the following night. "What can this grand resort offer me?" he asks with a smile. He's not sure why he's back. He flirts with the possibility of being admitted to the crisis unit again. He tells me that he slept under a bridge last night but doesn't want to do that again, emphasizing that he fears assault or theft of his belongings. His overall mental presentation is like yesterday's presentation.

I ask him how he lost his last apartment months ago. Gary is vague, simply stating that the property owner and he hated each other. He inappropriately laughs. His speech is somewhat loud as he describes feeling angry all the time. He doesn't give any reason for this. He seems guarded.

For a couple of seconds, he states something that makes no sense. He cannot clarify it. He whispers and mouths inaudibly at another point.

I ask him how he believes he could benefit from a stay on the crisis unit if there's a bed available there. "I don't know!" he yells.

I prompt him to take some deep breaths and remind him that I'm trying to help him. He takes a deep breath.

I ask him about hallucinations. Gary tells me he hasn't heard voices in a while. His thoughts are disorganized. Minutes later, he tells me that "Johnny" tells him that he's "a piece of shit and won't amount to anything." Sometimes, he hears Johnny instruct him to physically assault anyone whom he believes is "looking at me the wrong way." He reports not having acted on this recently.

I determined yesterday that Gary's reliability in reporting information was impaired. I cannot trust that he would safely function on a crisis unit. He needs more supervision and treatment than the crisis unit can offer. His recent crisis unit trials have not rendered him stable. His functioning seems to be worsening without medication. I suspect that he has been unmedicated outside of any inpatient or crisis unit for at least eight months. He was appointed a Rogers Monitor, which is ineffective outside of an inpatient unit.

He is at risk of harming others due to his psychosis and needs medication. Out of his view, I contact the police about the need for help to enforce a Section 12. I fax the Section 12 to them. They are familiar with Gary's history of violence. Though I did not ask for any number of officers to assist me, three officers arrive. They verbally persuade him to cooperate with ambulance staff members, which he does. It must be the uniforms and guns that again prevent aggression or elopement.

* * *

Approximately six days later, when I am at a hospital emergency department to evaluate another patient, the medical doctor asks me if there's any hope of securing a bed for Gary, since he has been there for six days. The patients who are most likely to become violent await admission to inpatient psychiatric units for days and even months at hospital emergency departments due to the shortage of inpatient beds and to discrimination. I remind the doctor about the shortage of inpatient beds, along with Gary's history of violence, and tell him that both factors inevitably extend the waiting period.

Meanwhile, a malingerer whom I evaluated at this same hospital emergency department yesterday has already been admitted to an inpatient unit. He will likely not become violent on the unit, likely won't present with barriers to a safe discharge, and likely will cooperate—at least to some degree—with the team. It becomes harder for well-meaning clinicians to not grant inpatient or crisis unit admission to the malingerer when administrators press them to do otherwise because the bed census happens to be low.

Patients discriminated against and waiting for admission to inpatient units eventually get admitted. I suspect this is due to either pressure from influential people or decreases of inpatient censuses that render desperation for revenue. The latter of these seems to occur much more frequently than the former. I witnessed both situations contributing to stuck patients eventually getting placed, on both inpatient and emergency settings.

Gary's six-day wait for inpatient placement is at once appalling and common. A recent study of ten hospital emergency departments, including community and academic hospitals in Massachusetts, examined the length of stays for psychiatric patients in a two-week period. In this study, the average length of stay for medical patients was 4.2 hours, while the average length of stay for psychiatric patients was 16.5 hours. The average length of stay for patients waiting to transfer to inpatient medical units was 3.9 hours, while the average length of stay of patients waiting to transfer to inpatient psychiatric units was 21.5 hours.[98] Another study compared waiting periods between five hundred five adult patients needing inpatient psychiatry and 18,768 adult patients needing inpatient medicine at a hospital emergency department from January 2007 to January 2008. The researchers found that the psychiatric patients waited 3.2 times longer than the medical patients for inpatient admission.[99]

The following day, I prepare to evaluate Gary at the hospital. When patients wait in hospital emergency departments during inpatient bed searches, they must be reassessed every twenty-four hours. Therefore, I naturally check the status of the bed search, with the assumption that this is a reassessment, since just yesterday the doctor and I discussed how long he had been waiting to be placed. But this is not a reassessment.

This is a new admission. The hospital emergency department discharged Gary to the streets last night, shortly after the doctor pressed me for resolution. Between these hospital emergency courses, Gary threatened to assault his aunt, who called the police. The police promptly authorized a Section 12 and escorted him back to the hospital. Perhaps the hospital's financial concerns contributed to the next premature discharge of Gary back to the streets. All the while, Gary doesn't fully grasp that he needs inpatient treatment.

CHAPTER 16

Anosognosia

Poor insight into psychosis is associated with poor treatment adherence, psychotic relapse, decreased psychosocial functioning (e.g., occupational status), and increased risk of violence toward self or others. Years ago, I gradually realized that inpatient cases involving the most severe psychosis had something in common. Many of these patients lacked awareness of their psychosis, especially regarding delusions. This is called anosognosia, a lack of insight into illness within oneself. It involves a lack of awareness of the signs and symptoms of an illness, along with an inability to comprehend the need for formal management and treatment of the illness.[100] Anosognosia often results in poor treatment compliance, which is why it warrants attention.

I have helped countless patients with delusions, medicated and unmedicated, and rarely have I seen a patient with insight into her delusions. I recall only one exceptional case in which a patient understood that he was delusional. Granted, I am most familiar with inpatient and emergency settings, which help many of the most disabled patients.

Thus, I cannot rule out the possibility of a higher rate of insight in other clinical settings.

Patients do not willfully induce anosognosia. Nor is this the same as denial. It involves a brain-based inability, likely on the right side of the brain, to understand that they are ill. Anosognosia probably involves abnormalities in the frontal and parietal lobes of the brain.[101] Using magnetic resonance imaging, researchers at McGill University in Canada compared the brains of sixty-six schizophrenic people with thirty-three healthy brains. They found that the schizophrenic brains had a significantly thinner insula cortex on the right side than the healthy brains. The insula cortex plays a role in self-awareness.[102]

Numerous studies reveal that approximately half of schizophrenic or bipolar-disordered people have anosognosia.[103] The peer-reviewed medical journal CNS *Drugs* documented that poor insight is a core feature of schizophrenia, and it occurs in 57 to 98 percent of patients.[104] In another study, researchers compared levels of awareness of having a serious mental illness among patients with schizophrenia, schizoaffective disorder, depression with psychosis, and mania as part of bipolar disorder. Out of all these groups, the schizophrenic patients had the least self-awareness of their serious mental illness.[105] With the high prevalence of anosognosia in schizophrenia, it is remarkable that anosognosia is not part of the diagnostic criteria for schizophrenia in the DSM-5.

Recovery is possible. A person with psychosis can gain insight and learn to take her medication, but this doesn't happen with all psychotic people. If someone with psychosis lacks awareness of her psychosis, she cannot understand that treatment is needed. I do not expect her to walk into a mental health agency and request help. I do not expect her to believe that the recommended medication would help.

Unless a patient wants to advocate for others whom she believes are mentally ill, she likely won't become actively involved in any advocacy organization designed to help her. When psychotic people lack the capacity to represent themselves, their families and friends need to advocate for them alongside mental health professionals. There are many professionals available to take on this role, but many patients lack a personal support network. Patients such as Lily, Earl, Drew, Adam, and thousands of others have only mental health professionals to speak for them.

Anosognosia often results in patients not adhering to their medication. Anosognosia is the most common reason that psychotic patients refuse to take their prescribed antipsychotic medication.[106] Medication nonadherence increases the risk of psychotic relapse.[107] Psychotic relapse typically leads to involuntary hospitalization. Therefore, increased anosognosia increases the risk of involuntary hospitalization.[108] One team of researchers completed a meta-analysis of fifty years of studies exploring the use of antipsychotic medication by schizophrenic patients. They found that patients who adhere to their prescribed antipsychotic medication are more likely to avoid psychotic relapse and hospitalization, refrain from violence, and have a decent quality of life.[109]

The following national study that shows the association between medication adherence and insight into illness was supported by the National Institute of Mental Health (NIMH), the National Institute of Drug Abuse, and the William T. Grant Foundation.[110] Researchers interviewed five hundred two seriously mentally ill people from ages eighteen to fifty-four about the extent to which they had either failed to receive treatment or dropped out of treatment over the immediately preceding twelve-month period. They explored the barriers and reasons for not receiving treatment or for dropping out of treatment. Among the people who didn't receive treatment, 55 percent reported that they didn't seek treatment because they didn't believe they had any problem, and 57.7 percent of the people who dropped out of treatment did so because they wanted to solve the problem on their own. These results seem to imply that anosognosia is a core reason for refusing to engage in treatment.

Researchers reviewed adherence to antipsychotic medication and insight into schizophrenia among sixty-eight schizophrenic adults on inpatient. They found a strong association between adherence to antipsychotic medication and having substantial insight into one's illness. They also found a strong association between adherence to antipsychotic medication and accepting the need for treatment.[111]

Anosognosia is a culprit in increasing the probability of violence among seriously mentally ill people. In Ohio, one hundred fifteen schizophrenic people with a history of being charged with violent offenses were compared with one hundred eleven schizophrenic people who had no history of violence. Researchers found that the patients with a history of violence had significantly poorer insight into their mental illness, less awareness of their mental illness, and less awareness of the purpose of their prescribed medication than did patients without a history of violence.[112] Five hundred three forensic patients on inpatient in England participated in a study exploring the relationship between violence and insight into mental illness. Poor insight was strongly associated with the highest levels of violence.[113]

A meta-analysis of nineteen studies shows that cognitive behavioral therapy and psychoeducation do not significantly help to reduce anosognosia.[114] Perhaps further scientific investigation into anosognosia could aid in the development of a new treatment to target this abnormality. No medication exists that specifically targets anosognosia.[115] The mental health system needs psychopharmacological development to alleviate anosognosia in seriously mentally ill patients.

Anosognosia can certainly interfere with a patient's ability to report information accurately to clinicians. When safety concerns are brought to my attention, perhaps by family members or police officers, and the patient does not acknowledge these concerns or minimizes them, it can be helpful to suspect that the patient is not reliable. When hints and clues exist, I must consider what is *not seen*. When gently pressed to explore and unmask the whole story, she might unveil a potential for violence, suicide, or poor self-care. The prevalence and consequences of anosognosia in serious mental illness—including an increased risk of violence—are extensive.

*AOT must not be the last resort ... It should be
offered before our loved ones' brains deteriorate.*

—G. G. Burns, tireless advocate for
people with serious mental illness

CHAPTER 17

Violence

IT'S WIDELY KNOWN THAT risk factors for violence include being male, misusing illicit drugs or alcohol, a history of imposing violence against others, a traumatic brain injury, and a history of being physically abused as a child. Environmental factors, such as geographical location, socioeconomic status, educational attainment, and unemployment influence the probability that violence will occur. Likewise, a history of engaging in antisocial behavior also seems to increase the chance of violence.[116]

I observe the signs that patients display indicating an increased risk of violence. These include restlessness, a history of traumatic brain injury, drug intoxication, a history of violence, and the presence of paranoid delusions while unmedicated.

Although there is a low prevalence of untreated psychosis among all mentally ill people, those with psychosis who are not receiving any psychotherapeutic treatment are more likely to be violent than the rest of the population. Unmanaged psychosis involving no medication is a risk factor for violence against others.[117] Research shows that 59 percent of one hundred eighty-five mass shootings in the United States from the years 1900 to 2017 were committed by either mentally ill people or those who showed signs of serious mental illness.[118]

Mother Jones analyzed sixty-two mass shootings over thirty years. In at least thirty-eight of these, the perpetrators displayed signs of mental illness, including delusions.[119] A study of 82,000 patients showed that violence decreased 45 percent among the subset of this group who complied with antipsychotic medication. Violence decreased 24 percent among the subset that accepted mood-stabilizing medication.[120]

In Sweden, 8,003 schizophrenic patients were studied immediately following their discharges from inpatient. Of this group, 13.2 percent engaged in at least one violent act, while 5.3 percent of the general population engaged in at least one violent act. However, much of the increased rate of violence was associated with increased use of illicit drugs and alcohol.[121]

Another study in Sweden looked at 2,005 people who were convicted of homicide or attempted homicide between the years 1988 and 2001. Eleven percent of this group was diagnosed with either schizophrenia or bipolar disorder. The highest rates of violence were among those who abused substances, were nonadherent with their medication, or both.[122]

When administrators and legislators emphasize that mentally ill people are no more likely to become violent than the general population, the most important part of the equation is missing. Although the percentage of the mentally ill population that is prone to violence toward others due to untreated psychosis is tiny, public safety is jeopardized when psychosis goes untreated. Most cancers don't originate in the head and neck, but the 3 percent of cancers that do occur in the head and neck are associated with higher rates of death.[123] If I were a medical student, I would want to learn about this first because it causes the most damage.

There have been instances when seriously mentally ill people who were untreated invoked mass violence in public places. A patient's inability to plan events is not part of the diagnostic criteria for any serious mental illness that involves psychosis. Although disorganized behavior and thinking can be part of psychosis, a meticulously planned act of violence does not rule out the possibility of serious mental illness as the culprit.[124]

On April 16, 2007, twenty-three-year-old Seung-Hui Cho, who was untreated for what probably was schizophrenia, killed thirty-two people and injured seventeen others at Virginia Polytechnic Institute and State University in Blacksburg, Virginia, before killing himself. Many psychiatrists suggested that Seung-Hui had emerging signs of schizophrenia and was probably delusional at the time of the murders and suicide. Even laypersons without clinical expertise who witnessed his disorganization and paranoia displayed in YouTube videos can understand that his thought process and content were abnormal. The video recordings he made of himself were seen by others only after the incident. Enraged by his perception that others harmed him, he ranted: "You had a hundred billion chances and ways to have avoided today. But you decided to spill my blood ... The decision was yours. Now you have blood on your hands that will never wash off ... You have vandalized my heart, raped my soul, and torched my conscience ... Thanks to you, I die like Jesus Christ to inspire generations of the weak and defenseless people ... Jesus loved crucifying me. He loved inducing cancer in my head, terrorizing my heart, and ripping my soul all this time."[125]

The link between violence and mental illness can appear unsubstantial when serious mental illness goes undetected. Seung-Hui was never formally diagnosed with a serious mental illness! When he expressed suicidal thinking with a peer at college, a licensed clinical social worker determined that he qualified for involuntary inpatient hospitalization and planned accordingly on December 13, 2005. The admitting documentation from Carilion Clinic Saint Albans Hospital shows only one diagnosis: mood disorder—not otherwise specified.

At that time, Virginia required a court hearing to determine a cause for continued commitment, immediately following involuntary admission. A psychologist and a psychiatrist evaluated Seung-Hui. Despite the odd nature of his largely mute presentation, neither of them contacted any outside source, including his parents and sister or other students, for assistance. The psychiatrist used privacy law as an excuse for this, even though the involuntary status of his case warranted no need for Seung-Hui's permission to initiate contact. Had this been done, perhaps his family would have voiced concern that something was amiss in the context of his baseline. The two evaluators submitted their recommendation that Seung-Hui be released from the hospital on December 14, 2005. The judge agreed to order his release, with the condition that Seung-Hui seek outpatient treatment. With the help of a staff member, Seung-Hui scheduled an appointment at the Cook Counseling Center for December 14, 2005. It was the last outpatient appointment he ever attended.[126]

When I first learned that Adam Lanza had killed his mother and then killed twenty children and six adults before killing himself at Sandy Hook Elementary School in Newtown, Connecticut, on December 14, 2012,[127] I wondered if he had psychosis at the time. Subsequently, I reviewed the analysis of Adam that the Office of the Child Advocate issued to the Connecticut government in 2014. I found insufficient evidence to conclude that he had psychosis at the time of this tragedy. Instead, I saw only a couple of weak indicators of the remote possibility of psychosis. Nevertheless, history has shown that government reports about patients' mental health status have not always been reliable. In September 2005, Adam had an emergency psychiatric evaluation at a hospital, but his mother refused to cooperate with the recommendation that he remain there for an additional evaluation by a hospital psychiatrist. He went home instead.[128]

On July 20, 2012, James E. Holmes killed twelve people and injured seventy others at a movie theater in Aurora, Colorado, while untreated for his serious mental illness.[129] His trial was an example of how flaws of the mental and legal systems have failed to protect and treat seriously mentally ill defendants. At James' trial, his defense attorney pursued the insanity plea. Public defense attorney Daniel King argued during the trial that twenty doctors who had evaluated James while he was in custody, in addition to a psychiatrist who had met with him before the shooting, all had diagnosed him with schizophrenia.[130] Based on her testimony, psychiatrist Lynne Fenton, who had treated James in psychotherapy just weeks before the shootings, appeared to suspect that he had psychosis. When James initiated termination of their relationship, she was so alarmed about the potential for danger that he displayed that she violated his confidentiality in the month before the shootings by contacting the police and his mother. But despite witnessing his homicidal threats, she didn't proceed with an involuntary hold.[131]

Confidentiality laws allow for exceptions. If I become alarmed enough to use the legal exception to honoring privacy because I suspect psychosis, a patient regularly makes homicidal threats, and treatment is refused, a Section 12 will be used. Despite psychiatrists' testimony that James had schizophrenia, the pursuit of NGRI failed. Jurors rejected the insanity plea.[132] James was found guilty of first-degree murder.[133]

The criteria for meeting the legal definition of insanity vary from state to state. The insanity defense is underutilized. The chance of a successful NGRI ruling is slim.[134] When NGRI is pursued, most cases don't go to trial by jury. After a defendant is charged with murder or attempted murder, the defendant, his lawyer, or the judge can request a psychiatric evaluation. The judge might determine that the defendant, due to his incompetence, is unable to participate in trial proceedings reasonably. If competence is not gained, he could be confined to inpatient for years. The defendant can gain competence with the assistance of psychiatric medication on an inpatient unit. If this occurs, a trial might ensue. If a trial is possible, the defendant can pursue the insanity plea with the goal of an NGRI verdict. When a judge rules that a defendant is NGRI, typically he is sentenced to a state inpatient psychiatric unit rather than to prison.

On March 30, 1981, John Hinckley, Jr. attempted to assassinate former President Ronald Reagan. John's defense attorney argued that John suffered from major depressive disorder and schizophrenia, and as a result, the attorney pursued the insanity plea. Before John engaged in this violence, he had become obsessed with the movie *Taxi Driver*, which involves a character plotting to assassinate a presidential candidate. One of the actresses in this movie, Jodie Foster, received a phone call and letters from John, in which he professed his love for her. His delusion involved his belief that she would return this love if he killed the President. In 1982, a judge ruled that John was NGRI, which resulted in his sentencing to an inpatient psychiatric unit rather than a prison.

The social, legal, and political backlash that arose from this ruling was fierce. Powerful members of the public, presumably connected to Reagan, disagreed with the ruling, leading to sweeping legislative changes. After the NGRI verdict, it became more difficult for lawyers and psychiatrists to succeed in their pursuit of NGRI because of the Insanity Defense Reform Act of 1984. In this Act, Congress restricted the legal definition of insanity, thus reserving this ruling for the sickest of the sick.[135] States restricted the criteria for which judges could deem a defendant charged with a violent crime as NGRI.[136] Also because of the backlash, Idaho, Montana, Utah, and Kansas eliminated the NGRI verdict as a possibility. Consequently, it seems likely that many defendants who commit violent offenses due to untreated psychosis are inappropriately sentenced to prison rather than to inpatient settings.

The consequences of restrictive NGRI criteria for defendants who need NGRI verdicts can include sentences of lifetime imprisonment or even the death penalty.[137] When the defendant is found guilty after an NGRI pursuit fails, he is sentenced to prison. The main purpose of prison is punishment. Thus, the extent of psychiatric treatment available is scant in prison compared with the treatment available at a psychiatric hospital. Although mental health courts allow judges to consider mental illness, and these courts exist in the states with or without NGRI, New England Public Radio quoted psychiatrist Camille LaCroix as stating that these courts usually do not manage cases involving violent offenses.[138]

One of the reasons for the scarcity of the NGRI verdict is that entering the insanity plea is financially costly for state governments. For instance, in California, entering an insanity plea increases both the length and cost of the trial.[139] Experts are hired to help the defense attorney. Evaluating the person with mental illness, reviewing his medical and psychiatric records, and testifying are all time-consuming. Because many seriously mentally ill defendants are also financially impoverished, they are typically unable to afford private defense counsel and psychiatric treatment providers. Therefore, public defenders and psychiatric professionals employed by state governments tend to take on these cases.

✳ ✳ ✳

The data collection period for the MacArthur Violence Risk Assessment Study, conducted by the Research Network on Mental Health & the Law and supported by the John D. and Catherine T. MacArthur Foundation and NIMH, spanned from the middle of 1992 to late 1995. The study involved interviews with nine hundred fifty-one men and women diagnosed with mental illness who were discharged from inpatient units to outpatient settings in Kansas City, Kansas; Pittsburgh, Pennsylvania; and Worcester, Massachusetts. Researchers interviewed five hundred sixty-four of them five times, approximately every ten weeks in the year immediately following their discharges from inpatient. The other participants were interviewed at least once. During this year, 27.5 percent of the participants engaged in physical violence toward others. In this group, substance-misuse was often present. Thirty-four percent of the participants had schizophrenia, bipolar disorder, or psychosis.

The MacArthur researchers determined that mentally ill people are not more likely to be aggressive than the rest of the population. However, most of the patients in this study were not psychotic. Most mentally ill people don't have untreated psychosis. Of the study participants, 17.2 percent were primarily diagnosed with schizophrenia. Of the study participants, 40.3 percent had depression, making this the most common primary diagnosis.[140] Depression is not associated with violence.

Those who refused to participate in the MacArthur study were more likely to have schizophrenia than were those who participated in the study. Toward the beginning of the study, 29 percent of the patients refused to participate. Fifty percent of the patients terminated their participation within the year. Among the patients who refused to participate, 43.7 percent were diagnosed with schizophrenia.[141]

The MacArthur study also excluded the schizophrenic patients who could not be found during the follow-up. These patients were more likely to be violent than those who cooperated with the researchers.[142] Among a variety of research studies, patients who cannot be found or who directly refuse to participate in longitudinal studies are more likely to act violently than those who cooperate with researchers.[143]

The MacArthur researchers eliminated those who were most likely to become violent. When Christian Joyal and colleagues reviewed the study, they believed that the prevalence of assaults would have been greater if the percentage of schizophrenic patients participating in the study were higher.[144] The researchers did not include prisoners or recent prisoners, anyone jailed, anyone involuntarily engaged in treatment, anyone in forensic hospitals, or anyone committed to extended-care inpatient units. These populations tend to be more violent than other populations.

The MacArthur study also excluded incidents of violence that did not result in bodily harm. In other words, if a potential target was confronted by someone attempting to assault him and the target ran away before being assaulted, this case was not included in the study. The researchers also didn't consider incidents of property destruction.[145] Eric N. Bertrand, homeless and showing signs of paranoid schizophrenia, set a fire in the Forbes Library in Northampton, Massachusetts, and the fire resulted in an estimated $100,000 worth of damage.[146] Eric would not be considered violent in this study.

Furthermore, the MacArthur study's control group involved neighborhoods that were more prone to violence than most neighborhoods in the United States. These neighborhoods were economically impoverished as well, and many seriously mentally ill people resided there. The prevalence of substance-misuse in these neighborhoods was high at the time, and countless studies have shown that substance-misuse increases the probability of violence. Psychiatrist Sally Satel and DJ Jaffe expressed the belief that many of the patients in the experimental group were discharged from inpatient units to these same violence-prone neighborhoods, which decreased the difference in the measure of violence.[147]

Within one year following the MacArthur study, researchers conducted a follow-up evaluation of the risk of violence. Over 50 percent of the patients engaged in menacing behavior within one year of discharge from inpatient units.[148] They found a weak association between violence and hallucinations among patients. However, at this time, a strong association was found between the continuance of delusions and violence.[149]

Professionals in the mental health industry and legislators use the MacArthur study to bolster the common conception that "mentally ill people are no more violent than the general population." In my own workplace, I read this statement in an email sent by one of the managers to all staff members immediately following a violent act inflicted by a person with a serious mental illness. A rehabilitative outreach services recipient who was paranoid delusional and not willing to take any professionally recommended medication had caused the serious injury of a clinician. In the email message, staff members were told that the media had exaggerated the injuries. There was no mention of the fact that people with unmanaged psychosis are more likely to be violent than the general population.

The director of the program told me that she didn't believe the patient's mental illness was related to this violent incident. To give her the benefit of the doubt, I wonder if this was what she was taught. Did she truly believe otherwise but had been taught to repeat this falsehood?

Two hundred four studies explored whether psychosis was a risk factor for violence and made a comparison between psychotic people and the general population. A meta-analysis of these studies shows that psychosis contributed to a 49 to 68 percent increase in the probability of engaging in violence, as compared with the group without mental illness.[150] Leading psychiatrist E. Fuller Torrey lists myriad violent incidents that were associated with or caused by untreated schizophrenia and bipolar disorder in his books, *American Psychosis: How the Federal Government Destroyed the Mental Illness Treatment System*[151] and *The Insanity Offense: How America's Failure to Treat the Seriously Mentally Ill Endangers Its Citizens.*[152]

Seena Fazel and colleagues analyzed the results of twenty studies between 1970 and February 2009 that compared the risk of violence between psychotic people and the general population.[153] The percentage of violence was higher among the group with schizophrenia or other psychoses than among the general population. These studies involved a total of 18,423 cases of schizophrenia or other psychoses. Of these cases, 1,832 involved violence. All clinical cases were compared with 1,714,904 people in the general population. Among this general population, 27,185 were violent.

In this analysis, 4.7 percent of the cases were from the United States.[154] Of the rest of these cases, 0.2 percent were from New Zealand,[155] 0.4 percent were from England and Wales,[156] 0.5 percent were from Finland,[157] 0.5 percent were from Israel,[158] 2.8 percent were from Switzerland,[159] 7.2 percent were from Austria,[160] 9 percent were from Germany,[161] 10.2 percent were from Denmark,[162] 15.5 percent were from Australia,[163] and 49 percent were from Sweden.[164]

This meta-analysis shows that people with substance-misuse are just as likely to commit violence whether they are psychotic or not psychotic. People with substance-misuse who are not psychotic are more likely to be violent than people with no substance-misuse who are psychotic.[165]

This meta-analysis also shows that homicide is more associated with schizophrenia and other psychoses than with the general population. Psychotic people were charged with two hundred sixty-one homicides. People in the general population sample were charged with 2,999 homicides. The risk of committing homicide was greater in the population with schizophrenia or other psychoses than in the general population sample.[166]

Delusions are associated more with violence than hallucinations are. Among psychotic people who are most violent, delusions often drive violence.[167] A study of 1,400 psychotic patients in the United States found that delusions were associated with incidents of serious violence.[168] Another study found that 40 percent of psychotic prisoners attributed their crimes to delusions, regardless of their levels of insight into these delusions.[169] A significant relationship was found between delusional drives and violence resulting in serious injuries in a sample of patients on a high-security inpatient unit. Seventy-five percent of these patients attributed their violence to delusions.[170]

Persecutory delusions are particularly associated with violence[171] and include the perception of being in danger, expecting to be harmed, and the sense of being controlled by an outside source.[172] The following types of delusional beliefs most increase the risk of violence:

+ the belief that others or outside forces are threatening to harm them

+ the belief that others or outside forces are controlling their minds

+ the belief that others or outside forces are inserting thoughts into their brains[173]

Among psychotic people who have the potential for violence, the probability of repeated violence is lessened with adherence to medication and beneficial response to medication.[174] Since anosognosia often results in nonadherence to medication, it would be prudent for professionals to consider this when planning treatment for psychotic patients.

CHAPTER 18

Stigma and Antipsychiatry

STIGMA TOWARD MENTAL ILLNESS embodies the belief that the mentally ill person caused her illness. It associates mental illness with shame, infamy, and disgrace. How much stigma exists toward mental illness? It's difficult to measure. Organizations that advocate for the mentally ill population, including the National Alliance on Mental Illness (NAMI), appear to overemphasize stigma.[175] They portray it as a massive problem and urgently promote campaigns to eradicate it. But is stigma less problematic than the media and certain organizations make it out to be? Is NAMI's claims about the extent of stigma a myth?

It is antiquated to apply shame to mental illness. The belief that mental illness is less serious than physical illness reinforces stigma. Of course, we shouldn't minimize the seriousness of brain abnormality. If mental illness weren't downplayed, there would be less stigma surrounding it. It is now uniformly understood in all scientific arenas that serious mental illness originates in the brain.[176] The brain is just as much a physical and tangible organ as the liver, heart, and stomach.

Breakdown

Leading research demonstrates that the greatest risk factor for bipolar disorder and schizophrenia lies in genetics,[177] which confirms that serious mental illness is biological in origin.

There are many reasons why psychotic people don't engage in treatment. They include:

+ inability to afford copays

+ not having any health insurance or having an inability to pay

+ side effects or fear of toxic effects of medications

+ lack of access to outpatient appointments

+ the belief that they can improve functioning without medication or other services

+ dissatisfaction with services (e.g., the psychiatrist was rude)

+ logistical inability to get to appointments (e.g., lack of transportation)

+ not knowing enough about the illness or treatment

+ substance-dependence

+ fear of being involuntarily hospitalized

+ lack of family support or encouragement

+ forgetting to follow through

+ intentional self-harm

+ apathy

✦ language barrier

✦ wanting to solve the problem on their own

✦ perceived lack of effectiveness of treatment

Although stigma associated with mental illness exists, it is not the greatest barrier to accessing treatment. No patient with psychosis ever reported to me that this was her reason for not seeking help.

The belief that mental illness doesn't exist and that medication is largely unhelpful runs amok throughout government-funded programs. In Massachusetts, the Recovery Learning Communities (RLCs) are groups largely dominated by peer specialists who endorse the possibility that signs of psychosis are normal. Besides running Reiki sessions that seem frivolous because no scientific evidence shows their effectiveness, the groups regularly lead classes titled "Hearing Voices" for their members. They advertise that "Hearing Voices groups do not pathologize the experience of hearing voices or experiencing other altered/extreme states. Instead, they ask, 'What does the experience mean to you?'"[178]

To pathologize a human experience means to view it as abnormal. Hearing voices that do not exist is certainly not normal. If an impressionable person in her early twenties is experiencing auditory hallucinations for the first time that involve commands to kill herself or someone else, and she attends one of these classes, the chance that she will seek appropriate treatment is reduced if she comes to believe that nothing abnormal is going on. Although encouraging members to explore the meaning of their voices and cope with them in healthy ways is acceptable, allowing too much self-determination can be dangerous. Conversations with the opposing camp revealed that if a member says she heard voices commanding her to kill herself, the trainer of the hearing-voices class will determine if this member views it as problematic. If I hypothetically insert myself into this situation, I would be more concerned about the member if she did not view the voices as problematic than if she did. This is because a person is less likely to seek help if she has anosognosia. It seems that they would be more concerned about the member if she viewed the voices as problematic than if she did not. Therein lies the crux of our differences. Anosognosia is real and a common barrier to treatment. But, they either minimize anosognosia or delegitimize it.

For months in 2017, Western Mass RLC advertised their seminars titled "Coming Off Psych Drugs," which supported people planning to reduce or stop taking their prescribed psychiatric medications.[179] Of course, seriously depressed people who are drug resistant are better off using psychotherapy, self-help, electroconvulsive shock therapy, transcranial magnetic stimulation, or light therapy. Regardless of the illness, people who are not authorized to prescribe medication should not teach people how to reduce or stop taking medication, especially in a formal setting. Advanced nurse practitioners, physician's assistants, or medical doctors do not lead these seminars. I cannot imagine that anyone who lacked awareness of her psychosis benefitted from this class.

The government allows antipsychiatry to infiltrate programs that it funds. The Massachusetts Department of Mental Health (DMH) has funded RLCs in recent years and continues to do so.[180] The DMH promotes RLCs.[181] The NAMI chapter of Massachusetts also promotes RLCs.[182]

In July 2017, I testified at the Boston State House in favor of a bill to implement Assisted Outpatient Treatment (AOT), which is described later. At the hearing, most of the opposition to AOT came from peer specialists. As I waited to testify, I heard their testimonies. Instead of identifying mental illness as pathology originating in the brain, they berated psychiatrists for labeling people with psychiatric diagnoses. Instead of referring to auditory hallucinations as being a sign of mental illness, they promoted the notion that hearing voices that are not there is simply an extreme state of altered reality.

A meta-analysis of eighteen studies involved 5,597 participants receiving a variety of services from peer specialists. The researchers found no significant benefits to using peer specialists to help the seriously mentally ill population.[183] The Centers for Medicare & Medicaid Services reports that the use of peer specialists does not demonstrate significant clinical benefits to the seriously mentally ill population.[184]

When they do not deny the existence of mental illness, RLCs minimize it. Minimizing mental illness is not far off from believing that it doesn't exist. Followers of RLCs are either persuaded to believe that no mental illness exists and that medication is largely unhelpful, or influenced to minimize mental illness and downplay the benefits of medication. Whenever mental illness and the importance of medication are minimized, psychiatry is devalued and considered less worthy of respect than other medical specialties. This is the essence of stigma.

And what kind of twisted "right" is it to stab or shoot to death yourself or some innocent bystander while in a psychotic frenzy directed by terrifying voices from a disordered and disabled mind—in the face of treatment which, because of lack of laws or lack of resources, cannot be given?

—Darold A. Treffert, M.D.[185]

CHAPTER 19

Reform

Malingerers are light years away from people who are prone to violence and anosognosia due to their serious mental illnesses and their caregivers who make genuine appeals for help. Malingerers are on the opposite end of the spectrum of psychiatric presentation. How can the prevalence of malingering be reduced? Not easily. I don't expect the entire problem to dissipate. There will always be patients who malinger, regardless of attempts to correct the problem. Unfortunately, all attempts by master-level clinicians to not enable malingerers at the hospital will not prevent all emergency medical doctors from being overly cautious. But some attempts at tackling the problem are better than no attempt at all.

When a staff member of a hospital or crisis unit must decide between admitting a malingerer and a patient with psychosis who is likely to become violent and refuse to accept all treatment offered, the former of these will be preferred. Inpatient staff members may find that attending to malingering patients is less difficult than attending to other patients. Malingerers are usually pleasant (especially when they get what they want) and not violent. Their thought processes are usually organized and clear, making it easy to understand them.

Hospitals and crisis units are financially profiting from these patients. If information that warrants inpatient and crisis unit criteria is conveyed to health insurance companies by clinicians, the units get reimbursed. For this reason, I suspect that many, if not all, of these facilities, would rally against any attempt to curtail malingering.

The United States Department of Health and Human Services and state governments could require that rates of malingering be tracked. Once the magnitude of the problem is understood, large-scale attempts to reduce it can be sanctioned. Agencies and hospitals that employ mobile emergency services teams could require clinicians to contribute to a database of names of patients discovered to be malingering. Mental health agencies, inpatient units, and hospital emergency departments could be required by their funding sources and regulatory agencies to track rates of malingering.

Whenever clinicians strongly suspect malingering, find evidence of it, or diagnose it, they could add the names of these patients to the database. The database would alert clinicians to the higher chances of malingering since past behaviors can predict future behaviors. Whenever clinicians are preparing to interview patients by reviewing electronic records, alerts could appear that warn that these patients have been known to malinger. By accessing the database, clinicians would then know whom they are about to interview, thus reducing the likelihood that inpatient hospitalization will be granted to those who don't need it and saving the beds for those most in crisis. This doesn't mean that the final treatment disposition cannot be an inpatient or crisis unit admission. I occasionally evaluate patients who have malingered and who apologize for that when they are truly in crisis.

University programs should include courses on malingering in their curriculums. Basic courses in psychology, social work, and other related fields should not begin with the premise that all patients are truthful. Students aspiring to begin careers in psychology and social work would benefit from knowing that malingerers regularly interact with mental health professionals. If I had been better educated on how to identify malingering at the beginning of my career, I would have been more prepared to refuse malingerers' requests for entry to inpatient or crisis units.

When searching for continuing education courses to maintain my license, I've never come across this topic. Continuing education companies that help clinicians maintain their licenses should offer more courses on malingering. More education about this population would likely lead to fewer cases of enabling them. This would free up inpatient beds for patients who truly need them.

The outpatient mental health system in the United States is inadequate[186] and has continuously declined in quality and overall funding support, both in the public and private sectors, for decades.[187] The Social Security Administration's Medicaid Institutions for Mental Diseases law is the main reason that state-operated hospitals have eliminated so many psychiatric beds. A part of deinstitutionalization and in existence since 1965, this law prohibits the federal government from financially reimbursing Medicaid for inpatient psychiatric facilities with more than sixteen beds for patients aged twenty-one, and in certain circumstances twenty-two, up to sixty-four years old. It discriminates against the seriously mentally ill population, who are more likely than the rest of the mentally ill population to need government-funded inpatient care. When Medicaid didn't have enough money to fund hospitals, state governments eliminated inpatient beds or closed hospitals.[188] The exclusion prevents hospitals from getting reimbursed for this population, which renders those institutions unwilling to hospitalize patients for extended periods of time. Medicaid should be allotted adequate federal funding to increase the number of beds. Federally sanctioned discrimination against the seriously mentally ill population is wrong. The law should be repealed because it excludes this population from getting proper inpatient funding.

The pendulum that symbolizes the mental health system is suspended at one end of its arc. Overly restrictive inpatient criteria and a severe shortage of inpatient beds mean that fewer seriously mentally ill people are hospitalized than ever before. It is not necessary to restore the number of inpatient beds that were available in the 1950s. The treatment advances since then make this unnecessary. But gravity should be allowed to pull the pendulum toward the middle. We need many more private and public inpatient psychiatric beds, both in Massachusetts and throughout the United States, to treat and protect the seriously mentally ill population. Inpatient criteria should be expanded so that it is no longer close to impossible for a person with psychosis, anosognosia, and a propensity to become violent to be helped.

Since February 1, 2018, in Massachusetts, all health insurance companies are expected to assist emergency services programs with inpatient bed searches for patients. If an inpatient bed hasn't been secured by the twenty-fourth hour since the start of the bed search, the program must notify the patient's insurance of this. When asking insurance for assistance, the emergency clinician is expected to convey information about the patient's clinical necessity for inpatient admission, barriers to inpatient units accepting him, evidence of the bed search, and reasons for inpatient units denying him admission. Insurance is expected to communicate with clinical and administrative leaders of hospitals about the case. Insurance clinicians can ask inpatient units to prioritize patients who are waiting the longest.[189]

If no bed has been found by the end of the fourth day of waiting, insurance must inform the Department of Mental Health (DMH) about the case and ask for DMH's assistance. If a barrier to securing a bed is clinical, a conference call is required between a hospital emergency physician, an insurance psychiatrist, and a DMH psychiatrist.[190] They can talk for hours upon hours about why the patient needs inpatient admission and describe the barriers to him getting accepted, but this doesn't change the fact that hospitals do not violate any law when they refuse to grant admission to patients. Of course, there are clinically appropriate reasons for not accepting patients for admission. For instance, if a patient is medically compromised, he would be better served on a psychiatric unit of a general hospital surrounded by an array of medical consultations than in a freestanding psychiatric hospital. But it's inappropriate to refuse to grant admission to a patient because they expect his length of stay to extend way beyond the typical week.

Perhaps the hospital emergency stays in Massachusetts will decline with the increase in advocacy efforts by emergency services teams, insurance companies, DMH, and inpatient units. Although these new mandates are intended to reduce the hospital emergency length of stays for patients needing inpatient care, not much is expected to change anytime soon. As long as it is legal for inpatient units to discriminate and there remains a severe shortage of inpatient beds, too many patients will continue to wait for weeks or even months for inpatient units to accept them. Armed with all the information about patients pertaining to why they are denied admission, insurance companies are limited in their capacity to influence hospitals. Ultimately, inpatient units are legally allowed to accept or deny for admission whoever they want, regardless of ethics.

* * *

Inpatient units are more likely to decline for admission those patients who don't want help, who are violent, who have no payment source, or who will likely need lengthy inpatient courses. When I worked on an inpatient unit, I accidentally overheard two administrators discussing their priority to remind the admissions department not to admit any patient who's "homeless, hard to place ... going to be stuck here forever ... going to seriously hurt one of us." Inpatient units should be held legally accountable for this type of discrimination because these are the patients who need inpatient admission the most.

There is no appropriate excuse for discrimination against this population. Inpatient units are all equipped with chemical and mechanical restraints as well as staff members who are sufficiently trained on how to use them. Inpatient units have staff members who are trained in verbal de-escalation techniques to try to prevent restraint. They are morally obligated to care for and contain violent and seriously mentally ill patients who don't want help but need inpatient treatment.

The government should require that inpatient admissions departments submit their censuses every six to twelve hours to all emergency services programs that conduct bed searches. All emergency staff members should have access to this listing of bed availability. Although many inpatient admissions departments already do this for marketing purposes, there's no legal accountability when they discriminate against the most challenging patients.

Let's suppose I am searching for an inpatient bed for Joe, but Joe is violent, without health insurance, unable to pay privately, does not want any help, and will likely need a transfer to a DMH inpatient unit that would render him stuck there for months. An inpatient admissions staff member tells me that there is no bed availability. But I see in the census list just forwarded to us that the unit has plenty of bed availability. I could then report this inconsistency to DMH. Citations and warnings could be issued, along with the threat of closure, to any inpatient unit that repeatedly discriminates against patients who are more challenging.

Although the federal law to protect patients' confidentiality, the Health Insurance Portability and Accountability Act (HIPAA), can occasionally appear excessive when it interferes with providing ideal care to patients in emergency psychiatry, it presents more challenges on inpatient. In emergency psychiatry, it is unnecessary to obtain release of confidentiality documents when Section 12s are in place. No release of confidentiality must be signed by patients to talk with their legal guardians or physician-invoked health care proxies. Although these legal aspects apply to inpatient units as well, including Section 7, inpatient cases typically last longer and involve more clinical exploration than emergency services cases. Inpatient units are designed to plan for discharges and aftercare much more efficiently than emergency services programs. It can be nearly impossible to obtain reliable information from a patient who is so disorganized that he can barely form a sentence, who is highly agitated, doesn't want to be there, or is paranoid. As a social worker on inpatient, my responsibilities included obtaining background information from family members or friends of the patients, updating them on progress, and gauging readiness for discharge based on their impressions of the patients' progress. The patient can refuse to allow the inpatient social worker to provide information to anyone on the outside who cares for him.

If the mental health system in the United States worked properly and if psychosis could be treated easily, HIPAA would not be as problematic as it is now. Because the system is very far from working properly and psychosis cannot be treated easily, I offer the following solution, in the meantime.

When anosognosia and psychosis render a patient unable to make sound judgments involving treatment recommendations, and unable to sign any release of confidentiality document, it warrants an exception to the conventional procedure. If the clinical record already includes the name of a family member or friend, relationship to the patient, and phone number or email address of the person, confidentiality law could allow for two psychiatrists to authorize an exception to confidentiality rules. The team would inform the patient of this override. This type of HIPAA authorization would enable the inpatient treatment team to have contact with the patient's closest family member or friend, which would enable safe discharge planning.

There are undoubtedly instances when the family member or friend who is listed in the record is not supportive, not reliable as a reporter of information, or both. Treatment team members would be expected to do their best to discern this and consider it when formulating and executing the treatment plan. Occasionally, I come across a patient's family member who appears unstable, shows poor judgment, does not speak supportively about the patient, or disagrees with me on all accounts. Such a family member can be disappointed with me. My job is not to please everyone when the safety of the patient is paramount.

* * *

Many patients with untreated psychosis deteriorate to the extent where they or others have been harmed and inpatient care is inevitable. Assisted Outpatient Treatment (AOT) helps seriously mentally ill patients who are at risk of not adhering to their recommended outpatient treatment plans. It helps them by preventing danger.

AOT can involve civil court orders or no court orders. In both types of AOT, mental health professionals attempt to persuade the recipients to adhere to their prescribed medications and attend their clinical outpatient appointments with psychotherapists, psychiatrists, and case managers. All AOT involves intensive case management services and comprehensive supervision. In court-ordered AOT, judges order seriously mentally ill patients to adhere to their outpatient treatment plans, which may or may not include medications.[191]

Laws allowing AOT do not increase costs for outpatient agencies because these agencies already provide services that AOT recipients can use. With AOT, admissions to inpatient units are more likely to be timely because recipients have already been supervised by the outpatient system. For seriously mentally ill people who don't immediately qualify for inpatient level of care, AOT can be used to prevent mental deterioration and danger. This preventive approach reduces the probability of future inpatient hospitalizations.[192]

Lack of treatment of psychosis escalates financial spending by governments with increased rates of homicides, fires, and arrests. AOT is proven to save money and lives by reducing homelessness, hospitalizations, rates of arrest, and criminalization of mentally ill people. Prison and hospital confinement are vastly costlier than outpatient treatment. AOT is an evidence-based treatment that is less financially costly than incarceration and inpatient treatment.

Farron was not the recipient of AOT, Involuntary Outpatient Commitment (IOC), or Conditional Release (CR) when he killed two police officers. If Farron had been court-ordered to take his prescribed medication to manage his schizophrenia, would it have prevented those deaths? The chance of this tragedy occurring would have been significantly reduced if he had been medicated.

William was not the recipient of AOT, IOC, or CR when he killed his mother, Amy. At the time of this tragedy, no AOT, no IOC, and no CR existed in Maine. If William had been court-ordered to take his prescribed medication to manage his schizophrenia, and if he had been discharged from the inpatient unit at the appropriate time, his mother would likely be alive. Even William himself acknowledged later to his father that this tragedy would not have happened if he had been properly medicated. The families of severely mentally ill people have the right to safety.

CR and court-ordered AOT are types of IOC. AOT is more inclusive than IOC because AOT includes plans that are not court-ordered. Per an inpatient court order, while involuntarily committed to an inpatient unit, a patient under CR can be discharged to a non-secured setting in the community under the regular supervision of the hospital, with the condition that if he mentally deteriorates, readmission to the inpatient unit can be enforced.[193] Literature also refers to IOC as mandatory community treatment or community treatment orders.[194] I largely use the term AOT because it is the most commonly used term to describe IOC in the media and in professional literature.

Massachusetts has no AOT, no IOC, and no CR. It is the only state without both CR and AOT. It has none of these legal means of improving care and preventing danger for the seriously mentally ill population. Recent Massachusetts bills have called for AOT, but no tragedy has motivated legislators enough to adopt it. AOT also does not exist in Connecticut and Maryland. All other states and the District of Columbia have laws that allow AOT.

If Massachusetts ever enacts AOT, it could be the best preventive strategy to fight the consequences of untreated schizophrenia and bipolar disorder with psychosis. Dr. Treffert brilliantly wrote, "Many of these 'dying with your rights on' cases demonstrate graphically, and tragically, that freedom can be a hazard—or another form of imprisonment—for persons who are obviously ill and in need of treatment, who are not yet dangerous but well on their way to being so, and who, because of that obviously and permeating illness, are unable to care for themselves."[195] Will the further loss of life due to serious mental illness motivate legislators to enact AOT? On January 20, 2011, Deshawn James Chappell, twenty-seven years old, with schizophrenia, killed twenty-five-year-old Stephanie Moulton, a counselor at a state-funded residential program for DMH recipients in Revere, Massachusetts. He beat her on the head and repeatedly stabbed her in the neck before leaving her partially nude body in a church parking lot.[196]

According to WBUR, Boston's National Public Radio news station, DMH reported that Deshawn had an extensive history of mental illness involving psychosis and violence beginning at twenty years old, and he often refused to take his medication.[197] His mother, Yvette Chappell, reported that he had psychosis involving paranoia and auditory hallucinations. She said that he told her the devil was ordering him to do things, and he spoke nonsensically.[198] Just a few days before he killed Stephanie, Deshawn's family members expressed their concerns to staff members who supervised him at his residential program. The family told them that he was not complying with his prescribed outpatient medication.[199] The court forensic psychologist on the case also found that Deshawn had psychosis.[200] Deshawn's lawyer pursued not guilty by reason of insanity (NGRI) because Deshawn experienced commanding auditory hallucinations instructing him to do things and he had stopped taking his medication just before the tragedy.[201]

On November 10, 1971, two women, ages twenty and twenty-six, stood staring at each other on a street corner in Michigan without saying a word to anyone for hours. The police noticed this and sought to connect them with psychiatric care. While the women were held at the police station, the police contacted city attorneys for advice on how to proceed. The attorneys' office told the police that unless the women presented signs of danger to themselves or anyone else, they should be released. The police released them. Thirty hours later, authorities found the two women on the floor of an apartment that was engulfed in a fire that they intentionally set to kill themselves. One of the women lived with severe burns. The other woman died "with her rights on."[202]

AOT is often used as a supportive tool for people who are transitioning into the community following discharges from inpatient care. It can be used as an alternative to involuntary hospitalization. With drastically fewer state inpatient beds than there were decades ago, people who need inpatient psychiatry commonly wait for treatment in hospital emergency departments or jail cells.[203] People who are actively psychotic and have no awareness of this are often left to suffer the consequences of not being formally treated. They lose their housing and become unemployed, malnourished, and sleep deprived. They languish in jails, prisons, hospital emergency departments, homeless shelters, family members' homes, nursing homes, and on the streets.

To qualify for AOT, a person must meet certain criteria such as extensive interactions with law enforcement; frequent inpatient hospitalizations; an extensive history of noncompliance with outpatient treatment, which renders him unlikely to adhere to treatment independently; and being prone to violence. Although AOT laws vary slightly from state to state, they dictate the following eligibility criteria:

+ The person must be at least eighteen years old.

+ The person must be diagnosed with a serious mental illness.

+ The person must be unlikely to meet ordinary demands of life outside of a secured setting without supervision.

+ The person must possess a history of not complying with treatment, which has led to either the need for inpatient hospitalization (including forensic units) or outpatient services due to mental illness, during incarceration at least twice within the thirty-six months immediately preceding AOT pursuit.

+ The person must have engaged in at least one incident of serious violence toward himself or others within the forty-eight months immediately preceding AOT pursuit.

+ The person must have refused a chance to voluntarily engage in outpatient treatment that would enable safe living outside of a secured setting.

+ The person must be significantly deteriorating psychiatrically.

+ The person must be unable to be stabilized in a less restrictive setting.

+ The person must be likely to benefit from the use of AOT.

+ The person must need AOT to prevent further instability that would likely result in becoming dangerous to himself or others.[204]

Many AOT recipients are likely to follow the orders of judges in court because of the black robe effect. That is, the judge is seen as a credible authority figure and thus should be obeyed. The Treatment Advocacy Center vastly favors the use of court orders in AOT, attributing their success to the black robe effect.[205] When a 2009 study in New York compared the clinical outcomes of court-ordered AOT recipients with the outcomes of AOT recipients without court orders who received the same type of treatment, the court-ordered AOT group experienced more robust outcomes. The court-ordered AOT recipients were less likely to be hospitalized or arrested, and they were more likely to engage in treatment than the AOT recipients without court orders. This apparently highlights the added benefit of the black robe effect.[206]

Some jurisdictions allow their AOT recipients to not be under court order. During a study evaluation period of AOT in San Francisco County, California, from November 2, 2015, to February 9, 2017, only six of sixty AOT recipients were court-ordered to receive such services. While all AOT recipients in the county received services from a psychologist with forensic experience, a master-level clinician, and two outreach workers focused on supporting patients and their family members or friends, the court-ordered AOT recipients also received enhanced services, including intensive clinical case management, support from a half-time peer specialist, and medications from a 60 percent-time nurse practitioner.[207]

If AOT recipients don't follow through with court-ordered treatment plans, courts are not required to order inpatient psychiatric admission automatically.[208] However, family members with relatives using AOT report that psychiatrists arrange for involuntary transfers to hospitals whenever their treatment plans, particularly medication orders, are not followed. Violating the court order usually leads to involuntary transfer to a hospital emergency department where inpatient admission is considered.[209]

AOT does not violate anyone's civil rights and instead improves access to treatment. It does not force medication upon mentally ill people. Securing mental health treatment for people who clearly need it does not violate their civil liberties. The New York State Court of Appeals determined in 2004 that AOT does not violate civil liberties and is not forced treatment.[210]

Overall, the use of AOT programs vastly improves the quality of life for recipients. AOT results in better compliance and cooperation with outpatient treatment, improved medication adherence, and a reduction in the number of involuntary transports to hospital emergency departments for containment. It also reduces homelessness, substance-misuse, admission to inpatient units, inpatient stays, arrests, incarcerations, and violence.[211] Effective use of AOT lowers the risk of violence because it enhances compliance with antipsychotic medication and reduces substance-misuse.[212]

AOT not only ensures that seriously mentally ill people adhere to treatment plans supervised by the court system, it also requires outpatient treatment providers to deliver the services that they are expected to provide to recipients. AOT appears to improve the chances that outpatient treatment providers will follow through on delivering treatment plans because it encourages them to prioritize the population receiving AOT.[213] AOT ensures prioritization of the subset of the seriously mentally ill population that needs it. This group is typically considered more difficult and expensive for agencies to treat, and thus the system often neglects them.[214]

County mental health departments typically petition the court to request AOT and develop treatment plans.[215] Psychiatric hospitals or outpatient mental health agencies can petition the court for AOT. Families can also petition the court for it although it can be expensive and difficult.[216] Families find it less difficult to access care for their seriously mentally ill relatives when AOT is in place as compared with attempting to access treatment without it.[217] Dr. Treffert recently wrote to me, "In our county, and many others in Wisconsin, the ninety-days settle agreements work well. In those, the patient, his or her attorney, the county corporation counsel and the judge agree to a ninety-day period where the patient will voluntarily agree to settlement agreements (appointments, medications if indicated, etc.) at the end of which, if completed satisfactorily, the whole commitment proceeding is dropped."

Some people who oppose AOT argue that the patient who refuses to accept help should not be forced into treatment because doing so might damage his trust in his caregiver. Studies indicate that most people who are involuntarily treated later realize that this intervention was needed and have positive attitudes toward it, especially if the treatment was effective.[218] When a seriously mentally ill person needs treatment but lacks the capacity to understand the need and seek treatment, he needs a professional to impose treatment respectfully.

Months after I authorized a Section 12 (involuntary hold due to danger) for someone with anosognosia regarding her psychosis, I reassessed her. Making direct eye contact with me, she acknowledged, "I wasn't in a right state of mind back then." Then she thanked me for sending her to the hospital when she didn't want to go. Weeks after a patient underwent Section 7 and 8b on inpatient, she thanked the psychiatrist, the nurses, and me for helping her. After she was discharged, the resident psychiatrist who'd worked with me on inpatient treated this woman on an outpatient basis and told me that she demonstrated favorable outcomes for many months after that. She continued to take her medication and was able to sustain employment at a supermarket because she didn't feel the need to guard her home from what she believed were people trying to break in and harm her.

Allowing psychotic people the right to further deteriorate in functioning is not liberating to anyone. Some people who oppose AOT argue that cancer patients have the right to refuse medical treatment. Cancer patients typically do not have anosognosia and thus know that they have cancer. A former clinical supervisor told me while we discussed a case involving psychosis, "He has the right to be psychotic." Does someone have the right to die from starvation because he falsely believes that his food is poisoned? I would do everything possible to prevent a patient from dying that way.

When I testified in favor of a bill authorizing AOT at the Massachusetts State House in 2013, some people who opposed AOT testified that it is not needed because of the existence of Rogers Monitors. This argument is neither sound nor logical. Outside of locked inpatient units, Rogers Monitors are meaningless. It doesn't take much thought to figure out that it's impossible to restrain and forcibly administer medication to an adult outside of a secured setting. The only setting in which Rogers authorizations are implemented and enforced is the locked inpatient unit. Even in this setting, I have witnessed Rogers authorizations not being implemented on several occasions. Not all nursing homes honor Rogers Monitors. I know this from past work at nursing homes, consulting with them in attempts to discharge their residents back from inpatient, and from consulting with administrators for emergency cases. Without the black robe effect of AOT or CR, a patient with psychosis who needs treatment but refuses to access it due to anosognosia will likely go without treatment.

First, we must try voluntary measures to connect psychotic people to treatment. If a person with a serious mental illness chooses to engage in treatment, AOT is not necessary. If a person with psychosis and anosognosia refuses to engage in treatment, AOT should be tried swiftly and without hesitation.

The unreasonable actions of Recovery Learning Communities (RLC) debase the system. The support that DMH and National Alliance on Mental Illness (NAMI) provide them is profoundly disquieting. By supporting an organization that promotes nonadherence to recommended psychiatric treatment, DMH and NAMI simultaneously undermine and discredit psychiatry. Besides, the funds that support RLCs could be put to effective use, such as expanding the number of inpatient beds or improving outpatient programs. The mental health industry could benefit from providing less support and giving less credit to peer specialists. If this is done, resources can be allocated instead to evidence-based treatments. The government should not support any group that upholds the notion that mental illness doesn't exist or that minimizes its seriousness.

An alternative to the recovery model is the medical model, which emphasizes biological etiology and treatment of mental illness. We would benefit from an enhancement of the medical model. To decrease the use of the recovery model and increase the use of the medical model, I recommend that the government lower the status of peer specialists. If the Substance Abuse and Mental Health Services Administration (SAMHSA) and state governments stop funding them, the power that they have could be eliminated.

The drastic reduction of inpatient beds in the United States since the beginning of the 1960s has trapped severely psychotic people in the revolving door of repeated admissions—often involuntary—to inpatient units, followed by premature discharges. Some states have addressed this problem by examining the reasons—other than economic interests—that inpatient length of stays are too short. One reason is that inpatient criteria are overly restrictive.

In 1996, Wisconsin enhanced the Wisconsin Mental Health Act by adding criteria for involuntary hold authorization and inpatient admission regardless of whether the person is acting dangerously. If a person with a known history of mental illness shows mental deterioration and thus needs treatment to prevent further deterioration that could result in behaviors that pose a danger to himself or others, a petition for his detainment can be approved by the attorney general's office within twelve hours of being filed.[219]

Furthermore, in Wisconsin, if someone is having difficulty attending to his basic biological needs and protecting himself from basic harm due to mental illness, lacks the capacity to understand his need for treatment to address it, or is unable or unwilling to access treatment, he can be involuntarily transferred to a hospital. If a person with mental illness displays concerning behaviors which, if not curtailed with treatment, could lead to his inability to function independently or his incapacity to control his actions, he could be involuntarily held as well.[220]

The Wisconsin commitment criteria stand in contrast to the Massachusetts requirement that danger be imminent or already in progress for the person to be involuntarily held. Although Section 12 addresses poor self-care due to psychosis, it neglects to consider whether a person needs treatment or can understand his mental illness. Regarding psychosis, Massachusetts calls for inpatient criteria that are too narrow. It does little to prevent physical danger by requiring that danger be imminent or in progress. If Massachusetts directly modeled Wisconsin's legislation regarding commitment criteria, this would vastly improve the lives of the seriously mentally ill population and their families and friends. Treatment access would be timely, which would prevent more frequent relapses.

Because legislators and administrators fail to consider anosognosia in laws to reduce the damage caused by untreated serious mental illnesses, psychiatry might appear unscientific to other medical specialties. Mental health professionals must be trained to recognize that untreated psychosis is a risk factor for violence. Omitting this fact when discussing serious mental illness reinforces stigma and marginalizes those most sick and their personal caregivers.

CHAPTER 20

The United States

MASSACHUSETTS IS NOT THE only state with a broken mental health system. Advocates whom I have befriended from other states report seeing strong opposition to AOT, especially from organizations dominated by peer specialists. Although the news has spread recently about the benefits of Assisted Outpatient Treatment (AOT) programs, they are widely underutilized when available. In the majority of states where AOT laws are in place, the programs are not applied nearly often enough to be adequate.[221] Fifteen out of all states that allow AOT almost never use it.[222] Many of the states that have enacted AOT laws do not provide sufficient outpatient treatment resources to allow for full implementation of the programs.[223] When AOT programs are implemented in the United States with adequate intensive outpatient services and court orders that last for at least six months, the outcomes for recipients are predominantly successful and positive.[224] AOT should be promoted throughout the country; it is needed to protect both the seriously mentally ill population and the public from danger.

* * *

In North Carolina, Duke University School of Medicine conducted the first randomized controlled trial study of IOC for seriously mentally ill patients.[225] All of the AOT plans referred to in this study were court-ordered but did not include court-ordered medication. Patients who had been involuntarily confined to inpatient units were randomly assigned upon discharge either to receive court-ordered AOT involving case management and clinical outpatient services, or to receive case management services and clinical outpatient services without AOT. The former group, which comprised one hundred twenty-nine patients, underwent AOT that ranged from ninety days to one year. The latter group was the control group. It included one hundred thirty-five patients who didn't receive any AOT in the twelve months of analysis. Another group of patients who had recent histories of violence received AOT upon discharge, but they were not randomly assigned. People in the group that received AOT for a sustained period (at least one hundred eighty days) were more likely to comply with outpatient treatment, had fewer readmissions to inpatient units, were less likely to engage in violence or be victimized, and encountered arrests less frequently than those in other groups.[226]

In this study, the probability of rehospitalization was analyzed monthly for twelve months. The patients receiving AOT were significantly less likely to be rehospitalized than those in the control group. The patients who received AOT for a sustained period, including case management and clinical outpatient services, experienced 57 percent fewer inpatient readmissions and twenty fewer inpatient days as compared with the control group. These clinically beneficial outcomes in AOT were most pronounced among psychotic patients without mood instability. The psychotic group showed 72 percent fewer inpatient readmissions and twenty-eight fewer inpatient days as compared with the control group.[227]

Furthermore, in this study, AOT recipients showed less violence over the twelve months than those in the control group. The rate of violence was 27 percent among patients receiving sustained AOT, while the rate of violence was 42 percent among patients receiving AOT for fewer than one hundred eighty days, regardless of psychosis. During the twelve months, patients receiving at least one hundred eighty days of AOT were less violent than both the patients in the control group and the patients who received fewer than one hundred eighty days of AOT. The benefits of sustained AOT were greater when AOT was combined with at least three clinical outpatient visits per month. The patients who received at least one hundred eighty days of AOT with at least three outpatient visits per month were less violent (at a rate of 24 percent) than the patients who received fewer than one hundred eighty days of AOT with less frequent outpatient appointments (at a rate of 48 percent). The lowest rate of violence was 13 percent. It was seen among patients who received at least one hundred eighty days of AOT, used clinical outpatient services at least three times per month, engaged in minimal to no substance-misuse, and adhered to medication.[228]

In Ohio, a study of AOT recipients found an increase in the attendance rate at outpatient psychiatric appointments. Prior to AOT, these patients attended appointments an average of 5.7 times per year; during AOT, they attended appointments thirteen times per year. Attendance at day treatment programs increased from twenty-three sessions per year prior to AOT involvement to sixty sessions per year during involvement. During the first twelve months of being enrolled in the AOT program, participants demonstrated reduced use of emergency psychiatric departments, decreased inpatient admission rates, and decreased inpatient length of stays as compared with the previous twelve months without AOT.[229]

* * *

New York's AOT law is also referred to as Kendra's Law because Andrew Goldstein, who had unmedicated schizophrenia, pushed Kendra Webdale in front of a subway train, killing her, on January 3, 1999.[230] Despite his defense lawyer pursuing the insanity plea, a judge found him criminally responsible for this act.[231] This is another example in which an NGRI pursuit failed because of flaws in the mental health and legal systems.

One of the earliest studies in New York compared markers of dysfunction in the immediate three years prior to AOT enrollment to the same markers during AOT enrollment, and found a 74 percent reduction in homelessness, a 77 percent reduction in psychiatric hospital admissions, an 83 percent reduction in arrests, and an 87 percent reduction in incarcerations. When lengths of inpatient courses in the immediate six months prior to AOT enrollment were compared with six months of AOT enrollment, researchers found a 56 percent decrease.[232] Current hospitalization rates are concerning because inpatient care is far more financially costly than outpatient care. More patients are hospitalized on inpatient for psychiatric illness than for any other medical problem.[233]

Researchers asked case managers to rate participants' engagement levels in outpatient treatment services in New York's AOT program. The results showed that the percentage of participants with admirable medication compliance rose from 34 percent at the onset of the AOT court order to 69 percent at the end of the first six-month period involving AOT. In comparing timeframes, the percentage of participants who had a favorable engagement in other services, such as psychotherapy, rose from 41 percent before AOT enrollment to 62 percent with AOT.[234]

Mood instability and psychosis can interfere with a person's ability to complete routine and simple tasks. The New York study participants' overall ability to meet the ordinary demands of life at the end of their first six months of receiving AOT was compared with their functioning in similar areas at the onset of receiving AOT. Regarding their ability to prepare meals, manage their medication, access transportation, manage personal hygiene, maintain an adequate diet, and manage their finances, along with other markers of self-care, they had a 23 percent average reduction in difficulty. Regarding their ability to maintain social networks and manage their leisure time and conflicts in social settings, along with other markers of social functioning, they had a 22 percent average reduction in difficulty. Regarding their ability to maintain attention and concentration, understand and remember instructions, perform routines near others, and other markers of task performance, they had a 23 percent average reduction in difficulty.[235]

In New York, the frequency with which study participants engaged in harmful behaviors by the end of their first six months of receiving AOT was compared with the frequency of engaging in these behaviors at the onset of receiving AOT. Study participants showed a 55 percent reduction in physically harming themselves, including suicide attempts; a 49 percent reduction in abusing alcohol; a 48 percent reduction in abusing drugs; a 47 percent reduction in physically harming others; and a 43 percent reduction in threatening to harm others.[236]

AOT participants commonly have positive perceptions of mental health treatment. In New York, a study looked at seriously mentally ill patients and their perceptions of mental health treatment. They were either receiving AOT, had recently received AOT, had relatively recently received AOT (immediately prior to the six months before the research interview), or had never received AOT. Study participants receiving AOT perceived decreased barriers to accessing treatment and increased benefits of AOT as compared with nonrecipients. Eighty-one percent of current recipients reported benefiting from AOT. Only 33 percent of recipients perceived barriers to accessing treatment. Ninety percent of patients who had recently received AOT perceived mental health treatment as beneficial. Only 30 percent of those who had recently received AOT perceived barriers to accessing treatment. Sixty percent of patients who had relatively recently undergone AOT viewed mental health treatment positively. Only 42 percent of those who had relatively recently received AOT perceived barriers to accessing treatment.[237]

The rate of intensive case management services received by AOT recipients in New York increased from 11 percent prior to AOT enrollment to 28 percent in the first six months of AOT enrollment. It further increased to 33 percent from seven to twelve months of enrollment. The rate of non-intensive case management by AOT recipients increased from 18 percent prior to AOT enrollment to 44 percent in the first six months of AOT enrollment. It further increased to 53 percent from seven to twelve months of enrollment.[238]

AOT recipients in New York were almost two-thirds less likely to be arrested than were seriously mentally ill people who qualified for AOT but had not yet enrolled.[239] The study compared arrest rates of AOT recipients in New York with their arrest rates prior to receiving AOT. Researchers found that the patients' odds of being arrested were 2.66 times greater prior to AOT involvement than during AOT involvement. More specifically, they found that the odds of being arrested for violence were 8.61 times higher prior to AOT involvement than during involvement. For the seriously mentally ill group that had never received AOT, the odds of being arrested were almost double that of AOT recipients.[240]

In New York City, the rate of violence over three years among seventy-six recipients of AOT with histories of violence was compared with a control group of mentally ill patients who did not meet AOT criteria due to a history of less violence or less frequent hospitalizations. The AOT recipients were four times less likely than the control group to engage in serious violent acts.[241]

The chances of AOT recipients being hospitalized were lowered by approximately 25 percent in the first six months of court-ordered AOT, compared with the chances of being hospitalized prior to this period. During subsequent renewals of AOT court orders for additional six-month periods, the chances of being hospitalized were reduced by more than one-third.[242] Among AOT recipients who were hospitalized on inpatient, the length of inpatient courses decreased on average from eighteen days in the six months immediately preceding AOT to eleven days in the first six months of AOT.[243]

The most recent AOT study outcomes in New York are just as promising as previous results since AOT's inception in 1999. In New York, AOT recipients experienced a 63 percent reduction in the frequency of hospital admissions during AOT enrollment, compared with before enrollment. AOT recipients experienced a 72 percent reduction in the rate of incarceration and a 67 percent decrease in homelessness during AOT enrollment when compared with before enrollment.[244]

Further recent AOT study outcomes in New York showed that participation in coordinated treatment services by AOT participants increased by 377 percent as compared with before AOT enrollment. Access to psychiatric medications increased by 210 percent as compared with before AOT enrollment.[245] Researchers found an increase in service engagement from 33 percent at the onset of AOT enrollment to 39 percent at the end of six months of enrollment. They found an increase in medication adherence from 55 percent at the onset of AOT enrollment to 63 percent at the end of six months of enrollment.[246] The prevalence of engaging in harmful behaviors (for example, creating a public disturbance; damaging property, inducing arson; or physically assaulting other people) declined among AOT recipients by 16 percent as compared with before their AOT enrollment.[247]

In New Jersey, outcomes were positive for an AOT program in fiscal year 2017 that involved fifty-two recipients. At the onset of AOT enrollment, nine of these patients were homeless. Due to AOT participation, seven of them resolved homelessness. This group of fifty-two AOT recipients was also 69 percent less likely to be readmitted to inpatient units one year following initial enrollment than it was in the year immediately preceding enrollment. This meant that the local and state governments saved approximately $4,800,336 with AOT. When comparing these same timeframes, the study participants were 100 percent less likely to be arrested or incarcerated if they were enrolled in AOT.[248]

AOT is beneficial to people who use it even after AOT court orders expire. In Iowa, a study showed that after the court order expired, three-fourths of recent AOT participants voluntarily remained in outpatient treatment.[249] In 2010, another New York study of seventy-six AOT recipients showed that they were four times less likely to engage in violent behavior over three years as compared with another group of seriously mentally ill patients without AOT.[250]

We cannot disregard the evidence demonstrating the overall success of AOT. Although many people attempt to dispute the arguments favoring it, their arguments are not reasonable because they are not based on facts. AOT research outcomes debunk arguments against it. I have not found any study that proves that AOT is ineffective. No AOT study shows that civil rights are violated or that AOT recipients' attitudes toward mental health professionals worsen. AOT research outcomes only fortify the need to promote it. Studies show that the use of AOT increases mental health treatment adherence and reduces rates of violence, arrest, inpatient admission, and homelessness. When professionally recommended treatment is followed, patients typically achieve greater functional gains in all domains of their lives.

On the federal level, former Member of Congress Timothy Murphy of Pennsylvania created the Helping Families in Mental Health Crisis Act, and Senator John Cornyn of Texas created the Mental Health and Safe Communities Act. These were rolled into the 21st Century Cures Act, which was signed into law by former President Barack Obama in December 2016.

The monumental 21st Century Cures Act restructured the SAMHSA, the government office that regulates mental health services. The Act vastly promotes AOT. It enabled SAMHSA to establish the Interdepartmental Serious Mental Illness Coordinating Committee (ISMICC), which is comprised of nationwide experts on serious mental illness.[251] The ISMICC involves leaders from the United States Department of Health and Human Services, Department of Justice, Department of Labor, Department of Veterans Affairs, Department of Defense, Department of Housing and Urban Development, Department of Education, Centers for Medicare and Medicaid Services, and the

Social Security Administration. It also comprises fourteen nonfederal members of the public.[252] These nonfederal members represent mental health, law enforcement, and legal professionals, advocates, an author, and family members of seriously mentally ill relatives. Another nonfederal member is John Snook, a Doctor of Jurisprudence who is the executive director of the Treatment Advocacy Center, an organization that researches serious mental illness and advocates for the seriously mentally ill population.[253]

The first ISMICC meeting was held on August 31, 2017,[254] and chaired by psychiatrist Elinore McCance-Katz.[255] She is the first assistant secretary for mental health and substance-use,[256] thanks to the 21st Century Cures Act. Other federal members of ISMICC include the secretary for mental health and substance abuse and the attorney general.[257] The ISMICC is beginning to initiate better federal coordination of government departments intended to serve the seriously mentally ill population.

Markers of dysfunction in this population include homelessness, criminalization, unemployment, suicide, violence, and frequent readmission to inpatient units. The ISMICC is using advanced research to promote evidence-based treatment for this population. Previously, SAMHSA's evidence-based treatment list for the seriously mentally ill population was insufficient.[258] In January 2018, I learned that SAMHSA, at the direction of ISMICC, terminated the contract with the company that managed their National Registry of Evidence-based Programs and Practices (NREPP).[259] Since 1997, the NREPP included hundreds of interventions and practices that the public and clinicians could learn about and formally adopt. Federally-funded workshops disseminated information about these practices. A profound majority of programs in NREPP were not geared toward helping the seriously mentally ill population.[260] Due to the new order, the list froze without growth beginning in September 2017. This is an excellent step toward shifting the focus of

SAMHSA from the "worried well" who usually function normally but are anxious, to the seriously mentally ill, who usually do not.

The ISMICC compiled a report to Congress on December 13, 2017, which listed the following goals:

- report on advances in research on prevention, diagnosis, intervention, and access to services as these pertain to serious mental illness

- evaluate the public outcomes of federal programs that are designed to alleviate serious mental illness

- recommend actions that federal departments can take to improve the coordination of services

- improve seriously mentally ill persons' access to treatment

- facilitate seriously mentally ill persons' ability to engage in quality treatment

- order local and state mental health agencies to offer treatment approaches that have been scientifically proven to be effective

- strengthen diversion efforts from the criminal justice system to the mental health system to reduce criminalization of the mentally ill population

- develop economic plans to increase the availability and affordability of treatment services[261]

The 21st Century Cures Act reauthorizes and enhances AOT grant programs by increasing federal funding to states for AOT implementation[262] and expanding the time allotment of these grants.[263] In September 2016, SAMHSA promoted AOT by allowing $13 million in grant programs.[264] The Act also allows states to use Department of Justice grants to fund AOT in civil courts, which decreases the probability of incarceration of seriously mentally ill people.[265]

In addition to SAMHSA's endorsement of AOT, the following powerhouses in the mental health industry formally endorse it: the American Psychiatric Association,[266] the National Sheriffs' Association,[267] the International Association of Chiefs of Police,[268] the Department of Justice,[269] and the Agency for Healthcare Research & Quality.[270] Yet three states lag.

Where does the National Alliance on Mental Illness (NAMI) stand in its effort to alleviate the suffering of the severely ill? Teresa Pasquini, a determined advocate for her family member with a serious mental illness, requested of NAMI's Chief Executive Officer, Mary Giliberti, that NAMI create a Families of Adult Serious Mental Illness Advisory Council. Currently, there are just four councils that advise the Board of Directors. These include peer specialists, executive directors of NAMI state organizations and affiliates, military veterans, and presidents of NAMI state organizations. Despite that Teresa presented a sound case involving the reasons for this need, NAMI disagreed with her.[271] By rejecting Teresa's proposal, NAMI marginalizes the strongest advocates for the seriously mentally ill population—families.

You may choose to look the other way but you can never again say that you did not know.

—William Wilberforce (1759–1833), politician who tried to abolish slavery in England

CHAPTER 21

Massachusetts

O<small>N</small> A<small>UGUST</small> 15, 2012, Jahvon Goodwin, twenty-one years old, homeless, with schizophrenia, stabbed twenty-four-year-old Rashad Lesley-Barnes to death in Roxbury, Massachusetts.[272] Jahvon reported to the press that he had followed Rashad when he got off a public bus. Jahvon told doctors that he had heard voices ordering him to kill Rashad. His legal team tried the insanity defense, but it was not successful. Instead of getting treatment in a psychiatric hospital, Jahvon was sentenced to prison.[273]

On October 14, 2014, Bodio Hutchinson physically attacked two people with a knife on the Boston Common. His lawyer described him as having paranoid schizophrenia. Bodio's history involved punching a woman twice without provocation at a McDonald's restaurant in 2013 and then biting the man who tried to help her.[274]

On August 20, 2015, Keven Blakemore, with bipolar disorder and schizophrenia, attempted to kill his brother by stabbing him many times in Boxborough, Massachusetts. Then Keven tied his brother's girlfriend to a chair and sexually assaulted her. Afterward, Keven forced both to ride in his car on a drive from Massachusetts to Ohio.[275]

The Boston Globe reported that Lee Chiero, thirty-five years old, stabbed his mother, Nancy Chiero, in the eyes with a knife, resulting in her death. Lee had been released from an inpatient unit less than a month before this incident. One of his delusions involved his belief that hospital doctors had raped him and his mother. Previously, he was frequently hospitalized with delusional thinking and repeatedly prematurely discharged. His sister later said that he had become adept at hiding his delusions when interacting with psychiatric hospital staff members. Immediately following these discharges, he refused to take any medication for his severe mental illness, which he didn't believe existed.[276]

Another of Lee's delusions involved his belief that agents working for a group called Asosa had broken into his home and kidnapped him. He was particularly paranoid toward his mother, which was evident in videotaped conversations with her. He believed that she was part of Asosa and conspiring to harm him. He disconnected computers and the electricity to assuage his belief that Asosa was spying on him. He started to take apart his basement's ceiling in search of secretly placed cameras that he believed were being used to spy on him. He believed that he had been abducted by aliens and abused by animals. When his mother said something unrelated to animals, he believed that she was referring to animals trying to harm him. As he killed her, he demanded that she confess, and he verbalized delusions. He recorded this incident on video. Lee was legally found NGRI.[277]

The Boston Globe investigated circumstances of homicides committed in Massachusetts from 2005 to 2016 and found a common theme in the homicides involving mental illness or suspected mental illness. Alleged perpetrators were often not engaged in outpatient treatment, not adhering to prescribed medication, or were abusing illicit drugs or alcohol during these violent incidents. In 2015, among the ninety-five homicides with known suspects, people with known or apparent mental illness allegedly committed approximately 15 percent of these.[278]

* * *

Perhaps the accounts of violence relating to untreated mental illness prompted some legislative change in favor of AOT. In 2015, Massachusetts began an Assisted Outpatient Treatment (AOT) pilot program that was funded by the Department of Mental Health (DMH). Funding for this pilot continued into the fiscal years 2016 and 2017. The title of this program changed from AOT pilot to Enhanced Outpatient Treatment pilot (EOTP), perhaps due to the degree of distaste toward AOT. In this program, an outpatient agency identified thirty people primarily suffering from mood disorders or psychosis who demonstrated some or all the following characteristics:

+ mental illness

+ difficulty engaging in treatment services, with inconsistent connections to outpatient providers

+ inability to follow through with referrals made by emergency or inpatient providers

+ excessive utilization of emergency services

+ current or past criminal justice system involvement

+ co-occurring substance-use disorder

+ frequent homelessness or unemployment

+ a high need for a variety of mental health services

✦ excessive use of inpatient psychiatric units and emergency personnel (e.g., 911 calls, ambulances, firefighters, police officers)

Sixty-five percent of this group had substance-use problems along with mental illness.[279] The use of illicit drugs or alcohol can impede a professional's ability to determine whether a patient is mentally ill. I recall as an inpatient psychiatric social worker occasionally submitting applications to DMH on behalf of patients with recent histories of heavy substance-misuse. Back then, more than a decade ago, DMH denied all these patients. In recent years, there has been an increase in the overall prevalence of substance-misuse in the United States. In emergency psychiatry, I witness some DMH recipients using illicit drugs or alcohol daily for many months in a row. This calls into question whether the state is prioritizing clinical demands in the most effective way possible. Of course, it's possible for patients to have co-occurring serious mental illnesses and substance-misuse problems. But many people who are highly psychotic lack the organizational skills "needed" to negotiate drug deals. Inappropriately allocating state funds neglects to serve those who are difficult to engage in treatment.

Because the EOTP program is completely voluntary and does not involve the courts, it likely neglects to serve many seriously mentally ill people who reluctantly accept their treatment or refuse to engage in needed treatment. As emphasized earlier, the prevalence of anosognosia in psychosis is remarkable. However, only 15 percent of EOTP program recipients had a primary diagnosis of psychosis. The EOTP program mimics the PACT model because of the emphasis on the constant availability of an interdisciplinary outreach team for its recipients. But instead of including a psychiatrist, EOTP employs an advanced nurse practitioner.

The EOTP program has shown the following successful outcomes among its recipients: an 82 percent decrease in legal involvement, a 62 percent decrease in suicidal ideation or self-harm, an 84 percent decrease in hospitalization, a 75 percent decrease in lack of stable housing, a 15 percent decrease in unemployment, and a 91 percent decrease in rates of treatment disengagement.[280] Successful functional outcomes would likely be even greater if the treatment were court-ordered, considering the grand benefit of the black robe effect in AOT seen in other states.

Unfortunately, the deaths of Stephanie and Nancy didn't result in Massachusetts enacting an AOT law. In recent years, several legislative bills have been introduced and deliberated in an attempt to bring AOT to Massachusetts. Despite the powerful endorsements and colossal scientific research evidencing the clinical benefits of AOT throughout the United States, Massachusetts has not adopted AOT. Massachusetts is still not aligned with the federal government's sanctioning and normalizing of AOT, nor is it aligned with the forty-six state governments that allow it.

Although the National Alliance on Mental Illness's (NAMI) national office endorses AOT,[281] the NAMI of Massachusetts apparently does not support AOT. NAMI was absent when AOT bills were debated in hearings at the Boston State House in 2013, 2015, and 2017. The DMH did not testify in favor of AOT at any of these hearings. Both the NAMI and Massachusetts DMH were expected to represent the subset of the seriously mentally ill population without the capacity to advocate for themselves. Instead, they fell silent. The neutrality of NAMI and DMH sent a message to the seriously mentally ill population and their caregivers—AOT was not important. Their silence allowed RLC to rise and crush the scientific backing of AOT.

Advocacy efforts to improve the system can be simple and effective. Place phone calls or mail letters to your state and federal Senators and Members of Congress, and to NAMI and DMH. Meet with them in real time. Mail this book to them. Ask them to stop ignoring the needs of the population that would benefit from AOT. Any citizen of Massachusetts is permitted to testify in support of AOT bills orally, in writing, or by using both means in legislative hearings led by committees such as the Joint Committee on Mental Health, Substance Use and Recovery, or the Joint Committee on the Judiciary. In Massachusetts, hearings can occur every two years, on odd-numbered years. To learn about the status of bills in Massachusetts, you can go online to www.malegislature.gov/bills and enter "assisted outpatient treatment" in the search engine. Change within the system is more likely to occur when concerned citizens pressure the government for it.

CHAPTER 22

Conclusion

EMERGENCY PSYCHIATRIC services work is akin to watching a train wreck without any ability to prevent it from happening. I am regularly engaged in trying to prevent tragedies among seriously mentally ill people. When will the next tragedy occur that involves serious injury or loss of life due to untreated serious mental illness? Tragedies inevitably occur because the mental health system is broken.

Governments are reactive. The mental health system has recently cycled back to the nineteenth century, when Dorothea Dix was appalled by what she witnessed in Massachusetts. She would be shocked, bewildered, terrified, and unimpressed with both the Massachusetts and United States systems if she were alive today.

Across the United States, state inpatient psychiatric hospitals emptied their beds, but the money saved didn't adequately flow to the outpatient mental health system. This forced many thousands of seriously mentally ill people to struggle for survival without protection from harm. The severe shortage of inpatient psychiatric beds, along with overly restrictive inpatient commitment criteria, often results in only the sickest of the sick population being admitted to inpatient units. This shortage of beds overcrowds hospital emergency departments, which results in treatment delays. For psychotic people who lack awareness of their psychosis, brain deterioration often occurs long before sufficient psychiatric treatment is obtained.

Seriously mentally ill people need our help. It is imperative that we advocate to improve their lives. In the throes of psychosis, patients often do not have the capacity to advocate for themselves. Some are lucky enough to have supportive family members or friends to speak for them, but others are not lucky. They need mental health professionals, police officers, and lawyers to advocate for them.

Discrimination against the patients who are the most challenging to manage, including those who are violent, further delays care. They excessively wait for inpatient admission because inpatient admissions departments inappropriately refuse to accept them. They are more likely to admit to inpatient the malingerer who doesn't need treatment than they are to admit the patient with psychosis who can cover up symptoms. Some hospital emergency medical doctors attending to patients awaiting this type of placement follow the appropriate path by patiently waiting for beds to become available. Other doctors look away from the potential or actual danger these patients pose and prematurely discharge them to their homes, jails, homeless shelters, family members' homes, or the streets. Emergency medical doctors are more likely to release a dangerous patient to the streets if she does not want any treatment than to discharge a dangerous patient who wants treatment. If patients are transferred to inpatient settings, the inpatient courses are brief. Inpatient commitment criteria dwindle—especially for those who don't want any help. Too often, they are discharged too soon.

There are not enough CIT-trained police officers. Law enforcement is burdened with the task of doing the necessary work that mental health professionals neglect to do. Although the CIT model is commendable, it appears to be a measure of damage control. If the mental health system functioned as it should, it would need fewer police officers.

Rates increase for the criminalization of the seriously mentally ill population, such as in the case of Farron. Rates increase for homelessness, violence, and readmission to inpatient units. Seriously mentally ill people who are not adequately treated die with their rights on. Or their loved ones are seriously hurt or killed, as in the case involving Amy, who was killed by her son William.

On the other end of the spectrum, the malingerers, who are just looking for food and shelter or a hiding place, access inpatient beds with apparent ease. They take away inpatient beds from patients who desperately need them, and the system allows this to happen. Their deception is evident in the rampant inconsistencies found in the stories they share. Hospitals and crisis units enable their lies to gain revenue. When the enabling of malingerers has gone on for years or sometimes decades, they expect their requests for admission to inpatient or crisis units to be granted. If malingerers were turned away from emergency settings or inpatient units more often, they would be less inclined to return. They cycle in and out of hospital doors just as frequently as some of the most seriously mentally ill people.

Borderline personality disorder stands out because it is the most common personality disorder that mental health professionals observe on inpatient and emergency settings. Borderline personality-disordered behavior can be reckless, impulsive, and unpredictable. When a person with borderline personality disorder inappropriately requests inpatient admission, her motive can be opaque. She may intentionally inflict superficial injuries upon herself, often without any intention to die. The descent into psychiatric erosion can quicken with every injury she inflicts on herself. Her death might be accidental. Indeed, this disorder warrants just as much attention as any serious mental illness.

AOT can be lifesaving. There is no doubt that if Massachusetts enacts an Assisted Outpatient Treatment (AOT) law, tragedies due to untreated serious mental illness will be prevented. With AOT, the quality of life would improve for the subset of the seriously mentally ill population that is most at risk of homelessness, inpatient readmission, violence, suicide, and poor self-care. Throughout the United States, AOT should be used whenever needed and without hesitation.

Schizophrenia and other illnesses involving psychosis cause the most destruction among mentally ill people. Laws are supposed to protect the civil rights of everyone. But in a zealous attempt to protect the rights of mentally ill people, legal limitations abandon their rights. A person with psychosis and anosognosia doesn't have the right to be evicted from her apartment repeatedly because of her delusions and to subsequently freeze on the streets. A person with psychosis doesn't have the right to be arrested and jailed countless times for crimes she committed because of her commanding hallucinations. She doesn't have the right to refuse to take her antipsychotic medication when this was the only treatment that prevented her from acting on delusions with violence toward others. With no social support, a person with psychosis doesn't have the right to own a total of $1.25 because her profound disorganization interferes with her ability to manage finances. She doesn't have the right to not shower for a year because of her delusion surrounding showers, leading to life-threatening skin infections involving maggots. A person with psychosis doesn't have the right to starve herself to death because she believes that aliens are poisoning her food. A person with psychosis should not be allowed to die with her rights on.

References

Preface

[1] Steadman, Henry J., and Eric Silver. "Immediate Precursors of Violence Among Persons with Mental Illness: A Return to a Situational Perspective." In *Violence Among the Mentally Ill: Effective Treatments and Management Strategies*, edited by Sheilagh Hodgins, 35–48. Dordrecht: Kluwer Academic Publishers, 2000.

Chapter 1: Introduction

[2] Japsen, Bruce. "US Psychiatrist Shortage Intensifies." Forbes Media LLC. June 06, 2017. https://bit.ly/2uKq47e.

[3] Stowell, Keith, Peter Florence, Herbert Harman, and Rachel Glick. "Psychiatric Evaluation of the Agitated Patient: Consensus Statement of the American Association for Emergency Psychiatry Project BETA Psychiatric Evaluation Workgroup." *Western Journal of Emergency Medicine* 13, no. 1 (2012): 11–16. doi:10.5811/westjem.2011.9.6868.

[4] Hoermann, Simone, Corrine Zupanick, and Mark Dombeck. "DSM-5: The Ten Personality Disorders: Cluster B." MentalHelp.net: Borderline Personality Disorder. April 26, 2016. https://bit.ly/2wXDUH1.

Quote and Chapter 3: Tribute to Farron

[5] Treffert, Darold A. "Letters to the Editor: Dying with Their Rights on." *American Journal of Psychiatry* 130, no. 9 (1973): 1041. doi:10.1176/ajp.130.9.1041.

[6] United States. NOAA/NWS/NCEP/TPC/National Hurricane Center, National Weather Service. National Oceanic and Atmospheric Administration. *The Deadliest, Costliest, and Most Intense United States Tropical Cyclones from 1851 to 2006 (and Other Frequently Requested Hurricane Facts)*. By Eric S. Blake, Edward N. Rappaport, and Christopher W. Landsea. April 2007. https://bit.ly/2x9Hr4f.

[7] University of North Carolina: Carolina Population Center. "Atlantic Hurricanes." Carolina Demography. August 03, 2015. https://unc.live/2jxm7Rp.

[8] "List of Florida Hurricanes." Wikipedia, Wikimedia Foundation. December 14, 2017. https://bit.ly/2ydKoiK.

[9] Wang, Cao, Quanwang Li, Long Pang, Aming Zou, and Long Zhang. "Hurricane Damage Assessment for Residential Construction Considering the Non-stationarity in Hurricane Intensity and Frequency." *Acta Oceanologica Sinica* 35, no. 12 (2016): 110–18. doi:10.1007/s13131-016-0828-7.

[10] United States. Department of Health and Human Services. National Institute of Mental Health. *Schizophrenia*. Accessed September 21, 2017. https://bit .ly/2vrB48J.

[11] United States. Department of Health and Human Services. National Institute of Mental Health. *Schizophrenia*. Accessed February 9, 2018. https://bit .ly/2nPuUOl.

[12] Torrey, E. Fuller, and Elizabeth Sinclair. "Hocus Pocus: How the National Institute of Mental Health Made Two Million People with Schizophrenia Disappear." Arlington: Treatment Advocacy Center. January 2018. https:// bit.ly/2Ca848m.

[13] United States. Department of Health and Human Services. National Institute of Mental Health. *Schizophrenia*. Accessed February 16, 2018. https://bit .ly/2nPuUOl.

[14] Associated Press. "Two Alabama Police Officers Shot Dead." Nytimes.com, January 04, 2004. https://nyti.ms/2hvwHbl.

[15] Friedman, L., D. Hrouda, S. Noffsinger, P. Resnick, and P. Buckley. "Psychometric Relationships of Insight in Patients with Schizophrenia Who Commit Violent Acts." *Schizophrenia Research* 60, no. 1 (2003): 81. doi:10.1016/ s0920-9964(03)80626-6.

[16] Arango, C., A. C. Barba, T. Gonzalez-Salvador, and A. C. Ordonez. "Violence in Inpatients with Schizophrenia: A Prospective Study." *Schizophrenia Bulletin* 25, no. 3 (1999): 493–503. doi:10.1093/oxfordjournals.schbul.a033396.

Chapter 4: Roots

[17] "Certified Peer Specialist Training (CPS)." Transformation Center. March 9, 2018. https://bit.ly/2tVb2yN.

[18] Fuller, Doris A., Elizabeth Sinclair, Jeffrey Geller, Cameron Quanbeck, and John Snook. "Going, Going, Gone: Trends and Consequences of Eliminating State Psychiatric Beds." Arlington: Treatment Advocacy Center. June 2016. https:// bit.ly/2wLHqDf; "Prevalence of Serious Mental Illness Among Adults, by State (2016)." Arlington: Treatment Advocacy Center. https://bit.ly/2xQbH1G;

United States. Department of Health and Human Services. National Institute of Mental Health. *Schizophrenia.* Accessed December 22, 2017. https://bit .ly/2vrB48J; United States. Department of Commerce. Census Bureau. *Statistical Abstract of the United States, 1955.* 76th ed. Washington, D.C., 1955. https://bit.ly/2gMdTAs.

19 Treffert, Darold A. "The MacArthur Coercion Studies: A Wisconsin Perspective." *Marquette Law Review* 82, no. 4 (1999): 759–85. Marquette University Law School. https://bit.ly/2vADly0.

20 Torrey, E. Fuller. "The Perfect Storm: 1981–1999." In *American Psychosis: How the Federal Government Destroyed the Mental Illness Treatment System*, 98. Oxford: Oxford University Press, 2014.

21 "Consequences of Non–treatment." Arlington: Treatment Advocacy Center. 2017. https://bit.ly/2vrXhna.

22 Bachrach, Leona L. "The State of the State Mental Hospital 1996 [published erratum appears in *Psychiatric Services* January 1997; 48(1):99]." *Psychiatric Services* 47, no. 10 (1996): 1071–078. doi:10.1176/ps.47.10.1071.

23 Torrey, E. Fuller. "Introduction: The Origins of a Disaster." In *The Insanity Offense: How America's Failure to Treat the Seriously Mentally Ill Endangers Its Citizens*, 2. New York: W.W. Norton & Company, Inc., 2012.

24 Fuller, Doris A., Jeffrey Geller, Cameron Quanbeck, John Snook, and Elizabeth Sinclair. "Going, Going, Gone: Trends and Consequences of Eliminating State Psychiatric Beds." Arlington: Treatment Advocacy Center. June 2016. https://bit.ly/2wLHqDf.

25 Ibid; "Prevalence of Serious Mental Illness Among Adults, by State (2016)." Arlington: Treatment Advocacy Center. https://bit.ly/2xQbH1G; United States. Department of Health and Human Services. National Institute of Mental Health. *Schizophrenia.* Accessed December 22, 2017. https://bit.ly/2vrB48J; United States. Department of Commerce. Census Bureau. *Statistical Abstract of the United States, 1955.* 76th ed. Washington, D.C., 1955. https://bit .ly/2gMdTAs.

26 Treffert, Darold A. "Letters to the Editor: Dying with Their Rights on." *American Journal of Psychiatry* 130, no. 9 (1973): 1041. doi:10.1176/ajp.130.9.1041.

27 Treffert, Darold A. "Dying with Their Rights on." *Prism* 2 (February 1974): 49–52.

28 Globe Spotlight Team, Jenna Russell, et al. "The Desperate and the Dead: Police Confrontation." *The Boston Globe*, July 6, 2016. https://bit.ly/2xEkLXb.

29 Department of Commerce. *US Census Bureau QuickFacts: Massachusetts; United States.* Accessed December 28, 2017. https://bit.ly/2wJzWyD.

30 Fuller, Doris A., Jeffrey Geller, Cameron Quanbeck, John Snook, and Elizabeth Sinclair. "Going, Going, Gone: Trends and Consequences of Eliminating State Psychiatric Beds." Arlington: Treatment Advocacy Center. June 2016. https://bit.ly/2wLHqDf.

31 The Pulitzer Prizes. "Finalist: Jenna Russell, Maria Cramer, Michael Rezendes, Todd Wallack and Scott Helman of *The Boston Globe*." The 2017 Pulitzer Prize Finalist in Local Reporting. https://bit.ly/2haePhW.

32 Globe Spotlight Team, Jenna Russell, et al. "The Desperate and the Dead: Police Confrontation." *The Boston Globe*, July 6, 2016. https://bit.ly/2xEkLXb.

33 Globe Spotlight Team, Michael Rezendes, et al. "The Desperate and the Dead: Families in Fear." *The Boston Globe*, June 23, 2016. https://bit.ly/2vZd78s.

Chapter 5: Schizophrenia

34 United States. Department of Health and Human Services. Substance Abuse and Mental Health Services Administration. *Results from the 2013 National Survey on Drug Use and Health: Mental Health Findings.* Center for Behavioral Health Statistics and Quality. 2014. https://bit.ly/2vSfewm.

35 United States. Department of Health and Human Services. National Institute of Mental Health. *Serious Mental Illness (SMI) Among US Adults.* Accessed December 28, 2017. https://bit.ly/2v7Euyi.

36 Green, M. F., and K. H. Nuechterlein. "Should Schizophrenia be Treated as a Neurocognitive Disorder?" *Schizophrenia Bulletin* 25, no. 2 (1999): 309–19. doi:10.1093/oxfordjournals.schbul.a033380; Green, M. F., R. S. Kern, D. L. Braff, and J. Mintz. "Neurocognitive Deficits and Functional Outcome in Schizophrenia: Are We Measuring the 'Right Stuff'?" *Schizophrenia Bulletin* 26, no. 1 (2000): 119–136. doi:10.1093/oxfordjournals.schbul.a033430; Young, Donald A., Konstantine K. Zakzanis, Carrie Bailey, Rafaela Davila, Judith Griese, Gudrun Sartory, and Anja Thom. "Further Parameters of Insight and Neuropsychological Deficit in Schizophrenia and Other Chronic Mental Disease." *The Journal of Nervous & Mental Disease* 186, no. 1 (1998): 44–50. doi:10.1097/00005053-199801000-00007.

37 United States. Department of Health and Human Services. National Institute of Mental Health. *Schizophrenia.* Accessed December 21, 2017. https://bit.ly/2vrB48J.

Chapter 6: On the Fence

38 Monahan, J., M. Swartz, and R. J. Bonnie. "Mandated Treatment in the Community for People with Mental Disorders." *Health Affairs* 22, no. 5 (2003): 28–38. doi:10.1377/hlthaff.22.5.28.

39 Sisti, Dominic A., Andrea G. Segal, and Ezekiel J. Emanuel. "Improving Long-term Psychiatric Care." *Journal of the American Medical Association* 313, no. 3 (2015): 243–44. doi:10.1001/jama.2014.16088.

40 "Criminalization: Serious Mental Illness (SMI) Prevalence in Jails and Prisons." Arlington: Treatment Advocacy Center. September 2016. https://bit.ly/2xRZext; Torrey, E. Fuller, Mary T. Zdanowicz, Aaron D. Kennard, H. Richard Lamb, Donald F. Eslinger, Michael C. Biasotti, and Doris A. Fuller. "The Treatment of Persons with Mental Illness in Prisons and Jails: A State Survey." Arlington: Treatment Advocacy Center. April 8, 2014. https://bit.ly/2EfemWG; United States. Department of Justice: Office of Justice Programs. Bureau of Justice Statistics. *Correctional Populations in the United States, 2014.* By Danielle Kaeble, Lauren Glaze, Anastasios Tsoutis, and Todd Minton. Edited by Lauren Glaze, E. Ann Carson, and Todd Minton. January 21, 2016. https://bit.ly/2fAsC0V.

41 Nicks, B. A., and D. M. Manthey. "The Impact of Psychiatric Patient Boarding in Emergency Departments." *Emergency Medicine International* 2012 (2012): 1–5. doi:10.1155/2012/360308.

42 Erickson, Steven K., J. Richard Ciccone, Steven B. Schwarzkopf, J. Steven Lamberti, and Michael J. Vitacco. "Legal Fallacies of Antipsychotic Drugs." *Journal of the American Academy of Psychiatry and the Law* 35, no. 2 (June 2007): 235–46. https://bit.ly/2vcov4r.

Chapter 7: Borderline Personality Disorder

43 Torgersen, Svenn, John Myers, Ted Reichborn-Kjennerud, Espen Roysamb, Thomas S. Kubarych, and Kenneth S. Kendler. "The Heritability of Cluster B Personality Disorders Assessed Both by Personal Interview and Questionnaire." *Journal of Personality Disorders* 26, no. 6 (December 2012): 848–66. doi:10.1521/pedi.2012.26.6.848; Kendler, K. S., J. Myers, and T. Reichborn-Kjennerud. "Borderline Personality Disorder Traits and Their Relationship with Dimensions of Normative Personality: A Web-based Cohort and Twin Study." *Acta Psychiatrica Scandinavica* 123, no. 5 (May 2010): 349–59. doi:10.1111/j.1600-0447.2010.01653.x.

44 Simeon, D., B. Stanley, A. Frances, J. J. Mann, and M. Stanley. "Self-mutilation in Personality Disorders: Psychological and Biological Correlates." *American Journal of Psychiatry* 149, no. 2 (1992): 221–26. doi:10.1176/ajp.149.2.221.

45 Linehan, Marsha. *Cognitive-behavioral Treatment of Borderline Personality Disorder.* New York: Guilford Press, 1993; Brown, Milton Z., Katherine Anne Comtois, and Marsha M. Linehan. "Reasons for Suicide Attempts and Nonsuicidal Self-injury in Women with Borderline Personality

Disorder." *Journal of Abnormal Psychology* 111, no. 1 (2002): 198–202. doi:10.1037//0021-843x.111.1.198.

46 Gunderson, John G., and Perry D. Hoffman. "Suicidal and Self-injurious Behavior in Borderline Personality Disorder: A Self-regulation Model." In *Understanding and Treating Borderline Personality Disorder: A Guide for Professionals and Families*, edited by John G. Gunderson and Perry D. Hoffman, 43–63. Washington, D.C.: American Psychiatric Publishing, 2005.

47 Gunderson, John G., and Maria E. Ridolfi. "Borderline Personality Disorder. Suicidality and Self-mutilation." *Annals of the New York Academy of Sciences* 932, no. 1 (April 2001): 61–77. doi:10.1111/j.1749-6632.2001.tb05798.x; Kolla, N., and P.S. Links. "Assessing and Managing Suicide Risk." In *American Psychiatric Publishing Textbook of Personality Disorders*, edited by J. M. Oldham, Andrew E. Skodol, and Donna S. Bender, 449–62. Washington, D.C.: American Psychiatric Publishing, 2005; Paris, Joel. "Chronic Suicidality Among Patients with Borderline Personality Disorder." *Psychiatric Services* 53, no. 6 (2002): 738–42. doi:10.1176/appi.ps.53.6.738; Stanley, B., and B. S. Brodsky. "Dialectical Behavior Therapy." In *American Psychiatric Publishing Textbook of Personality Disorders*, edited by J. M. Oldham, Andrew E. Skodol, and Donna S. Bender, 307–320. Washington, D.C.: American Psychiatric Publishing, 2005; Paris, Joel. "Is Hospitalization Useful for Suicidal Patients with Borderline Personality Disorder?" *Journal of Personality Disorders* 18, no. 3 (2004): 240–47. doi:10.1521/pedi.18.3.240.35443; Paris, Joel. "Half in Love with Easeful Death: The Meaning of Chronic Suicidality in Borderline Personality Disorder." *Harvard Review of Psychiatry* 12, no. 1 (2004): 42–48. doi:10.1080/714044399; Gerson, Jessica, and Barbara Stanley. "Suicidal and Self-injurious Behavior in Personality Disorder: Controversies and Treatment Directions." *Current Psychiatry Reports* 4, no. 1 (2002): 30–38. doi:10.1007/s11920-002-0009-6.

48 Linehan, Marsha. *Cognitive-behavioral Treatment of Borderline Personality Disorder.* New York: Guilford Press, 1993; Livesley, W. John. *Practical Management of Personality Disorder.* New York: Guilford Press, 2003; Paris, Joel. *Treatment of Borderline Personality Disorder: A Guide to Evidence-based Practice.* New York: Guilford Press, 2008.

49 Boggild, Andrea K., Marnin J. Heisel, and Paul S. Links. "Social, Demographic, and Clinical Factors Related to Disruptive Behaviour in Hospital." *The Canadian Journal of Psychiatry* 49, no. 2 (2004): 114–18. doi:10.1177/070674370404900206; Soliman, Alaa El-Din, and Hashim Reza. "Risk Factors and Correlates of Violence Among Acutely Ill Adult Psychiatric Inpatients." *Psychiatric Services* 52, no. 1 (2001): 75–80. doi:10.1176/appi.ps.52.1.75.

Chapter 8: No Intention to Die

50 Stone, Michael H. *The Fate of Borderline Patients: Successful Outcome and Psychiatric Practice*. New York: Guilford Press, 1990; Paris, Joel, R. Brown, and D. Nowlis. "Long-term Follow-up of Borderline Patients in a General Hospital." *Comprehensive Psychiatry* 28, no. 6 (1987): 530–35. doi:10.1016/0010-440x(87)90019-8; Paris, Joel, and Hallie Zweig-Frank. "A 27-year Follow-up of Patients with Borderline Personality Disorder." *Comprehensive Psychiatry* 42, no. 6 (2001): 482–87. doi:10.1053/comp.2001.26271; Kullgren, Gunnar. "Factors Associated with Completed Suicide in Borderline Personality Disorder." *The Journal of Nervous and Mental Disease* 176, no. 1 (1988): 40–44. doi:10.1097/00005053-198801000-00005.

51 Perry, J. C. "Longitudinal Studies of Personality Disorders." *Journal of Personality Disorders*, Supplement No. 1, 7, no. 3 (January 1993): 63–85. https://bit.ly/2wAYzOB; Black, Donald W., Nancee Blum, Bruce Pfohl, and Nancy Hale. "Suicidal Behavior in Borderline Personality Disorder: Prevalence, Risk Factors, Prediction, and Prevention." *Journal of Personality Disorders* 18, no. 3 (2004): 226–39. doi:10.1521/pedi.18.3.226.35445; Oldham, John M. *Practice Guideline for the Treatment of Patients with Borderline Personality Disorder*. Washington, D.C.: American Psychiatric Association, 2001; American Psychiatric Association. "Practice Guideline for the Treatment of Patients with Borderline Personality Disorder." *American Journal of Psychiatry* 158 (October supplement 2001): 1–52.

52 Soloff, P. H. "Characteristics of Suicide Attempts of Patients with Major Depressive Episode and Borderline Personality Disorder: A Comparative Study." *American Journal of Psychiatry* 157, no. 4 (2000): 601–08. doi:10.1176/appi.ajp.157.4.601.

53 Gunderson, John G. *Borderline Personality Disorder: A Clinical Guide*. Washington, D.C.: American Psychiatric Press, 2001.

54 Ibid.

55 United States. Department of Health and Human Services. National Institute of Mental Health. *Borderline Personality Disorder*. December 2017. https://bit.ly/2xZw90c.

Quote and Chapter 9: Police

56 Treffert, Darold A. "An Opposing View: Don't Let 'Rights' Block Needed Protection." *USA Today*, March 5, 1987, 10A.

57 Globe Spotlight Team, Jenna Russell, et al. "The Desperate and the Dead: Police Confrontation." *The Boston Globe*, July 6, 2016. https://bit.ly/2xEkLXb.

58 Bayne, Michaeliam C. "Furor Sparks Call for Crisis Team." *Metro: The Commercial Appeal*, September 30, 1987, B1.

59 Codispoti, Amanda. "Dealing with Mentally Ill a Police Focus: Roanoke Police Officers Are Trained in Intervention Techniques for Dealing with the Mentally Ill." *Roanoke Times*, July 19, 2009. https://bit.ly/2u05D5K.

60 Globe Spotlight Team, Jenna Russell, et al. "The Desperate and the Dead: Police Confrontation." *The Boston Globe*, July 6, 2016. https://bit.ly/2xEkLXb.

61 Ibid.

62 Ibid.

63 Dupont, Randolph, Major Sam Cochran, and Sarah Pillsbury. *Crisis Intervention Team Core Elements*. Department of Criminology and Criminal Justice—CIT Center, 2007. University of Memphis—School of Urban Affairs and Public Policy. https://bit.ly/2wgfK7G.

64 Globe Spotlight Team, Jenna Russell, et al. "The Desperate and the Dead: Police Confrontation." *The Boston Globe*, July 6, 2016. https://bit.ly/2xEkLXb.

Chapter 10: Deterioration

65 "Consequences of Non-treatment." Arlington: Treatment Advocacy Center. 2017. https://bit.ly/2vrXhna.

66 Walsh, E., P. Moran, C. Scott, K. McKenzie, T. Burns, F. Creed, P. Tyrer, R. M. Murray, and T. Fahy. "Prevalence of Violent Victimisation in Severe Mental Illness." *The British Journal of Psychiatry* 183, no. 3 (2003): 233–38. doi:10.1192/bjp.183.3.233; Chapple, Benjamin, David Chant, Patricia Nolan, Sue Cardy, Harvey Whiteford, and John McGrath. "Correlates of Victimisation Amongst People with Psychosis." *Social Psychiatry and Psychiatric Epidemiology* 39, no. 10 (2004): 836–40. doi:10.1007/s00127-004-0819-4; Teplin, Linda A., Gary M. McClelland, Karen M. Abram, and Dana A. Weiner. "Crime Victimization in Adults with Severe Mental Illness." *Archives of General Psychiatry* 62, no. 8 (2005): 911–21. doi:10.1001/archpsyc.62.8.911.

67 Treffert, Darold A. "The MacArthur Coercion Studies: A Wisconsin Perspective." *Marquette Law Review* 82, no. 4 (1999): 759–85. Marquette University Law School. https://bit.ly/2vADly0.

Chapter 11: Three Hots and a Cot

68 Rissmiller, David J., Al Wayslow, Harry Madison, Paul Hogate, Frances R. Rissmiller, and Robert A. Steer. "Prevalence of Malingering in Inpatient Suicide Ideators and Attempters." *Crisis* 19, no. 2 (1998): 62–66. doi:10.1027/0227-5910.19.2.62; Rissmiller, David A., Robert A. Steer, Michael Friedman, and Robert Demercurio. "Prevalence of Malingering in Suicidal Psychiatric

Inpatients: A Replication." *Psychological Reports* 84, no. 3 (1999): 726–30. doi:10.2466/pr0.1999.84.3.726; Yates, B. D., C. R. Nordquist, and R. A. Schultz. "Feigned Psychiatric Symptoms in the Emergency Room." *Psychiatric Services* 47, no. 9 (1996): 998–1000. doi:10.1176/ps.47.9.998.

Chapter 12: Tribute to Amy

[69] United States. Department of Health and Human Services. Substance Abuse and Mental Health Services Administration. *SAMHSA's Working Definition of Recovery Updated.* By Paolo Del Vecchio. March 23, 2012. https://bit .ly/2xofRyd.

[70] Jaaskelainen, E., P. Juola, N. Hirvonen, J. J. McGrath, S. Saha, M. Isohanni, J. Veijola, and J. Miettunen. "A Systematic Review and Meta-analysis of Recovery in Schizophrenia." *Schizophrenia Bulletin* 39, no. 6 (2012): 1296–306. doi:10.1093/schbul/sbs130.

[71] Joyal, Christian, Jean-Luc Dubreucq, Catherine Gendron, and Frederic Millaud. "Major Mental Disorders and Violence: A Critical Update." *Current Psychiatry Reviews* 3, no. 1 (2007): 33–50. doi:10.2174/157340007779815628; Joyal, C. C., A. Putkonen, P. Paavola, and J. Tiihonen. "Characteristics and Circumstances of Homicidal Acts Committed by Offenders with Schizophrenia." *Psychological Medicine* 34, no. 3 (2004): 433–42. doi:10.1017/s0033291703001077; Steadman, Henry J., Edward P. Mulvey, John Monahan, Pamela Clark Robbins, Paul S. Appelbaum, Thomas Grisso, Loren H. Roth, and Eric Silver. "Violence by People Discharged from Acute Psychiatric Inpatient Facilities and by Others in the Same Neighborhoods." *Archives of General Psychiatry* 55, no. 5 (1998): 393–401. doi:10.1001/archpsyc.55.5.393.

[72] Bernstein, Elizabeth, and Nathan Koppel. "A Death in the Family." *The Wall Street Journal* (New York), August 16, 2008. https://on.wsj.com/2uoVdz7.

Chapter 13: Bipolar Disorder, with or without Psychosis

[73] Kessler, Ronald C., Wai Tat Chiu, Olga Demler, and Ellen E. Walters. "Prevalence, Severity, and Comorbidity of 12-month DSM-IV Disorders in the National Comorbidity Survey Replication." *Archives of General Psychiatry* 62, no. 6 (June 1, 2005): 617–27. doi:10.1001/archpsyc.62.6.617.

[74] United States. Department of Health and Human Services. National Institute of Mental Health. *Bipolar Disorder Among Adults.* Accessed July 30, 2017. https://bit.ly/2vrxhbm.

Chapter 14: Revolving Door

[75] Appleby, L., D. J. Luchins, P. N. Desai, R. D. Gibbons, P. G. Janicak, and R. Marks. "Length of Inpatient Stay and Recidivism Among Patients with

Schizophrenia." *Psychiatric Services* 47, no. 9 (1996): 985–90. doi:10.1176/ps.47.9.985; Appleby, L., P. N. Desai, D. J. Luchins, R. D. Gibbons, and D. R. Hedeker. "Length of Stay and Recidivism in Schizophrenia: A Study of Public Psychiatric Hospital Patients." *American Journal of Psychiatry* 150, no. 1 (1993): 72–76. doi:10.1176/ajp.150.1.72.

[76] Treffert, Darold A. "Dying with Their Rights on." *Prism* 2 (February 1974): 49–52.

[77] Fuller, Doris A., Elizabeth Sinclair, and John Snook. "Released, Relapsed, Rehospitalized: Length of Stay and Readmission Rates in State Hospitals, a Comparative State Survey." Arlington: Treatment Advocacy Center. November 2016. https://bit.ly/2ePVMwe.

[78] Ibid.

[79] Pearlmutter, Mark D., Kristin H. Dwyer, Laura G. Burke, Niels Rathlev, Louise Maranda, and Greg Volturo. "Analysis of Emergency Department Length of Stay for Mental Health Patients at Ten Massachusetts Emergency Departments." *Annals of Emergency Medicine* 70, no. 2 (2017): 193–202. doi:10.1016/j.annemergmed.2016.10.005.

Chapter 15: Dangerously Unaware

[80] Yesavage, J. A. "Inpatient Violence and the Schizophrenic Patient: An Inverse Correlation Between Danger-related Events and Neuroleptic Levels." *Biological Psychiatry* 17 (November 1982): 1331–337.

[81] Kasper, J. A., S. K. Hoge, T. Feucht-Haviar, J. Cortina, and B. Cohen. "Prospective Study of Patients' Refusal of Antipsychotic Medication under a Physician Discretion Review Procedure." *American Journal of Psychiatry* 154, no. 4 (1997): 483–89. doi:10.1176/ajp.154.4.483.

[82] Bartels, S. J., R. E. Drake, M. A. Wallach, and D. H. Freeman. "Characteristic Hostility in Schizophrenic Outpatients." *Schizophrenia Bulletin* 17, no. 1 (1991): 163–71. doi:10.1093/schbul/17.1.163.

[83] Holloman, Garland, and Scott Zeller. "Overview of Project BETA: Best Practices in Evaluation and Treatment of Agitation." *Western Journal of Emergency Medicine* 13, no. 1 (2012): 1–2. doi:10.5811/westjem.2011.9.6865.

[84] Nordstrom, Kimberly, Leslie Zun, Michael Wilson, Victor Stiebel, Anthony Ng, Benjamin Bregman, and Eric Anderson. "Medical Evaluation and Triage of the Agitated Patient: Consensus Statement of the American Association for Emergency Psychiatry Project BETA Medical Evaluation Workgroup." *Western Journal of Emergency Medicine* 13, no. 1 (2012): 3–10. doi:10.5811/westjem.2011.9.6863.

[85] Weiss, Anthony P., Grace Chang, Scott L. Rauch, Jennifer A. Smallwood, Mark Schechter, Joshua Kosowsky, Eric Hazen, Florina Haimovici, David F. Gitlin, Christine T. Finn, and Endel J. Orav. "Patient and Practice-related Determinants of Emergency Department Length of Stay for Patients with Psychiatric Illness." *Annals of Emergency Medicine* 60, no. 2 (2012). doi:10.1016/j.annemergmed.2012.01.037.

[86] Parsons, Taft. "Length of Stay: Managed Care Agenda or a Measure of Clinical Efficiency?" *Matrix Medical Communications* 3, no. 6 (June 2006): 46–52. https://bit.ly/2wqN76T.

[87] Nicks, B. A., and D. M. Manthey. "The Impact of Psychiatric Patient Boarding in Emergency Departments." *Emergency Medicine International* 2012 (2012): 1–5. doi:10.1155/2012/360308.

[88] Pines, Jesse M., Robert J. Batt, Joshua A. Hilton, and Christian Terwiesch. "The Financial Consequences of Lost Demand and Reducing Boarding in Hospital Emergency Departments." *Annals of Emergency Medicine* 58, no. 4 (2011): 331–40. doi:10.1016/j.annemergmed.2011.03.004.

[89] Globe Spotlight Team, Michael Rezendes, et al. "The Desperate and the Dead: Families in Fear." *The Boston Globe*, June 23, 2016. https://bit.ly/2vZd78s.

[90] "Consequences of Non–treatment." Arlington: Treatment Advocacy Center. 2017. https://bit.ly/2vrXhna.

[91] Drake, R. J., C. J. Haley, S. Akhtar, and S. W. Lewis. "Causes and Consequences of Duration of Untreated Psychosis in Schizophrenia." *The British Journal of Psychiatry* 177, no. 6 (2000): 511–15. doi:10.1192/bjp.177.6.511; Dell'Osso, Bernardo, Ira D. Glick, David S. Baldwin, and A. Carlo Altamura. "Can Long-term Outcomes be Improved by Shortening the Duration of Untreated Illness in Psychiatric Disorders? A Conceptual Framework." *Psychopathology* 46, no. 1 (2013): 14–21. doi:10.1159/000338608.

[92] Ascher-Svanum, Haya, Baojin Zhu, Douglas E. Faries, David Salkever, Eric P. Slade, Xiaomei Peng, and Robert R. Conley. "The Cost of Relapse and the Predictors of Relapse in the Treatment of Schizophrenia." *BioMed Central Psychiatry* 10, no. 2 (January 7, 2010). doi:10.1186/1471-244x-10-2.

[93] Busch, Alisa B., Anthony F. Lehman, Howard Goldman, and Richard G. Frank. "Changes Over Time and Disparities in Schizophrenia Treatment Quality." *Medical Care* 47, no. 2 (2009): 199–207. doi:10.1097/mlr.0b013e31818475b7.

[94] Wyatt, R. J. "Neuroleptics and the Natural Course of Schizophrenia." *Schizophrenia Bulletin* 17, no. 2 (1991): 325–51. doi:10.1093/schbul/17.2.325.

[95] Lieberman, J. A., J. M. Alvir, A. Koreen, S. Geisler, M. Chakos, B. Sheitman, and M. Woerner. "Psychobiologic Correlates of Treatment Response in

Schizophrenia." *Neuropsychopharmacology* 14, no. 3 (supplement) (1996): 13S–21S. doi:10.1016/0893-133x(95)00200-w.

96 Conus, Philippe, Sue Cotton, Benno G. Schimmelmann, Patrick D. McGorry, and Martin Lambert. "Rates and Predictors of 18-months Remission in an Epidemiological Cohort of 661 Patients with First-episode Psychosis." *Social Psychiatry and Psychiatric Epidemiology* 52, no. 9 (May 5, 2017): 1089–099. doi:10.1007/s00127-017-1388-7.

97 Globe Spotlight Team, Michael Rezendes, et al. "The Desperate and the Dead: Families in Fear." *The Boston Globe*, June 23, 2016. https://bit.ly/2vZd78s.

98 Pearlmutter, Mark D., Kristin H. Dwyer, Laura G. Burke, Niels Rathlev, Louise Maranda, and Greg Volturo. "Analysis of Emergency Department Length of Stay for Mental Health Patients at Ten Massachusetts Emergency Departments." *Annals of Emergency Medicine* 70, no. 2 (2017): 193–202. doi:10.1016/j.annemergmed.2016.10.005.

99 Nicks, B. A., and D. M. Manthey. "The Impact of Psychiatric Patient Boarding in Emergency Departments." *Emergency Medicine International* (2012): 1–5. doi:10.1155/2012/360308.

Chapter 16: Anosognosia

100 David, A. S. "Insight and Psychosis." *The British Journal of Psychiatry* 156, no. 6 (1990): 798–808. doi:10.1192/bjp.156.6.798.

101 Torrey, E. Fuller. "God Does Not Take Medication." In *The Insanity Offense: How America's Failure to Treat the Seriously Mentally Ill Endangers Its Citizens*, 116. New York: W.W. Norton & Company, Inc., 2012.

102 Emami, Seema, Synthia Guimond, M. Mallar Chakravarty, and Martin Lepage. "Cortical Thickness and Low Insight into Symptoms in Enduring Schizophrenia." *Schizophrenia Research* 170, no. 1 (2016): 66–72. doi:10.1016/j.schres.2015.10.016.

103 Torrey, E. Fuller. "God Does Not Take Medication." In *The Insanity Offense: How America's Failure to Treat the Seriously Mentally Ill Endangers Its Citizens*, 112. New York: W.W. Norton & Company, Inc., 2012; "Serious Mental Illness and Anosognosia." Arlington: Treatment Advocacy Center. 2016. https://bit.ly/2uByAs3; Prigatano, George P. *The Study of Anosognosia*. Oxford: Oxford University Press, 2010; Fennig, Shmuel, Elyse Everett, Evelyn J. Bromet, Lina Jandorf, Silvana R. Fennig, Marsha Tanenberg-Karant, and Thomas J. Craig. "Insight in First-admission Psychotic Patients." *Schizophrenia Research* 22, no. 3 (1996): 257–63. doi:10.1016/s0920-9964(96)00077-1.

[104] Buckley, Peter F., Donna A. Wirshing, Prameet Bhushan, Joseph M. Pierre, Seth A. Resnick, and William C. Wirshing. "Lack of Insight in Schizophrenia." *CNS Drugs* 21, no. 2 (2007): 129–41. doi:10.2165/00023210-200721020-00004.

[105] Amador, Xavier F. "Awareness of Illness in Schizophrenia and Schizoaffective and Mood Disorders." *Archives of General Psychiatry* 51, no. 10 (1994): 826–36. doi:10.1001/archpsyc.1994.03950100074007.

[106] "Serious Mental Illness and Anosognosia." Arlington: Treatment Advocacy Center. 2016. https://bit.ly/2uByAs3; Prigatano, George P. *The Study of Anosognosia*. Oxford: Oxford University Press, 2010; Fennig, Shmuel, Elyse Everett, Evelyn J. Bromet, Lina Jandorf, Silvana R. Fennig, Marsha Tanenberg-Karant, and Thomas J. Craig. "Insight in First-admission Psychotic Patients." *Schizophrenia Research* 22, no. 3 (1996): 257–63. doi:10.1016/s0920-9964(96)00077-1; Lehrer, Douglas, and Jennifer Lorenz. "Anosognosia in Schizophrenia: Hidden in Plain Sight." *Innovations in Clinical Neuroscience* 11, no. 5–6 (2014): 10–17. https://bit.ly/2xbUiTN; Lacro, Jonathan P., Laura B. Dunn, Christian R. Dolder, Susan G. Leckband, and Dilip V. Jeste. "Prevalence of and Risk Factors for Medication Nonadherence in Patients with Schizophrenia." *The Journal of Clinical Psychiatry* 63, no. 10 (2002): 892–909. doi:10.4088/jcp.v63n1007.

[107] Lehrer, Douglas, and Jennifer Lorenz. "Anosognosia in Schizophrenia: Hidden in Plain Sight." *Innovations in Clinical Neuroscience* 11, no. 5–6 (2014): 10–17. https://bit.ly/2xbUiTN.

[108] Shad, Mujeeb U., Matcheri S. Keshavan, Carol A. Tamminga, C. Munro Cullum, and Anthony David. "Neurobiological Underpinnings of Insight Deficits in Schizophrenia." *International Review of Psychiatry* 19, no. 4 (2007): 437–46. doi:10.1080/09540260701486324.

[109] Leucht, Stefan, Magdolna Tardy, Katja Komossa, Stephan Heres, Werner Kissling, Georgia Salanti, and John M. Davis. "Antipsychotic Drugs versus Placebo for Relapse Prevention in Schizophrenia: A Systematic Review and Meta-analysis." *The Lancet* 379, no. 9831 (2012): 2063–071. doi:10.1016/s0140-6736(12)60239-6.

[110] Kessler, R. C., P. A. Berglund, M. L. Bruce, J. R. Koch, E. M. Laska, P. J. Leaf, R. W. Manderscheid, R. A. Rosenheck, E. E. Walters, and P. S. Wang. "The Prevalence and Correlates of Untreated Serious Mental Illness." *Health Services Research* 36, no. 6 (December 2001): 987–1007. https://bit.ly/2vmK6YB.

[111] Faruqui, R. A., M. D. Andrews, R. Oyewole, and T. R. Barnes. "Clinical Correlates of Adherence to Antipsychotic Treatment in Pre-discharge Patients with Schizophrenia." *Schizophrenia Research* 60, no. 1, supplement (March 15, 2003): 322. doi:10.1016/s0920-9964(03)80281-5.

[112] Buckley, Peter F., Debra R. Hrouda, Lee Friedman, Stephen G. Noffsinger, Philip J. Resnick, and Kelly Camlin-Shingler. "Insight and Its Relationship to Violent Behavior in Patients with Schizophrenia." *American Journal of Psychiatry* 161, no. 9 (2004): 1712–714. doi:10.1176/appi.ajp.161.9.1712.

[113] Woods, P., V. Reed, and M. Collins. "The Relationship between Risk and Insight in a High-security Forensic Setting." *Journal of Psychiatric and Mental Health Nursing* 10, no. 5 (2003): 510–17. doi:10.1046/j.1365-2850.2003.00548.x.

[114] Pijnenborg, Gerdina H., Rozanne J. van Donkersgoed, Anthony S. David, and A. Aleman. "Changes in Insight during Treatment for Psychotic Disorders: A Meta-analysis." *Schizophrenia Research* 144, no. 1–3 (2013): 109–17. doi:10.1016/j.schres.2012.11.018.

[115] Lehrer, Douglas, and Jennifer Lorenz. "Anosognosia in Schizophrenia: Hidden in Plain Sight." *Innovations in Clinical Neuroscience* 11, no. 5–6 (2014): 10–17. https://bit.ly/2xbUiTN.

Chapter 17: Violence

[116] Joyal, Christian, Jean-Luc Dubreucq, Catherine Gendron, and Frederic Millaud. "Major Mental Disorders and Violence: A Critical Update." *Current Psychiatry Reviews* 3, no. 1 (2007): 33–50. doi:10.2174/157340007779815628.

[117] Jaffe, DJ. "Introduction: Overview of Everything." In *Insane Consequences: How the Mental Health Industry Fails the Mentally Ill*, 21, 247. Amherst: Prometheus Books, 2017.

[118] Duwe, Grant, and Michael Rocque. "Actually, There is a Clear Link Between Mass Shootings and Mental Illness." *Los Angeles Times*, February 23, 2018. https://lat.ms/2oIMi7g; Duwe, Grant. *Mass Murder in the United States: A History*. Jefferson: McFarland & Company, 2007.

[119] Follman, Mark. "Mass Shootings: Maybe What We Need is a Better Mental-health Policy." *Mother Jones*, June 24, 2017. https://bit.ly/2GTsfdp.

[120] Fazel, Seena, Johan Zetterqvist, Henrik Larsson, Niklas Langstrom, and Paul Lichtenstein. "Antipsychotics, Mood Stabilisers, and Risk of Violent Crime." *The Lancet* 384, no. 9949 (October 3, 2014): 1206–214. doi:10.1016/s0140-6736(14)60379-2.

[121] Fazel, Seena. "Schizophrenia, Substance Abuse, and Violent Crime." *Journal of the American Medical Association* 301, no. 19 (May 20, 2009): 2016–023. doi:10.1001/jama.2009.675.

[122] Fazel, Seena. "Psychiatric Morbidity Among Homicide Offenders: A Swedish Population Study." *American Journal of Psychiatry* 161, no. 11 (November 2004): 2129–131. doi:10.1176/appi.ajp.161.11.2129; Fazel, Seena, Petra Buxrud, Vladislav Ruchkin, and Martin Grann. "Homicide in Discharged Patients

with Schizophrenia and Other Psychoses: A National Case-control Study." *Schizophrenia Research* 123, no. 2–3 (November 2010): 263–69. doi:10.1016/j .schres.2010.08.019.

[123] Siegel, Rebecca L., Kimberly D. Miller, and Ahmedin Jemal. "Cancer Statistics, 2017." *CA: A Cancer Journal for Clinicians* 67, no. 1 (2017): 7–30. doi:10.3322/ caac.21387.

[124] Birnes, William J., and John A. Liebert. "Introduction." In *SUICIDAL MASS MURDERERS: A Criminological Study of Why They Kill*, xii–iii. Boca Raton: CRC Press/Taylor & Francis Group, 2011.

[125] Babylon616. "Seung-Hui Cho Full Video Virginia Tech Shooter." YouTube. April 24, 2007. https://bit.ly/2oAFQzK.

[126] Virginia Polytechnic Institute and State University. *Mass Shootings at Virginia Tech: Report of the Virginia Tech Review Panel*. TriData, a Division of System Planning Corporation, April 16, 2007. https://bit.ly/2F2sMgY. Presented to Governor Timothy M. Kaine, Commonwealth of Virginia, August 2007.

[127] "Connecticut Shootings Fast Facts." Cable News Network. December 7, 2017. https://cnn.it/2gqcnrl.

[128] United States. Connecticut State Office of the Child Advocate. *Shooting at Sandy Hook Elementary School: Report of the Office of the Child Advocate*. November 21, 2014. https://bit.ly/2vzk015.

[129] O'Neill, Ann. "Psychiatrist: Holmes Thought Daily About Killing." Cable News Network. June 17, 2015. https://cnn.it/2yxnup1.

[130] Gurman, Sadie. "Defense: 20 Doctors Agree James Holmes Has Schizophrenia." *CBS Corporation—Denver, Associated Press*. April 27, 2015. https://cbsloc .al/2znQmhu.

[131] Ingold, John, Matthew Nussbaum, and Jordan Steffen. "Aurora Theater Shooting Gunman Told Doctor: 'You Can't Kill Everyone.'" *The Denver Post*, April 22, 2016. https://dpo.st/2kXgg8M.

[132] McClelland, Mac. "When 'Not Guilty' is a Life Sentence." *The New York Times Magazine*, September 27, 2017. https://nyti.ms/2gBZuYb.

[133] Cevallos, Danny. "Insanity Defense? Forget About It (Opinion)." Cable News Network. July 17, 2015. https://cnn.it/2xGnOhi.

[134] Jacewicz, Natalie. "After Hinckley, States Tightened Use of the Insanity Plea." New England Public Radio. July 28, 2016. https://n.pr/2kKArqc; McClelland, Mac. "When 'Not Guilty' is a Life Sentence." *The New York Times Magazine*, September 27, 2017. https://nyti.ms/2gBZuYb.

[135] Ibid.

[136] Jacewicz, Natalie. "After Hinckley, States Tightened Use of the Insanity Plea." New England Public Radio. July 28, 2016. https://n.pr/2kKArqc.

[137] Jacewicz, Natalie. "With No Insanity Defense, Seriously Ill People End Up in Prison." New England Public Radio. August 5, 2016. https://n.pr/2iafELV.

[138] Ibid.

[139] Tindula, Rob. "The Rarity of the Insanity Defense." HuffPost/Oath, Inc. December 02, 2015. https://bit.ly/2wWmiry.

[140] Steadman, Henry J., Edward P. Mulvey, John Monahan, Pamela Clark Robbins, Paul S. Appelbaum, Thomas Grisso, Loren H. Roth, and Eric Silver. "Violence by People Discharged from Acute Psychiatric Inpatient Facilities and by Others in the Same Neighborhoods." *Archives of General Psychiatry* 55, no. 5 (1998): 393–401. doi:10.1001/archpsyc.55.5.393; Monahan, John. *Rethinking Risk Assessment: The MacArthur Study of Mental Disorder and Violence.* Oxford: Oxford University Press, 2001.

[141] Steadman, Henry J., Edward P. Mulvey, John Monahan, Pamela Clark Robbins, Paul S. Appelbaum, Thomas Grisso, Loren H. Roth, and Eric Silver. "Violence by People Discharged from Acute Psychiatric Inpatient Facilities and by Others in the Same Neighborhoods." *Archives of General Psychiatry* 55, no. 5 (1998): 393–401. doi:10.1001/archpsyc.55.5.393; Monahan, John. *Rethinking Risk Assessment: The MacArthur Study of Mental Disorder and Violence.* Oxford: Oxford University Press, 2001.

[142] Steadman, Henry J., Edward P. Mulvey, John Monahan, Pamela Clark Robbins, Paul S. Appelbaum, Thomas Grisso, Loren H. Roth, and Eric Silver. "Violence by People Discharged from Acute Psychiatric Inpatient Facilities and by Others in the Same Neighborhoods." *Archives of General Psychiatry* 55, no. 5 (1998): 393–401. doi:10.1001/archpsyc.55.5.393; Monahan, John. *Rethinking Risk Assessment: The MacArthur Study of Mental Disorder and Violence.* Oxford: Oxford University Press, 2001.

[143] Joyal, Christian, Jean-Luc Dubreucq, Catherine Gendron, and Frederic Millaud. "Major Mental Disorders and Violence: A Critical Update." *Current Psychiatry Reviews* 3, no. 1 (2007): 33–50. doi:10.2174/157340007779815628.

[144] Ibid.

[145] Satel, Sally, and DJ Jaffe. "Violent Fantasies." *National Review,* July 1998, 36–38.

[146] Contrada, Fred. "Homeless Man Arraigned for Setting Fire in Forbes Library." MassLive LLC. July 16, 2014. https://bit.ly/2uFqRbY.

[147] Satel, Sally, and DJ Jaffe. "Violent Fantasies." *National Review,* July 1998, 36–38.

[148] Torrey, E. F., J. Stanley, J. Monahan, and H. J. Steadman. "The MacArthur Violence Risk Assessment Study Revisited: Two Views Ten Years After Its Initial Publication." *Psychiatric Services* 59, no. 2 (2008): 147–52. doi:10.1176/appi.ps.59.2.147.

[149] Monahan, John. *Rethinking Risk Assessment: The MacArthur Study of Mental Disorder and Violence.* Oxford: Oxford University Press, 2001; Appelbaum, Paul S., Pamela Clark Robbins, and Roumen Vesselinov. "Persistence and Stability of Delusions over Time." *Comprehensive Psychiatry* 45, no. 5 (2004): 317–24. doi:10.1016/j.comppsych.2004.06.001.

[150] Douglas, Kevin S., Laura S. Guy, and Stephen D. Hart. "Psychosis as a Risk Factor for Violence to Others: A Meta-analysis." *Psychological Bulletin* 135, no. 5 (September 2009): 679–706. doi:10.1037/a0016311.

[151] Torrey, E. Fuller. *American Psychosis: How the Federal Government Destroyed the Mental Illness Treatment System.* Oxford: Oxford University Press, 2014.

[152] Torrey, E. Fuller. *The Insanity Offense: How America's Failure to Treat the Seriously Mentally Ill Endangers Its Citizens.* New York: W.W. Norton & Company, Inc., 2012.

[153] Fazel, Seena, Gautam Gulati, Louise Linsell, John R. Geddes, and Martin Grann. "Schizophrenia and Violence: Systematic Review and Meta-analysis." *PLOS Medicine* 6, no. 8 (August 11, 2009). doi:10.1371/journal.pmed.1000120.

[154] Elbogen, Eric B., and Sally C. Johnson. "The Intricate Link Between Violence and Mental Disorder." *Archives of General Psychiatry* 66, no. 2 (2009): 152–61. doi:10.1001/archgenpsychiatry.2008.537; Monahan, John, and Paul D. Appelbaum. "Reducing Violence Risk: Diagnostically Based Clues from the MacArthur Violent Risk Assessment Study." In *Violence Among the Mentally Ill: Effective Treatments and Management Strategies,* edited by Sheilagh Hodgins, 19–34. Dordrecht: Kluwer Academic Publishers, 2000; Corrigan, Patrick W., and Amy C. Watson. "Findings from the National Comorbidity Survey on the Frequency of Violent Behavior in Individuals with Psychiatric Disorders." *Psychiatry Research* 136, no. 2–3 (2005): 153–62. doi:10.1016/j .psychres.2005.06.005; Swanson, Jeffrey W., Charles E. Holzer, Vijay K. Ganju, and Robert Tsutomu Jono. "Violence and Psychiatric Disorder in the Community: Evidence from the Epidemiologic Catchment Area Surveys." *Psychiatric Services* 41, no. 7 (1990): 761–70. doi:10.1176/ps.41.7.761; Sosowsky, L. "Crime and Violence Among Mental Patients Reconsidered in View of the New Legal Relationship between the State and the Mentally Ill." *American Journal of Psychiatry* 135, no. 1 (1978): 33–42. doi:10.1176/ajp.135.1.33.

[155] Arseneault, Louise, Terrie E. Moffitt, Avshalom Caspi, Pamela J. Taylor, and Phil A. Silva. "Mental Disorders and Violence in a Total Birth Cohort." *Archives of General Psychiatry* 57, no. 10 (2000): 979–86. doi:10.1001/archpsyc.57.10.979.

[156] Hodgins, Sheilagh, Jane Alderton, Adrian Cree, Andrew Aboud, and Timothy Mak. "Aggressive Behaviour, Victimisation and Crime Among Severely Mentally Ill Patients Requiring Hospitalisation." *The British Journal of Psychiatry* 191, no. 4 (2007): 343–50. doi:10.1192/bjp.bp.106.06.029587; Coid, J., M. Yang,

A. Roberts, S. Ullrich, P. Moran, P. Bebbington, T. Brugha, R. Jenkins, M. Farrell, G. Lewis, and N. Singleton. "Violence and Psychiatric Morbidity in a National Household Population—A Report from the British Household Survey." *American Journal of Epidemiology* 164, no. 12 (2006): 1199–208. doi:10.1093/ aje/kwj339.

[157] Tiihonen, Jari, M. Isohanni, P. Rasanen, M. Koiranen, and J. Moring. "Specific Major Mental Disorders and Criminality: A 26-year Prospective Study of the 1966 Northern Finland Birth Cohort." *American Journal of Psychiatry* 154, no. 6 (June 1997): 840–45. doi:10.1176/ajp.154.6.840; Rasanen, P., J. Tahonen, M. Isohanni, P. Rantakallio, J. Lehtonen, and J. Moring. "Schizophrenia, Alcohol Abuse, and Violent Behavior: A 26-year Follow-up Study of an Unselected Birth Cohort." *Schizophrenia Bulletin* 24, no. 3 (1998): 437–41. doi:10.1093/ oxfordjournals.schbul.a033338; Elonheimo, Henrik, Solja Niemela, Kai Parkkola, Petteri Multimaki, Hans Helenius, Ari-Matti Nuutila, and Andre Sourander. "Police-registered Offenses and Psychiatric Disorders Among Young Males." *Social Psychiatry and Psychiatric Epidemiology* 42, no. 6 (April 21, 2007): 477–84. doi:10.1007/s00127-007-0192-1.

[158] Stueve, Ann, and Bruce G. Link. "Violence and Psychiatric Disorders: Results from an Epidemiological Study of Young Adults in Israel." *Psychiatric Quarterly* 68, no. 4 (December 1997): 327–42. https://bit.ly/2vTdyBM; Stueve, A., and B. G. Link. "Gender Differences in the Relationship between Mental Illness and Violence: Evidence from a Community-based Epidemiological Study in Israel." *Social Psychiatry and Psychiatric Epidemiology* 33, no. Supplement 1 (1998): S61–67. doi:10.1007/s001270050211.

[159] Modestin, Jiri, and Roland Ammann. "Mental Disorders and Criminal Behaviour." *The British Journal of Psychiatry* 166, no. 05 (1995): 667–75. doi:10.1192/ bjp.166.5.667; Modestin, Jiri, and Othmar Wuermle. "Criminality in Men with Major Mental Disorder with and without Comorbid Substance Abuse." *Psychiatry and Clinical Neurosciences* 59, no. 1 (2005): 25–29. doi:10.1111/j.1440– 1819.2005.01327.x; Modestin, J., and R. Ammann. "Mental Disorder and Criminality: Male Schizophrenia." *Schizophrenia Bulletin* 22, no. 1 (1996): 69–82. doi:10.1093/schbul/22.1.69.

[160] Haller, Reinhard, Georg Kemmler, Esther Kocsis, Walter Maetzler, R. Prunlechner, and Hartmann H. Hinterhuber. "Schizophrenia and Violence Results of an Overall Survey in an Austrian State." *Der Nervenarzt* 72 (November 2001): 859–66. https://bit.ly/2xFlY1g.

[161] Soyka, Michael, Christian Graz, Ronald Bottlender, Peter Dirschedl, and Heinz Schoech. "Clinical Correlates of Later Violence and Criminal Offences in Schizophrenia." *Schizophrenia Research* 94, no. 1–3 (2007): 89–98. doi:10.1016/j .schres.2007.03.027.

References

[162] Ortmann, J. *Mental Disorder and Criminal Behaviour. An Investigation of 11,533 Men Born in 1953 in Copenhagen Metropolitan Area*. Copenhagen: Justitsministeriet, 1981; Brennan, Patricia A., Sarnoff A. Mednick, and Sheilagh Hodgins. "Major Mental Disorders and Criminal Violence in a Danish Birth Cohort." *Archives of General Psychiatry* 57, no. 5 (2000): 494–500. doi:10.1001/archpsyc.57.5.494.

[163] Wallace, Cameron, Paul E. Mullen, and Philip Burgess. "Criminal Offending in Schizophrenia Over a 25-year Period Marked by Deinstitutionalization and Increasing Prevalence of Comorbid Substance-use Disorders." *American Journal of Psychiatry* 161, no. 4 (2004): 716–27. doi:10.1176/appi.ajp.161.4.716.

[164] Eriksson, A. *Schizophrenia and Criminal Offending: Risk Factors and the Role of Treatment*. Stockholm: Karolinska Institutet, 2008; Lindqvist, P., and P. Allebeck. "Schizophrenia and Crime. A Longitudinal Follow-up of 644 Schizophrenics in Stockholm." *The British Journal of Psychiatry* 157, no. 3 (September 1990): 345–50. doi:10.1192/bjp.157.3.345; Fazel, Seena, N. Langstrom, A. Hjern, M. Grann, and P. Lichenstein. "Schizophrenia, Substance Abuse, and Violent Crime." *Journal of the American Medical Association* 301, no. 19 (May 20, 2009): 2016–023. doi:10.1001/jama.2009.675.

[165] Fazel, Seena, Gautam Gulati, Louise Linsell, John R. Geddes, and Martin Grann. "Schizophrenia and Violence: Systematic Review and Meta-analysis." *PLOS Medicine* 6, no. 8 (August 11, 2009). doi:10.1371/journal.pmed.1000120.

[166] Wallace, Cameron, Paul E. Mullen, Philip Burgess, Simon Palmer, David Ruschena, and Chris Browne. "Serious Criminal Offending and Mental Disorder." *The British Journal of Psychiatry* 172, no. 06 (1998): 477–84. doi:10.1192/bjp.172.6.477; Fazel, Seena, and Martin Grann. "The Population Impact of Severe Mental Illness on Violent Crime." *American Journal of Psychiatry* 163, no. 8 (2006): 1397–403. doi:10.1176/ajp.2006.163.8.1397; Nielssen, Olav, B. D. Westmore, M. M. Large, and R. A. Hayes. "Homicide during Psychotic Illness in New South Wales between 1993 and 2002." *Medical Journal of Australia* 186, no. 6 (March 19, 2007): 301–04. https://bit.ly/2v0Lu2X; Haller, Reinhard, Georg Kemmler, Esther Kocsis, Walter Maetzler, R. Prunlechner, and Hartmann H. Hinterhuber. "Schizophrenia and Violence Results of an Overall Survey in an Austrian State." *Der Nervenarzt* 72 (November 2001): 859–66. https://bit.ly/2xFlY1g; Modestin, J., and R. Ammann. "Mental Disorder and Criminality: Male Schizophrenia." *Schizophrenia Bulletin* 22, no. 1 (1996): 69–82. doi:10.1093/schbul/22.1.69.

[167] Taylor, Pamela J. "Psychosis and Violence: Stories, Fears, and Reality." *The Canadian Journal of Psychiatry* 53, no. 10 (2008): 647–59. doi:10.1177/070674370805301004.

[168] Swanson, Jeffrey W., Marvin S. Swartz, Richard A. Van Dorn, Eric B. Elbogen, H. Ryan Wagner, Robert A. Rosenheck, T. Scott Stroup, Joseph P. McEvoy,

and Jeffrey A. Lieberman. "A National Study of Violent Behavior in Persons with Schizophrenia." *Archives of General Psychiatry* 63, no. 5 (2006): 490–99. doi:10.1001/archpsyc.63.5.490.

[169] Taylor, P. J. "Motives for Offending Among Violent and Psychotic Men." *The British Journal of Psychiatry* 147, no. 5 (1985): 491–98. doi:10.1192/bjp.147.5.491.

[170] Taylor, Pamela J., Morven Leese, Deborah Williams, Martin Butwell, Rachel Daly, and Emmet Larkin. "Mental Disorder and Violence: A Special (High-security) Hospital Study." *The British Journal of Psychiatry* 172, no. 03 (March 1998): 218–26. doi:10.1192/bjp.172.3.218.

[171] Bjorkly, S. "Psychotic Symptoms and Violence Toward Others—A Literature Review of Some Preliminary Findings." *Aggression and Violent Behavior* 7, no. 6 (2002): 617–31. doi:10.1016/s1359-1789(01)00050-7.

[172] Arseneault, Louise, Terrie E. Moffitt, Avshalom Caspi, Pamela J. Taylor, and Phil A. Silva. "Mental Disorders and Violence in a Total Birth Cohort." *Archives of General Psychiatry* 57, no. 10 (2000): 979–86. doi:10.1001/archpsyc.57.10.979; Hodgins, Sheilagh, Ulrika L. Hiscoke, and Roland Freese. "The Antecedents of Aggressive Behavior Among Men with Schizophrenia: A Prospective Investigation of Patients in Community Treatment." *Behavioral Sciences & the Law* 21, no. 4 (July 29, 2003): 523–46. doi:10.1002/bsl.540; Junginger, John, Judith Parks-Levy, and Lynanne McGuire. "Delusions and Symptom-consistent Violence." *Psychiatric Services* 49, no. 2 (February 1998): 218–20. doi:10.1176/ps.49.2.218; Taylor, Pamela J., Morven Leese, Deborah Williams, Martin Butwell, Rachel Daly, and Emmet Larkin. "Mental Disorder and Violence: A Special (High-security) Hospital Study." *The British Journal of Psychiatry* 172, no. 03 (March 1998): 218–26. doi:10.1192/bjp.172.3.218; Link, Bruce G., John Monahan, Ann Stueve, and Francis T. Cullen. "Real in Their Consequences: A Sociological Approach to Understanding the Association between Psychotic Symptoms and Violence." *American Sociological Review* 64, no. 2 (1999): 316–32. doi:10.2307/2657535; Stompe, T., G. Ortwein-Swoboda, and H. Schanda. "Schizophrenia, Delusional Symptoms, and Violence: The Threat/Control-override Concept Reexamined." *Schizophrenia Bulletin* 30, no. 1 (2004): 31–44. doi:10.1093/oxfordjournals.schbul.a007066; Link, Bruce G., and Ann Stueve. "Psychotic Symptoms and the Violent/Illegal Behavior of Mental Patients Compared to Community Controls." In *Violence and Mental Disorder: Developments in Risk Assessment*, edited by John Monahan and Henry J. Steadman, 137–59. Chicago: University of Chicago Press, 1994.

[173] Ibid.

[174] Joyal, C. C., A. Putkonen, P. Paavola, and J. Tiihonen. "Characteristics and Circumstances of Homicidal Acts Committed by Offenders with Schizophrenia." *Psychological Medicine* 34, no. 3 (June 30, 2004): 433–42. doi:10.1017/s0033291703001077.

Chapter 18: Stigma and Antipsychiatry

[175] "NAMI." StigmaFree | NAMI: National Alliance on Mental Illness. Accessed January 19, 2018. https://bit.ly/2AaGvie.

[176] *Mental Disorders as Brain Disorders: Thomas Insel at TEDxCaltech*. Performed by Thomas R. Insel. YouTube / TEDxTalks. February 08, 2013. https://bit.ly/2vLb6hu.

[177] McCarroll, Steve, Mark Daly, Alysa Doyle, Ben Neale, Shaun Purcell, Roy Perlis, and Jordan Smoller. "Genetics of Bipolar and Schizophrenia." Cambridge: Stanley Center for Psychiatric Research at Broad Institute. November 18, 2016. https://bit.ly/2eP0ZnR; United States. Department of Health and Human Services. National Institute of Mental Health. *Recovery After an Initial Schizophrenia Episode (RAISE)*. Accessed January 6, 2018. https://bit.ly/2tLz7aQ.

[178] Western Mass Recovery Learning Community. "Western Mass RLC | Healing and Recovery Through Peer Support." Calendar. January 06, 2018. https://bit.ly/2yFc5Fc.

[179] Western Mass Recovery Learning Community. "Western Mass RLC | Healing and Recovery Through Peer Support." Coming Off Psych Drugs. Accessed 28 July 2017. https://bit.ly/2vfutCo.

[180] United States. Commonwealth of Massachusetts Executive Office of Health and Human Services. Department of Mental Health. *Recovery Learning Communities*. 2010. https://bit.ly/2uGyRcd; "Recovery Learning Communities (RLCs)." Transformation Center. Accessed January 06, 2018. https://bit.ly/2u5TESW; United States. Commonwealth of Massachusetts Executive Office of Health and Human Services. Department of Mental Health. *Search Results*. 2017. https://bit.ly/2yFDQNW.

[181] Ibid.

[182] "Peer Support Resources." Peer Support Resources | NAMI Massachusetts. Accessed January 06, 2018. https://bit.ly/2iD6wMt.

[183] Lloyd-Evans, Brynmor, Evan Mayo-Wilson, Bronwyn Harrison, Hannah Istead, Ellie Brown, Stephen Pilling, Sonia Johnson, and Tim Kendall. "A Systematic Review and Meta-analysis of Randomised Controlled Trials of Peer Support for People with Severe Mental Illness." *BioMed Central Psychiatry* 14, no. 1 (February 14, 2014). doi:10.1186/1471-244x-14-39.

[184] Landers, Glenn, and Mei Zhou. "The Impact of Medicaid Peer Support Utilization on Cost." *Medicare & Medicaid Research Review* 4, no. 1 (2014): E1–E14. doi:10.5600/mmrr.004.01.a04.

Quote and Chapter 19: Reform

[185] Darold A. Treffert, "An Opposing View: Don't Let 'Rights' Block Needed Protection," *USA Today* (March 5, 1987), 10A.

[186] Fuller, Doris A., Elizabeth Sinclair, Jeffrey Geller, Cameron Quanbeck, and John Snook. "Going, Going, Gone: Trends and Consequences of Eliminating State Psychiatric Beds." Arlington: Treatment Advocacy Center. June 2016. https://bit.ly/2wLHqDf.

[187] Sisti, Dominic A., Andrea G. Segal, and Ezekiel J. Emanuel. "Improving Long-term Psychiatric Care." *Journal of the American Medical Association* 313, no. 3 (2015): 243–44. doi:10.1001/jama.2014.16088.

[188] United States. Social Security Administration. *Compilation of the Social Security Laws.* Accessed January 6, 2018. https://bit.ly/2y71e2I; Legal Action Center. *The Medicaid IMD Exclusion: An Overview and Opportunities for Reform.* Accessed January 6, 2018. https://bit.ly/2eWz7uJ; "The Medicaid IMD Exclusion and Mental Illness Discrimination." Arlington: Treatment Advocacy Center. 2016. https://bit.ly/2w9BAx5.

[189] United States. Executive Office of Health and Human Services. Department of Mental Health, Department of Public Health, Office of MassHealth, Executive Office of Housing and Economic Development, Division of Insurance. *Expedited Psychiatric Inpatient Admission Policy.* January 10, 2018. https://bit.ly/2ExjLeG.

[190] Ibid.

[191] Gerbasi, J. B., R. J. Bonnie, and R. L. Binder. "Resource Document on Mandatory Outpatient Treatment." *Journal of the American Academy of Psychiatry and the Law* 28, no. 2 (2000): 127–44. https://bit.ly/2feMjvz; Monahan, J., M. Swartz, and R. J. Bonnie. "Mandated Treatment in the Community for People with Mental Disorders." *Health Affairs* 22, no. 5 (2003): 28–38. doi:10.1377/hlthaff.22.5.28.

[192] Swartz, Marvin S., Steven K. Hoge, Debra A. Pinals, Eugene Lee, Li-Wen Lee, Mardoche Sidor, Tiffani Bell, Elizabeth Ford, and R. Scott Johnson. *APA Official Actions: Resource Document on Involuntary Outpatient Commitment and Related Programs of Assisted Outpatient Treatment.* Washington, D.C.: American Psychiatric Association, October 2015.

[193] Swartz, Marvin S., Steven K. Hoge, Debra A. Pinals, Eugene Lee, Li-Wen Lee, Mardoche Sidor, Tiffani Bell, Elizabeth Ford, and R. Scott Johnson. *APA*

Official Actions: Resource Document on Involuntary Outpatient Commitment and Related Programs of Assisted Outpatient Treatment. Washington, D.C.: American Psychiatric Association, October 2015.

[194] Ibid.

[195] Treffert, Darold A. "The MacArthur Coercion Studies: A Wisconsin Perspective." *Marquette Law Review* 82, no. 4 (1999): 759–85. Marquette University Law School. https://bit.ly/2vADly0.

[196] Deborah Sontag. "A Schizophrenic, a Slain Worker, Troubling Questions." *The New York Times*, June 16, 2011. https://nyti.ms/2xYDeOC.

[197] Becker, Deborah. "Report Raises Questions About Mass. Mental Health System." 90.9 WBUR: Boston's NPR News Station. December 10, 2013. https://wbur.fm/2jmfCRt.

[198] Deborah Sontag. "A Schizophrenic, a Slain Worker, Troubling Questions." *The New York Times*, June 16, 2011. https://nyti.ms/2xYDeOC.

[199] Johnson, Akilah, and John R. Ellement. "Man Convicted in Murder of Group Home Worker." *The Boston Globe*, October 28, 2013. https://bit.ly/2wW0Giv.

[200] Deborah Sontag. "A Schizophrenic, a Slain Worker, Troubling Questions." *The New York Times*, June 16, 2011. https://nyti.ms/2xYDeOC.

[201] Peter Schworm. "Murder Scene Described as 'Blood Bath' as Trial Begins." *The Boston Globe*, October 12, 2013. https://bit.ly/2eUsBEG.

[202] Treffert, Darold A. "Dying with Their Rights on." *Prism* 2 (February 1974): 49–52.

[203] Fuller, Doris A., Elizabeth Sinclair, Jeffrey Geller, Cameron Quanbeck, and John Snook. "Going, Going, Gone: Trends and Consequences of Eliminating State Psychiatric Beds." Arlington: Treatment Advocacy Center. June 2016. https://bit.ly/2wLHqDf.

[204] United States. San Francisco, California Department of Public Health. *San Francisco's Assisted Outpatient Treatment Program: 2017 Annual Report.* March 2017. https://bit.ly/2x5K6N8; United States. New York State Office of Mental Health. *Summary: An Explanation of Kendra's Law.* Accessed January 7, 2018. https://on.ny.gov/2CCVJuy.

[205] "No Relevance to Assisted Outpatient Treatment (AOT) in the OCTET Study of English Compulsory Treatment." Arlington: Treatment Advocacy Center. 2016. https://bit.ly/2wxWwJo.

[206] Swartz, Marvin S. and Jeffrey W. Swanson of Duke University School of Medicine, Henry J. Steadman and Pamela Clark Robbins of Policy Research Associates, and John Monahan of the University of Virginia School of Law. *New York State Assisted Outpatient Treatment Program Evaluation.* Charlottesville: University of Virginia—MacArthur Research Network. June 30, 2009.

https://at.virginia.edu/2vDwqcs. Submitted under Contract with the New York Office of Mental Health.

207 United States. San Francisco, California Department of Public Health. *San Francisco's Assisted Outpatient Treatment Program: 2017 Annual Report.* March 2017. https://bit.ly/2x5K6N8.

208 Torrey, E. Fuller, and John Snook. "Assisted Outpatient Treatment Enters the Mainstream." *Psychiatric Times, UBM Medica, LLC,* April 29, 2017. https://bit.ly/2u2bMhQ.

209 Stettin, Brian. "An Advocate's Observations on Research Concerning Assisted Outpatient Treatment." *Current Psychiatry Reports* 16, no. 3 (February 16, 2014): 1–6. doi:10.1007/s11920-013-0435-7.

210 Matter of K.L., No. 00961 (New York State Court of Appeals 2004) (New York State Law Reporting Bureau, Dist. file). https://bit.ly/2tyKE8l.

211 Segal, Steven P., and Philip M. Burgess. "The Utility of Extended Outpatient Civil Commitment." *International Journal of Law and Psychiatry* 29, no. 6 (2006): 525–34. doi:10.1016/j.ijlp.2006.09.001; United States. Department of Health and Human Services. *Management Strategies to Reduce Psychiatric Readmissions.* Agency for Healthcare Research and Quality, 2015. https://bit.ly/2vpHSs3; Segal, Steven P., and Philip Burgess. "Extended Outpatient Civil Commitment and Treatment Utilization." *Social Work in Health Care* 43, no. 2–3 (2006): 37–51. doi:10.1300/j010v43n02_04; Torrey, E Fuller, and John Snook. "Assisted Outpatient Treatment Enters the Mainstream." *Psychiatric Times, UBM Medica, LLC,* 29 Apr. 2017, bit.ly/2u2bMhQ.

212 Swanson, Jeffrey W., Marvin S. Swartz, H. Ryan Wagner, Barbara J. Burns, Randy Borum, and Virginia A. Hiday. "Involuntary Out-patient Commitment and Reduction of Violent Behaviour in Persons with Severe Mental Illness." *The British Journal of Psychiatry* 176, no. 4 (2000): 324–31. doi:10.1192/bjp.176.4.324.

213 Swartz, Marvin S., Christine M. Wilder, Jeffrey W. Swanson, Richard A. Van Dorn, Pamela Clark Robbins, Henry J. Steadman, Lorna L. Moser, Allison R. Gilbert, and John Monahan. "Assessing Outcomes for Consumers in New York's Assisted Outpatient Treatment Program." *Psychiatric Services* 61, no. 10 (2010): 976–81. doi:10.1176/ps.2010.61.10.976.

214 Torrey, E. Fuller, and Mary Zdanowicz. "Outpatient Commitment: What, Why, and for Whom." *Psychiatric Services* 52, no. 3 (2001): 337–41. doi:10.1176/appi.ps.52.3.337.

215 Torrey, E. Fuller, and John Snook. "Assisted Outpatient Treatment Enters the Mainstream." *Psychiatric Times, UBM Medica, LLC,* April 29, 2017. https://bit.ly/2u2bMhQ.

[216] Jaffe, DJ. "What Science Tells Us About Treatment that Should be Reflected in Policy." In *Insane Consequences: How the Mental Health Industry Fails the Mentally Ill*, 93. Amherst: Prometheus Books, 2017.

[217] Copeland, Darcy Ann, and Marysue V. Heilemann. "Getting 'to the Point.'" *Nursing Research* 57, no. 3 (2008): 136–43. doi:10.1097/01.nnr.0000319500.90240. d3.

[218] Kane, John M., F. Quitkin, A. Rifkin, J. Wegner, G. Rosenberg, and M. Borenstein. "Attitudinal Changes of Involuntarily Committed Patients Following Treatment." *Archives of General Psychiatry* 40, no. 4 (1983): 374–77. doi:10.1001/archpsyc.1983.01790040028004; Bradford, B., S. McCann, and H. Merskey. "A Survey of Involuntary Patients' Attitudes Toward Their Commitment." *Psychiatric Journal of the University of Ottawa* 11, no. 3 (1986): 162–65; Toews, J., N. El-Guebaly, A. Leckie, and D. Harper. "Change with Time in Patients' Reactions to Committal." *The Canadian Journal of Psychiatry* 31, no. 5 (1986): 413–15. doi:10.1177/070674378603100505; Schwartz, Harold I., William Vingiano, and Carol Bezirganian Perez. "Autonomy and the Right to Refuse Treatment: Patients' Attitudes After Involuntary Medication." *Psychiatric Services* 39, no. 10 (1988): 1049–054. doi:10.1176/ps.39.10.1049; Adams, Nicholas, and R. Julian Hafner. "Attitudes of Psychiatric Patients and Their Relatives to Involuntary Treatment." *Australian and New Zealand Journal of Psychiatry* 25, no. 2 (1991): 231–37. doi:10.3109/00048679109077739.

[219] Treffert, Darold A. "1995 Wisconsin Act 292: Finally, the Fifth Standard." *Wisconsin Medical Journal* 95, no. 8 (August 1996): 537–40; Treffert, Darold A. "The MacArthur Coercion Studies: A Wisconsin Perspective." *Marquette Law Review* 82, no. 4 (1999): 759–85. Marquette University Law School. https://bit.ly/2vADly0.

[220] United States. Wisconsin State Legislature. *Chapter 51: State Alcohol, Drug Abuse, Developmental Disabilities and Mental Health Act*. Vol. Sections 15 and 20. https://bit.ly/2iBcwIG; Treffert, Darold A. "The MacArthur Coercion Studies: A Wisconsin Perspective." *Marquette Law Review* 82, no. 4 (1999): 759–85. Marquette University Law School. https://bit.ly/2vADly0.

Chapter 20: The United States

[221] United States. Department of Health and Human Services. Substance Abuse and Mental Health Services Administration. *SAMHSA's National Registry of Evidence-based Programs and Practices: Assisted Outpatient Treatment (AOT)*. 2015. https://bit.ly/2wQoJjf.

[222] Torrey, E. Fuller, and John Snook. "Assisted Outpatient Treatment Enters the Mainstream." *Psychiatric Times, UBM Medica, LLC*, April 29, 2017. https://bit.ly/2u2bMhQ.

[223] Morrissey, Joseph P., Sarah L. Desmarais, and Marisa E. Domino. "Outpatient Commitment and Its Alternatives: Questions Yet to be Answered." *Psychiatric Services* 65, no. 6 (2014): 812–15. doi:10.1176/appi.ps.201400052; Swanson, Jeffrey W., and Marvin S. Swartz. "Why the Evidence for Outpatient Commitment is Good Enough." *Psychiatric Services* 65, no. 6 (2014): 808–11. doi:10.1176/appi.ps.201300424.

[224] Ibid.

[225] Swartz, Marvin, Jeffrey W. Swanson, H. Ryan Wagner, Barbara J. Burns, Virginia A. Hiday, and Randy Borum. "Can Involuntary Outpatient Commitment Reduce Hospital Recidivism?: Findings from a Randomized Trial with Severely Mentally Ill Individuals." *American Journal of Psychiatry* 156, no. 12 (1999): 1968–975. https://bit.ly/2gXCDJx; Swanson, Jeffrey W., Marvin S. Swartz, H. Ryan Wagner, Barbara J. Burns, Randy Borum, and Virginia A. Hiday. "Involuntary Out-patient Commitment and Reduction of Violent Behaviour in Persons with Severe Mental Illness." *The British Journal of Psychiatry* 176, no. 4 (2000): 324–31. doi:10.1192/bjp.176.4.324; Swartz, Marvin S., Jeffrey W. Swanson, Virginia A. Hiday, H. Ryan Wagner, Barbara J. Burns, and Randy Borum. "A Randomized Controlled Trial of Outpatient Commitment in North Carolina." *Psychiatric Services* 52, no. 3 (2001): 325–29. doi:10.1176/appi.ps.52.3.325.

[226] Swartz, Marvin, Jeffrey W. Swanson, H. Ryan Wagner, Barbara J. Burns, Virginia A. Hiday, and Randy Borum. "Can Involuntary Outpatient Commitment Reduce Hospital Recidivism?: Findings from a Randomized Trial with Severely Mentally Ill Individuals." *American Journal of Psychiatry* 156, no. 12 (1999): 1968–975. https://bit.ly/2gXCDJx; Swanson, Jeffrey W., Marvin S. Swartz, H. Ryan Wagner, Barbara J. Burns, Randy Borum, and Virginia A. Hiday. "Involuntary Out-patient Commitment and Reduction of Violent Behaviour in Persons with Severe Mental Illness." *The British Journal of Psychiatry* 176, no. 4 (2000): 324–31. doi:10.1192/bjp.176.4.324; Swartz, Marvin S., Jeffrey W. Swanson, Virginia A. Hiday, H. Ryan Wagner, Barbara J. Burns, and Randy Borum. "A Randomized Controlled Trial of Outpatient Commitment in North Carolina." *Psychiatric Services* 52, no. 3 (2001): 325–29. doi:10.1176/appi.ps.52.3.325.

[227] Swartz, Marvin, Jeffrey W. Swanson, H. Ryan Wagner, Barbara J. Burns, Virginia A. Hiday, and Randy Borum. "Can Involuntary Outpatient Commitment Reduce Hospital Recidivism?: Findings from a Randomized Trial with Severely Mentally Ill Individuals." *American Journal of Psychiatry* 156, no. 12 (1999): 1968–975. https://bit.ly/2gXCDJx; Swartz, Marvin S., Jeffrey W. Swanson, Virginia A. Hiday, H. Ryan Wagner, Barbara J. Burns, and Randy Borum. "A Randomized Controlled Trial of Outpatient Commitment in North

Carolina." *Psychiatric Services* 52, no. 3 (2001): 325–29. doi:10.1176/appi .ps.52.3.325.

[228] Swanson, Jeffrey W., Marvin S. Swartz, H. Ryan Wagner, Barbara J. Burns, Randy Borum, and Virginia A. Hiday. "Involuntary Out-patient Commitment and Reduction of Violent Behaviour in Persons with Severe Mental Illness." *The British Journal of Psychiatry* 176, no. 4 (2000): 324–31. doi:10.1192/bjp.176.4.324; Swartz, Marvin S., Jeffrey W. Swanson, Virginia A. Hiday, H. Ryan Wagner, Barbara J. Burns, and Randy Borum. "A Randomized Controlled Trial of Outpatient Commitment in North Carolina." *Psychiatric Services* 52, no. 3 (2001): 325–29. doi:10.1176/appi.ps.52.3.325.

[229] Munetz, M. R., T. Grande, J. Kleist, and G. A. Peterson. "The Effectiveness of Outpatient Civil Commitment." *Psychiatric Services* 47, no. 11 (November 1996): 1251–253. doi:10.1176/ps.47.11.1251.

[230] Bennett, Chuck. "Homeless Crazies Can't be Rounded Up—Until They Attack." *New York Post*, December 10, 2012. https://nyp.st/2gEOGZs.

[231] Buettner, Russ. "Mentally Ill, but Insanity Plea is Long Shot." *The New York Times*, April 3, 2013. https://nyti.ms/2yoyPY6.

[232] United States. New York State Office of Mental Health. *Kendra's Law: Final Report on the Status of Assisted Outpatient Treatment: Longer Term Findings: Outcomes of AOT Recipients Beyond the Initial Six Months.* 2005. https://on.ny .gov/2vDzR2H.

[233] Lee, Sungkyu, Aileen B. Rothbard, and Elizabeth L. Noll. "Length of Inpatient Stay of Persons with Serious Mental Illness: Effects of Hospital and Regional Characteristics." *Psychiatric Services* 63, no. 9 (2012): 889–95. doi:10.1176/ appi.ps.201100412.

[234] United States. New York State Office of Mental Health. *Kendra's Law: Final Report on the Status of Assisted Outpatient Treatment Outcomes for Recipients During the First Six Months of AOT.* 2005. https://on.ny.gov/2vfo5rB.

[235] Ibid.

[236] Ibid.

[237] Swartz, Marvin S. and Jeffrey W. Swanson of Duke University School of Medicine, Henry J. Steadman and Pamela Clark Robbins of Policy Research Associates, and John Monahan of University of Virginia School of Law. *New York State Assisted Outpatient Treatment Program Evaluation.* Charlottesville: University of Virginia and MacArthur Research Network. June 30, 2009. https://at.virginia.edu/2vDwqcs. Submitted under contract with the New York Office of Mental Health.

[238] Ibid.

[239] Gilbert, Allison R., Lorna L. Moser, Richard A. Van Dorn, Jeffrey W. Swanson, Christine M. Wilder, Pamela Clark Robbins, Karli J. Keator, Henry J. Steadman, and Marvin S. Swartz. "Reductions in Arrest Under Assisted Outpatient Treatment in New York." *Psychiatric Services* 61, no. 10 (2010): 996–99. doi:10.1176/ps.2010.61.10.996.

[240] Link, Bruce G. "Arrest Outcomes Associated with Outpatient Commitment in New York State." *Psychiatric Services* 62, no. 5 (2011): 504–08. doi:10.1176/appi.ps.62.5.504.

[241] Phelan, Jo C., Marilyn Sinkewicz, Dorothy M. Castille, Steven Huz, and Bruce G. Link. "Effectiveness and Outcomes of Assisted Outpatient Treatment in New York State." *Psychiatric Services* 61, no. 2 (2010): 137–43. doi:10.1176/ps.2010.61.2.137.

[242] Swartz, Marvin S., Christine M. Wilder, Jeffrey W. Swanson, Richard A. Van Dorn, Pamela Clark Robbins, Henry J. Steadman, Lorna L. Moser, Allison R. Gilbert, and John Monahan. "Assessing Outcomes for Consumers in New York's Assisted Outpatient Treatment Program." *Psychiatric Services* 61, no. 10 (2010): 976–81. doi:10.1176/ps.2010.61.10.976.

[243] Swartz, Marvin S. and Jeffrey W. Swanson of Duke University School of Medicine, Henry J. Steadman and Pamela Clark Robbins of Policy Research Associates, and John Monahan of University of Virginia School of Law. *New York State Assisted Outpatient Treatment Program Evaluation.* Charlottesville: University of Virginia–MacArthur Research Network. June 30, 2009. https://at.virginia.edu/2vDwqcs. Submitted under contract with the New York Office of Mental Health.

[244] United States. New York State Office of Mental Health. *Recipient Outcomes: Significant Events.* 2017. https://on.ny.gov/2wLlqGf.

[245] United States. New York State Office of Mental Health. *Recipient Outcomes: Service Participation.* 2017. https://on.ny.gov/2j7ia5W.

[246] United States. New York State Office of Mental Health. *Recipient Outcomes: Engagement and Adherence.* 2017. https://on.ny.gov/2wM1Exv.

[247] United States. New York State Office of Mental Health. *Recipient Outcomes: Harmful Behavior.* 2017. https://on.ny.gov/2wbRLoL.

[248] Nono, James. "CarePlus AOTS Team Demonstrates the Benefits of Court Ordered Treatment." CarePlus New Jersey, Inc. August 24, 2017. https://bit.ly/2xGJAW5.

[249] Rohland, B. M. *The Role of Outpatient Commitment in the Management of Persons with Schizophrenia.* Iowa City: Iowa Consortium for Mental Health, Services, Training, and Research, May 1998.

250 Phelan, Jo C., Marilyn Sinkewicz, Dorothy M. Castille, Steven Huz, and Bruce G. Link. "Effectiveness and Outcomes of Assisted Outpatient Treatment in New York State." *Psychiatric Services* 61, no. 2 (2010): 137–43. doi:10.1176/ps.2010.61.2.137.

251 United States. Department of Health and Human Services. Substance Abuse and Mental Health Services Administration. *Establishment of the Interdepartmental Serious Mental Illness Coordinating Committee (ISMICC).* By Carlos Castillo. Washington, D.C.: Federal Register: The Daily Journal of the United States Government, May 1, 2017. https://bit.ly/2exMAg3.

252 United States. Department of Health and Human Services. *Public Members Appointed to New Federal Effort to Address Serious Mental Illness.* August 16, 2017. https://bit.ly/2wwrsLJ; United States. Department of Health and Human Services. Substance Abuse and Mental Health Services Administration. *Interdepartmental Serious Mental Illness Coordinating Committee (ISMICC).* December 14, 2017. https://bit.ly/2AFjWQp.

253 "John Snook Appointed to Interdepartmental Serious Mental Illness Coordinating Committee." Arlington: Treatment Advocacy Center. 2017. https://bit.ly/2x0ulHK; United States. Department of Health and Human Services. Substance Abuse and Mental Health Services Administration. *Interdepartmental Serious Mental Illness Coordinating Committee (ISMICC).* December 14, 2017. https://bit.ly/2AFjWQp.

254 United States. Department of Health and Human Services. *Public Members Appointed to New Federal Effort to Address Serious Mental Illness.* August 16, 2017. https://bit.ly/2wwrsLJ.

255 Earley, Pete. "Sec. Price Calls Serious Mental Illnesses a 'Silent Epidemic': Phone Call About Violence Sparks Debate." Pete Earley. September 01, 2017. https://bit.ly/2vTHeym.

256 United States. Department of Health and Human Services. *Elinore F. McCance-Katz, M.D., Ph.D.* August 28, 2017. https://bit.ly/2x0QSUE.

257 United States. Department of Health and Human Services. Substance Abuse and Mental Health Services Administration. *Interdepartmental Serious Mental Illness Coordinating Committee (ISMICC).* December 14, 2017. https://bit.ly/2AFjWQp.

258 United States. Department of Health and Human Services. *Public Members Appointed to New Federal Effort to Address Serious Mental Illness.* August 16, 2017. https://bit.ly/2wwrsLJ.

259 Sun, Lena H., and Juliet Eilperin. "Trump Administration Freezes Database of Addiction and Mental Health Treatments." *The Washington Post*, January 10, 2018. https://wapo.st/2oLyLvy.

[260] United States. Department of Health and Human Services. Substance Abuse and Mental Health Services Administration. *All Programs.* Accessed March 03, 2018. https://bit.ly/2thqg0y.

[261] United States. Department of Health and Human Services. Substance Abuse and Mental Health Services Administration. *The Way Forward: Federal Action for a System that Works for All People Living with SMI and SED and Their Families and Caregivers: Executive Summary.* Interdepartmental Serious Mental Illness Coordinating Committee, 2017. https://bit.ly/2mc0BzS.

[262] Treatment Advocacy Center. "A Closer Look at Elements of the 21st Century Cures Act." *Catalyst*, Spring 2017.

[263] United States Congress. House of Representatives: Energy and Commerce, Ways and Means; Senate: Health, Education, Labor, and Pensions. *H.R.6: 21st Century Cures Act / Library of Congress.* By Fred Upton. 114 Cong. H. 6. Accessed January 8, 2018. https://bit.ly/2xEN8EC.

[264] Torrey, E. Fuller, and John Snook. Assisted Outpatient Treatment Enters the Mainstream. *Psychiatric Times,* UBM Medica, LLC, April 29, 2017. https://bit.ly/2u2bMhQ.

[265] Treatment Advocacy Center. "A Closer Look at Elements of the 21st Century Cures Act." *Catalyst*, Spring 2017.

[266] Binder, Renee. *Psychiatric News, Assisted Outpatient Treatment: APA's Position Statement.* Washington, D.C.: American Psychiatric Association, February 29, 2016. https://bit.ly/2iBuvyP.

[267] *National Sheriffs' Association Supports the Mission of the Treatment Advocacy Center.* Alexandria: National Sheriffs' Association, March 2013. https://binged.it/2w8iTXf.

[268] State Associations of Chiefs of Police. "Psychological Services Section and Police Physicians Section SACOP.010.T14." In *International Association of Chiefs of Police.* Proceedings of 2014 Resolutions Adopted at the 121st Annual Conference in Orlando, Florida. October 21, 2014. https://bit.ly/2wKgwMB.

[269] United States. National Institute of Justice. Office of Justice Programs: Crime Solutions. *Program Profile: Assisted Outpatient Treatment (AOT).* March 26, 2012. https://bit.ly/2vkGVNu.

[270] United States. Department of Health and Human Services. Effective Health Care Program. *Technical Brief Number 21: Management Strategies to Reduce Psychiatric Readmissions.* By RTI-UNC Evidence-based Practice Center. May 2015. https://bit.ly/2xgJOjT. Prepared for the Agency for Healthcare Research and Quality.

271 Earley, Pete. "Advocate Called on NAMI to Create Separate Advisory Council to Focus on Individuals with Serious Mental Illnesses. Answer: No." Pete Earley. July 11, 2018. https://bit.ly/2LjSegI.

Chapter 21: Massachusetts

272 McKee, Megan. Jahvon Goodwin Sentenced to Life in Stabbing Death of Rashad Lesley-Barnes. Northeastern University. Homicide Watch Boston. July 2, 2015. https://bit.ly/2tROUjs; Lowery, Wesley. "Homeless Man, 21, Charged in Fatal Roxbury Stabbing." *The Boston Globe,* August 29, 2012. https://bit.ly/2vNWMEg.

273 Cramer, Maria. "Man Gets Life in Prison for Killing MBTA Passenger." *The Boston Globe,* June 10, 2015. https://bit.ly/2tBIuda.

274 Ellement, John R. "Man Recalls Brutal Fight with Park Ranger Stabbing Suspect." *The Boston Globe,* October 15, 2014. https://bit.ly/2vyuf6l; Walker, Adrian. "Why Couldn't Anyone Stop Bodio Hutchinson?" *The Boston Globe,* October 16, 2014. https://bit.ly/2uNVQSS.

275 Redmond, Lisa. "Boxboro Man Gets 10–12 Years in 'Horrific' Attack." *Lowell Sun—Digital First Media,* March 8, 2016. https://bit.ly/2uW1ymL.

276 Globe Spotlight Team, Rezendes, Michael, et al. "The Desperate and the Dead: Families in Fear." *The Boston Globe,* June 23, 2016. https://bit.ly/2vZd78s.

277 Ibid.

278 Ibid.

279 United States. Commonwealth of Massachusetts Executive Office of Health and Human Services. Department of Mental Health. *Legislative Reports: Enhanced Outpatient Treatment Pilot Fiscal Year 2017.* March 2017. https://bit.ly/2HioQsM.

280 Ibid.

281 "Involuntary Commitment/Court-ordered Treatment." National Alliance on Mental Illness: Policy Platform 9. Legal Issues. 1995. https://bit.ly/2wXS0YT.

CPSIA information can be obtained
at www.ICGtesting.com
Printed in the USA
LVHW01s0734221018
594371LV00002B/92/P